MW00918120

The Life of
Louis Claude de Saint-Martin

The Life of Louis Claude de Saint-Martin
The Unknown Philosopher
and the Substance of his Transcendental Doctrine
by Arthur Edward Waite
Originally published in 1901
Copyright 2018 by Iugis Publishing
ISBN: 978-1-387-85610-7

THE LIFE OF

LOUIS CLAUDE DE SAINT-MARTIN

THE UNKNOWN PHILOSOPHER

AND THE SUBSTANCE OF HIS TRANSCENDENTAL DOCTRINE

BY

ARTHUR EDWARD WAITE

AUTHOR OF "DEVIL-WORHIP IN FRANCE"
AND TRANSLATOR OF ÉLIPHAS LÉVI

"Expliquer les choses par l'homme, et non pas l'homme par les choses."—*Des Erreurs et de la Vérité.*
"L'homme est le mot de tous les énigmes."—*De l'Esprit des Choses.*

IUGIS PUBLISHING
2018

"M. de Saint-Martin was in the last analysis a man of extraordinary merit, and of a noble and independent character. When his ideas were comprehensible they were exalted and altogether of a superior kind."—CHATEAUBRIAND

"The most instructed, the wisest, and the most elegant of modern theosophists, Saint-Martin."—COUNT JOSEPH DE MAISTRE

"It is just to recognise that never had mysticism possessed in France a representative more complete, an interpreter more profound and eloquent, or one who exercised more influence than Saint-Martin."—VICTOR COUSIN

"A French writer who has sublime gleams."—MADAME DE STAËL

"The feet of Saint-Martin are on earth, but his head is in heaven."—JOUBERT

"M. de Saint-Martin calls for study, or at least for superficial knowledge, even on the part of those who, profane like ourselves, do not presume to penetrate into what is obscure, occult, and reserved, as they say, for the initiates, in his doctrine."—SAINTE-BEUVE

"Saint-Martin has not as yet taken the place which is due to him in modern literature."—M. MATTER

"Saint-Martin should have his rank, a rank certainly among the most honourable in the history of the mystics."—M. CARO

Contents

Contents

BOOK IV

THE DOCTRINE OF THE REPAIRER

BOOK V

THE WAY OF REINTEGRATION

Contents

Book VI

Minor Doctrines of Saint Martin

Book VII

The Mystical Philosophy of Numbers

Contents

APPENDICES

Preface

AMIDST THE FEVER of the French Revolution we find certain men, whether actively or not participating in the turmoil of the time, whose intellectual eyes were fixed far off amidst the luminous peace of another and truer order. Here it is the Marquis de Condorcet, while the chaotic forces of the Reign of Terror are surging madly round his quiet study. Again, it is the author of *Obermann,* forlorn philosophic exile amidst "the scented pines of Switzerland." And, once more, it is Louis Claude de Saint-Martin, as isolated amongst the peaks of his spiritual aspirations as ever was Etienne Pivert de Sénancour amidst the Alpine snows. Of these three, all after their manner illustrious, Saint-Martin only had a message of permanent importance to the human race. Condorcet was a materialist, and, in the restricted sense, an infidel, who looked to the State for salvation; his considerable gifts were useful perhaps in their day, and he has passed with it, not untenderly remembered, but still to be classed among those whose prophecies have been made void and those whose tongues have failed. The ice of intellectual despair had enervated the soul of Sénancour before he went to dwell under the shadow of Jaman, and he, who rightly called himself *un solitaire inconnu,* had no anodyne for himself or his age. Too sad and too lonely, perhaps in a measure too exalted, to connect with the admitted interests of the reading and thinking world, he remains, as he was, unknown rather than forgotten, and it would therefore serve no purpose to exhibit the singular parallel which subsists, somewhat deep down, between the pessimist of Leman, who, after some undetermined manner, looked for a refuge in Eternity, and the gentle, melancholy, hopeful mystic who looked for a refuge from himself in a union between God and man, and an answer to all enigmas in the spiritual advent of the Word of God in the soul. On the surface, however, the Unknown Solitary recalls readily enough the Unknown Philosopher, and precisely the same spirit which took Sénancour to the mountains caused Saint-Martin to lead the hidden life at Paris, at Lyons, at Strasbourg, neither solitary nor unknown, but a prominent figure in high circles of society.

In France itself *le philosophe inconnu* is not inadequately remembered, though that remembrance is of the man rather than the mystic, and might be regarded by his admirers, who are still numerous, as standing in the place of knowledge. His chief works circulated far and wide at their period, and some of them were often reprinted. Within comparatively recent years he has been the subject of four notable biographies* of which one at least has high literary claims, and a fifth has been promised us from the pen of Gérard Encausse, better known under the occult pseudonym of Papus, and the actual president of the Martinist Order of France, in which capacity he has access to many precious unpublished documents.

In England Saint-Martin is chiefly known to Mystics by two rare translations, the work of the late Mr. Edward B. Penny, who so long and ably represented the higher aspects of the tradition of William Law. But the "Ministry of Man the Spirit" and the "Theosophic Correspondence," important and valuable as they are, which were

---

* *Saint-Martin, la Philosophe Inconnu, sa Vis et ses* Écrits, *son Maitre Martinez et leurs Groupes. D'apres des Documents inédits.* Par M. Matter, Conseiller honoraire de l'Université de France, &c. Paris, 1862, and second edition, 1864.

Du Mysticiscme au Dixhuitième Siècle. Par E. M. Caro. Paris 1852.

Le Philosophe Inconnu, Réflexions sur les Idées de Louis Claude de Saint Martin, le Théosophe; suivies de fragments d'une Correspondence inédite entre Saint-Martin et Kirchberger. Par L. Moreau. Paris 1850.

La Philopophie Mystique en Frace à la Fin du Dixhuitième Siècle. Saint-Martin et son Maître Martinez Pasqualis. Par Adolphe Franck. Paris, 1866.

thus made accessible for a season, are not in themselves sufficient. We have in the one case a development of the teaching of Saint-Martin under the influence of Jacob Böhme's theosophy, which presupposes an acquaintance with most of the earlier works, while on the other we have a single side only of the writer's personality—rich, indeed, in the things of the spirit, yet requiring elucidation almost at every page from the side of his outward life and from his formal philosophic treatises. It is, therefore, an unattempted as well as a pleasant task to offer in English vesture the story and the message of this saintly and illuminated thinker, which many transcendental interests have at the present moment combined to make possible; and more even than possible, for they would appear to indicate a special and felicitous opportunity. One of these interests, and the one only which calls for any mention in this place, is in connection with that school of Martinism which was referred to in the preceding paragraph. Connected, as its name indicates, with Saint-Martin himself, this unobtrusive body of esoteric students has of late years spread far beyond the confines of its native country, having branches established in England, but finding its widest diffusion in America. To the members of this Order the claim of the work which I have undertaken will scarcely need advertisement; but for all students of mystic thought the personality and the philosophy of the French Mystic possess real interest, as they will also on acquaintance for many persons who, without being consciously mystics, know something of the joys and sorrows of the life within.

As regards the work itself and the manner in which it has been accomplished, I must not shrink from saying that it has been done zealously and sincerely within its own lines. It should be observed that the writings of Saint-Martin would be considerable in a collected form, and would, in fact, if completely translated, fill something like twelve large volumes. For an enterprise of this kind, with all regard to Mystic interests, there is no public at this day, nor is a diffuse author, who also frequently fails in clearness, best presented at full length. It has been possible, therefore, to give only the substance of his doctrine, and in performing this task I have had two ends chiefly in view—in the first place, to provide a clear introduction to the theosophical system of Saint-Martin for the guidance of those who would prosecute the study of the originals; and, in the second place, to furnish that much more numerous class who have no opportunities for such a study with a synopsis which will serve for the whole. Whatsoever has seemed to me of value is represented here to the best of my ability; where it stands in my own words, it does not deviate from the spirit of the originals, and these portions have been supplemented throughout by direct translation. It may well be that in some points my faculty of appreciation has erred, and here I must ask the lenience of those who know Saint-Martin in their judgment upon a difficult undertaking.

It may be well, in conclusion, to advise those readers who will make their first acquaintance with Saint-Martin in these pages, that he was a Christian Mystic, whose original inspiration was drawn from the mysticism of the Latin Church, which, however, repudiated his views by placing one at least of the works which contained them on the Index of forbidden books. That he was not consciously separated from the Church is said to have been sufficiently witnessed by the keenness with which he felt this condemnation. At the same time he retracted nothing, and discerning as he did the evil days upon which official religion had fallen, he remained ostensibly within its circle, though perhaps no longer of it, but was in all respects the most enlightened, most liberal, and most catholic of the later Christian transcendentalists.

Book I

The Life of Saint-Martin

I

In The World Without

THE NAME OF Saint-Martin never appeared in his lifetime on the title-page of any one of the numerous works with which that name is now connected. He wrote, in most instances, under the pseudonym of "The Unknown Philosopher," once as a "Lover of Secret Things," when the publication pretended to be posthumous, and once quite anonymously, if the attribution in the instance referred to must be regarded as correct.* Furthermore, at the beginning of his literary career, he took other steps for the concealment of his identity; by example, two books which were issued in reality at Lyons bear the imprint of Edinburgh, and one of them has a publisher's advertisement describing the MS. as obtained from an unknown person, and pretending to distinguish a dual authorship therein. The grounds for this secrecy, and the excuse for these evasions, so opposed to the modern spirit and too frequently connected in the past with the devices of quackery, must be sought, firstly, in the writer's affiliation with occult societies, which enjoined, and could perhaps enforce, reserve in their disciples; secondly, in the dangers of the time, for Saint-Martin lived at the period, and was a figure on the scene, of

---

* In the case of *Le Livre Rouge,* concerning which the reader may consult the bibliography in the third section of the Appendix. I should add that *Ecce Homo, Le Nouvel Homme,* and some political pamphlets do not bear the pseudonym on their titles, but as it transpires in the text that they are the work of the Unknown Philosopher, they belong to the pseudonym series.

the French Revolution; thirdly, in social and family considerations, which would, perhaps, weigh more strongly than all with a member of the "privileged" and also proscribed classes at that period. It was, therefore, in the absence of any such extrinsic advantages as the name and position of their author that the books of Saint-Martin acquired such extensive appreciation, criticism, and opposition; that his first treatise, "Of Errors and of Truth," had forged sequels and false keys supplied to it, after the best manner of the school of Voltaire; or that his books, passing into Germany, were not only translated by admirers who knew nothing of the Unknown Philosopher, but were made the subject of elaborate commentaries, not without interest, and perhaps some value, even at the present day. It should be added that in his private life Saint-Martin did nothing to evade his literary connections, though he sometimes counselled caution to the admirers who approached him, and certainly for many years before he died there was no doubt as to the identity of the philosopher. The publication of his posthumous works in the year 1809, though it first avowed the authorship, did little more than register an open secret.

The precautions of Saint-Martin were unnecessary; in no recorded instance did he experience any inconvenience for philosophical opinions, though he suffered confiscation of property because of his social rank.

Louis Claude de Saint-Martin was born at Amboise, in the province of Touraine, on January 18, 1743. He was the son of pious and noble parents, and though he lost his mother a few days after his birth, her place was filled by the second marriage of his father so completely and so tenderly that, as he tells us himself, filial respect and affection became for him a sacred sentiment.* He was brought up strictly in the faith of the Catholic Church, devotion to God and the love of men being impressed ineffaceably on his mind, over which his second mother seems to have exercised an especial influence. "I owe her," he says, "my entire felicity, since it was from her that I derived the first elements of that sweet, solicitous, and pious education by which I was led alike to the love of God and of men. I

---

* *Portrait Historique et Philosophique de M. de Saint-Martin, fait par lui-méme. Œuvres Posthumes,* vol. i. p. 10.

recall having experienced in her society a great interior detachment, alike instructive and healthful. My thought was set free in her presence, and it would have been thus always, had we been subject to no interference; but there were, unhappily, other witnesses from whom we were forced to hide ourselves, as though our intent were evil."[*]

He was of fragile physique and extreme constitutional delicacy, which is, perhaps, all that we need infer from the one other statement concerning his early childhood that we owe to his own record: "I changed skins seven times in my suckling, and it is possibly to these accidents that I owe the deficiency of my astral part."[†] This weakness, whatever its origin, remained with him as a defect of his manhood: he was little capable of fatigue, unfitted for any exposure, and could not risk travelling, even by easy stages, during an inclement season. He was not the less a man of physical as well as great intellectual activity, by no means disposed to spare himself, or to shrink from the duties of his station.

He was sent at an early age to the College of Pontlevoi; but of this period we possess only one memorial—it is that in reality of his first introduction to the mystic life. It was there, as he tells us, that a work on Self-Knowledge by Abadie fell into his hands. He read it with delight, and seems to have understood it, even at that early age, which, he adds, should not seem surprising, as it was sentimental rather than profound. It was in either case to this forgotten, and in some respects inconsiderable, treatise that he ascribes his life-long detachment from the world.[‡]

Destined by his father for the law, Saint-Martin proceeded from Pontlevoi to a school of jurisprudence, probably at Orleans, where he imbibed from the writings of Burlamaqui his taste for the natural foundations of human justice and human reason,[§] but found little to engage him in administrative rules and technicalities. Though he completed his course, receiving his bonnet as King's Advocate at the High Court of Tours, and had everything to expect from the influ-

---

[*]   Ibid. p. 15.

[†]   *Portrait Historique et Philosophique de M. de Saint-Martin, fait par lui-méme. Œuvres Posthumes*, vol. i. p. 4.

[‡]   Ibid. p. 58   [§] Ibid. p. 58

ential offices of the Duc de Choiseul, a friend of his family, he was conscious not only of distaste, but of incompetence, and he besought the permission of his parents to retire from a profession which, at the best, must have absorbed his whole time without commanding any of his higher interests. It was not improbably the equal influence of the same patron over promotion in the military service which induced the elder Saint-Martin to consent that the profession of law should be exchanged for that of arms, and in 1766 the Duc de Choiseul procured for his protégé a lieutenant's commission in the regiment of Foix, then garrisoned at Bordeaux. To the inclinations of Saint-Martin it is certain that the new calling conceded nothing, but in the time of peace which followed the Treaty of Versailles it left him abundant leisure, which he devoted to his engrossing studies, namely, religion and philosophy. He was not yet twenty-four years of age, and he had already exhausted everything that the fashionable speculation of the period could offer to his understanding; he had been dazzled by the brilliance of Voltaire, he had been fascinated by the natural magician of Geneva, but he had been misled by neither.* Through what mental processes he had passed since he fell under the influence of Abadie does not transpire, but as the "Art of Self-Knowledge" had led him to renounce the world, and as Burlamaqui had attached him to the principles of sovereign justice, so to another master he owed his entrance into what he terms the "superior truths." On this occasion, however, his authority was not a book, but the oracles of a living teacher.

When Saint-Martin joined his regiment we have seen that it was stationed at Bordeaux. Thither in the late spring of the year 1767 came Don Martines de Pasqually de la Tour, otherwise Martinez de Pasquales, an initiate of the Rose Cross, a transfigured disciple of Swedenborg, and the propagator and Grand Sovereign of a rite of Masonic Illuminism which probably was of his own foundation,

---

* His admiration for Rousseau remained with him through all his life. Had the author of the "Confessions" fallen into enlightened hands he believed that his fruit would have been truly great. More than once he compared Rousseau with himself, to the advantage of the former, and was struck with the similarity of their tastes and the resemblance between the judgments formed of them. He observed also some likeness in their temporal vicissitudes, due allowance being made for the difference of their positions.

namely, the Order of the Elect Cohens. The researches of Dr. Gérard Encausse* already mentioned in the preface to this work, have cleared up many points in the life of this extraordinary personage: they have done something to show that he was a Spaniard rather than a Portuguese, as previously believed; they have established that he was not a member of the Jewish faith, nor also, so far as can be told, even of Jewish extraction, but that he was a Christian who, at least officially speaking, conformed to the observances of the Catholic Church; they have given us the date of his marriage, the date of his son's birth, and as much as we are likely to know concerning the circumstances of his death at Port-au-Prince, island of St. Domingo, in 1774. The essential mysteries of his life, his early history, the sources of his occult knowledge, the meaning which we are to attach to the statement that he was a Rosicrucian—these points, on which documentary evidence seems wanting, they have not cleared up. We learn upon earlier authority† that so far back as the year 1754, while Saint-Martin was still in his childhood, spelling over the first words of Self-Knowledge in the primer of Abadie, his future instructor was establishing a centre of Illuminism at Paris. There can be no doubt that this organised centre was identical with the Order which thirteen years later he brought to Bordeaux, invested with all the majesty of a sovereign tribunal, and affiliated with many Masonic lodges of Eastern France.

The purpose of Pasqually was not political, nor is there any trace of a financial motive in his proceedings, though there is evidence of financial embarrassments.‡ The order of the Elect Cohens was devoted to the practical study of an occult science and the application of the principles of an occult philosophy, of which Pasqually was the depositary, and of which also he does not seem to have divulged the final secrets. It is claimed, however, and appears on the face of the documents, that the initiations he imparted offered practical results

---

* *L'Illuminisme en France. Martines de Pasqually; sa vie, ses practicues magiques, son œuvre, ses disciples, &c.* Par Papus (*i.e.* Gérard Encausse) Paris, 1895. The term Cohen signifies priest.

† *Saint-Martin le Philosophe Inconnu, sa vie et ses écrits.* Par M. Matter. 2ⁿᵈ edition, Paris, 1864, p. 9.

‡ Papus, *Martines de Pasqually.* See especially the letter of Willermoz, cited *in extenso,* p. 42, *et seq.* Also pp. 49, 53, 55, 59.

to his disciples, and in this case they were genuine so far as they went. It remains further to be said that they exercised a conspicuous influence over many persons who received them, and among these over the young subaltern in the regiment of Foix, for Saint-Martin was admitted into the Order between August 3rd and October 2nd, 1768. According to the plan of this notice, his occult experiences are reserved for particular consideration in another section; we are here concerned only with the manifest results of an initiation which proved a turning-point in the life of its most illustrious recipient.

As already seen, he believed himself to be on the path of the superior truths. More accurately, this was the view which found expression in his private memoranda over twenty years after.* In 1768 he would have spoken possibly with greater enthusiasm concerning the secret knowledge in which he became a participant. That knowledge affected him in two ways at the moment: it drew him to the person of his initiator, who mentions in one of his letters that "the Master de Saint-Martin labours incessantly in our cause";† and it inspired him evidently with that sense of mission which ruled all his subsequent life. Of this inspiration the first specific result was the abandonment of the military profession, which occurred in 1771. As yet, however, he had planned no active propaganda. We find him at Paris, at Lyons, and again at Bordeaux; at Bordeaux chiefly, which the presence of the Grand Sovereign constituted the headquarters of the Order. In all these places Saint-Martin is in frequent communication with other initiated brethren-with the Comte d'Hauterive, the Abbé Fournié, and the Marquise de la Croix; possibly also with Cazotte.

A great blow was, however, destined to fall upon the Elect Cohens. In the early part of the year 1772 the private affairs of Martines de Pasqually called him to St. Domingo, from which place he never returned, if we except his manifestations in the spirit to one of his favoured disciples.‡ The path of initiation thus became closed to Saint-Martin in common with the other members of the Order. On this point we have the evidence of Saint-Martin's own conviction,

---

* *Portrait Historique et Philosophique, Œuvres Posthumes* vol. i. p. 58.

† Papus, *Matrines de Pasqually,* p. 56.

‡ The Abbé Fournié, of whom an account will be found in the next section.

that higher mysteries were known to their master, but that they were withheld in view of the weakness of his disciples.* Apart from his death, the departure of the adept into another hemisphere, with his work uncompleted, must itself have left the mystic Orients and lodges very much to their own resources; in those days communication from such a distance was exceedingly slow, and the acting chief, Willermoz, received only three letters for his guidance. Before the decease of Pasqually, Saint-Martin had begun already to follow his own line, which was destined to take him far away from the operations and ambitions of Elected Cohens. In the earlier stages of its development his mission, however, seems to have been the public propagation, within certain limits and with definite reservations, of the secret knowledge entrusted to him, or rather of original considerations derived from those doctrines, and calculated to lead reflecting minds on the way to their discovery. In this, as in other respects, Saint-Martin offers a sharp contrast to his teacher, whose methods were those of the hierophant guarding his secrets jealously from the world at large.

The mode of propagation adopted was of two kinds: by books published pseudonymously and by the personal influence of a man of birth, education, and genius, mixing in the higher circles of society. In the year 1774, being that of the death of Pasqually, we find the disciple engaged seriously in both directions; he is writing at Lyons his first and in some respects most important treatise, "Of Errors and of Truth," designed to recall man to the real principles of knowledge; and as to his social relations, there is a passage in his personalia concerning his circle of acquaintance at Paris which will speak for itself.† It was part spiritual, part worldly; above all, it was the circle of his friends Lucien and Lucrece de Lusignan, also initiates of his Order. His enumeration includes the Modenas, the Laurans, the Turpins, Montulés, Suifrens, Choiseuls, and Ruifés; the Puymandans, the Nieuls, the Dulans, and Bulabres; the Abbé de Darnpierre, the younger Clermont, MM. la Riviére, de Worms, and de Marjolai; M.

---

*   *Correspondance Inédite de L.C. de Saint-Martin, dit le Philosophe Inconnu, et Kirchberger, Baron de Liebistorf,* Lettre xcii. See also English translation by Penny, "Theosophic Correspondence." p. 318.

†   It is suppressed in the *Portrait Historique* by the editor of the "Posthumous Works," but is given by Matter, *Saint-Martin le Philosophe Inconnu,* p.74.

Duvivier d'Argenton, the Abbé Daubez, and M. de Thiange; the gene-alogist Chérin, the Sieur Rissi, and Madame la Maréchale de Noailles; with others almost innumerable, with all of whom he seems to have been on terms more or less intimate and not accidentally acquainted. In a word, as his biographer, Matter, remarks: "At the age of thirty years M. de Saint-Martin found himself very favourably placed in the world. An expressive countenance and polished manners, marked by great distinction and considerable reserve, presented him to the best advantage. His demeanour announcing not only the desire to please but something to bestow, he soon became known widely and was in request everywhere."* But while he certainly took pleasure in society and was gratified at his success, it was still in view of his philosophical mission; and the character which he always maintained was that of a mystic of exalted spirituality and fervent religion.

There is no need to say that it was a time of disillusion and unbe-lief, of expectancy which had at least a touch of awe, for the Revolu-tion was already at hand, and so also it was a time of wonder-seeking, of portents, and prophets, and marvels; it was the day of Cagliostro and of Mesmer, of mystic Masonry and wild Transcendentalism. It was the worst of all times for the message of true mysticism to be heard with much effect, but there were yet many persons, anxious, willing, and sincere up to a certain point, if not wholly capable, who turned readily enough towards Louis Claude de Saint-Martin. It is true that in his absence they might most of them have been content with Cagliostro, but, all things considered, I think that he was as much heard and put to heart as a mystic could expect then or would anticipate under reason now. And assuredly he drew to himself many choice or at least elegant minds. Among these, in the first flush of his reputation, there were the Marquise de Clermont-Tonnerre and the Marquise de la Croix, as a little later there were the Marquise de Chabanais and the Duchesse de Bourbon. No doubt, as years went on, and as the circumstances of the period became aggravated to-wards the catastrophe of the House of Capet and the Days of Terror, Saint-Martin came to see that his missionary work could be accom-plished better by his books than by his personal influence in a social

---

* Matter, *Saint-Martin le Philosophe Inconnu*, p. 67.

order which was being rent rather than dissolved. He therefore wrote more and was less in visible evidence; M. de Saint-Martin gave place to some extent, though not to his exclusion or effacement, to the Unknown Philosopher. In 1778 he published his "Natural Table of the Correspondences between God, Man, and the Universe," which is homogeneous with his first work, and is in a sense its sequel or extension. It was written at Paris and Luxembourg, partly under the eyes of Madame de la Croix and partly under those of Madame de Lusignan.

After the appearance of this work there is a lacuna which it is difficult to fill in the life of Saint-Martin. The period was perhaps divided between Paris, Lyons, and a mysterious journey to Russia. In 1787 his mystic interests drove him to London, where his friendship with Madame la Marquise de Coislin, wife of the French ambassador, assured his introduction into the highest circles. He made here a memorable and fruitful acquaintance with disciples of William Law, who is in some respects the Saint-Martin of England. Among the distinguished names which he mentions in connection with this visit are the astronomer Herschel, Lord Beauchamp, who was in sympathy with his transcendental objects; and, above all, the Russian Prince Galitzin, who declared some time after, that he had never been really a man until he knew M. de Saint-Martin.

From England in the same year, and everywhere with the same object, he travelled into Italy, where again the most distinguished names, cardinals, princes, bishops figure in his memorial notes. But there were no mystics, and there was no mystic interest. Cagliostro only was in the hands of the Inquisition, and his process was near at hand.

About 1788 we find Saint-Martin at Montbéliard, the residence of the Duchesse de Wurtemberg, whose sympathies in his mystic pursuits had been previously enlisted; and then for the space of three years he resided at Strasbourg, still, as it would seem, exclusively in the circles of aristocracy, and this period seems to have been the happiest of his life. It was here, under the auspices of the transcendentalist Rodolph Salzmann and of Madame de Boecklin, his most valued female friend, that he first made acquaintance with the writings of Jacob Böhme; here he became intimate with the Chevalier de Silferhielm, a nephew of Swedenborg; here also his literary activity was at its greatest; here, finally, the limits of his intellectual horizon were enlarged in an extraordinary degree. The explanation of the last point must not be referred to any single cause. We have it on his own authority[*] that he owed to Jacob Böhme his most important progress in those higher truths to which he had been introduced by Martines de Pasqually, and the influence of the "Teutonic Theosopher" upon all his later life and all his thoughts may be found on every leaf of his correspondence, perhaps on too many pages of his latest works. Yet there are many facts in his intellectual development which cannot be traced to that influence, nor perhaps altogether to the source suggested by Matter, the totality of the ideas and of the movement in the midst of which he was living during his sojourn in the old city on the banks of the Rhine.[†]

It was at Paris that he completed "The Man of Aspiration," which he had begun in London, the most exalted and inspired of his compositions; and this also was the period of the "New Man," which represents the extreme development of his philosophical system prior to his acquaintance with Böhme. The first of these works was undertaken at the suggestion of Thieman, an ardent mystic, with whom, in England and Italy, he had formed the closest ties of friendship; to the second he was urged by Silferhielm. It was also at Strasbourg and Paris that he wrote *Ecce Homo,* a simplified presentation of the "New Man," designed especially for the spiritual necessities of the Duchesse de Bourbon.

In the summer of 1791 he was called from Strasbourg to Amboise, his native place, by the illness of his father, and from that time till the death of the latter in February 1793, he was either there or at Paris, where he witnessed the terrors of the 10th of August 1792. "The streets near the house I was in were a field of battle; the house itself"—probably the palace of the Duchesse de Bourbon—"was a hospital where the wounded were brought, and, moreover, was every moment threatened with invasion and pillage. In the midst of all this I had to go, at the risk of my life, to take care of my sister, half a league from my dwelling." So he writes in the most memorable, the most beautiful,

---

[*]   *Portrait Historique et Philosophique, Œuvres Posthumes* vol. i. p. 69.

[†]   *Saint-Martin,* p. 171.

the most fascinating of all theosophic correspondences, which was begun on the 22nd of May 1792, and continued for five years, between himself and the Swiss Baron Kirchberger de Liebistorff.*

The death of Saint-Martin's father was almost coincident with the execution of Louis XVI, and was followed speedily by that of Philippe Egalité, the brother of his friend the Duchesse; and it is one of the minor marvels of those terrific days that his frequent sojourns at her palace, or at her chateau at Petit-Bourg, did not somehow cost him his head. His correspondence fell under suspicion, and he was once called to account for its mysterious phraseology. He helped to ensure his safety by various gifts in money towards the equipment of the soldiers of the republic. In 1794, the decree which exiled the nobility from Paris compelled him to retire to Amboise, where he was permitted to remain without molestation, and was indeed deputed to catalogue the books and manuscripts which had been seized in the suppressed monastic houses of his district. A little later on he was called to the Ecole Normale, which was intended to train teachers for public instruction; and he is even said to have formed one of the guard at the Temple when the Dauphin, Louis XVII was confined there. On his return to Amboise, he was chosen a member of the electoral assembly of that department. It was possibly these unsought duties which directed his mind once more to the political aspects of his transcendental system, and produced as a result his famous "Letter to a Friend on the French Revolution," which resumes and extends a memorable section of his first work, "Of Errors and of Truth." The Letter appeared in 1796, and was followed the next year by an "Elucidation of Human Association," designed to amplify and complete the former thesis. In the stress of the time these pamphlets, which, it must be confessed, involved much that was impossible of application, impressed only the choicer and mystic minds of his own circle. Perhaps even less can be said for a publication of 1798, entitled "The Crocodile," a satirical prose poem of trying dimensions, of which only one adventitious section possesses any interest to the admirers of Saint-Martin at this, if at any, day. That section is an essay on the "Influence of Signs upon Ideas," and there are two evidences that Saint-Martin himself weighed

---

* *Correspondance,* Lettre viii; Penny, "Theosophic Correspondence," pp. 31, 32.

the entire performance at its proper worth; in the first place, it did not appear under his usual pseudonym of the "Unknown Philosopher," and, in the second place, he detached the essay which is of value from the bizarre context which is not, and issued it separately as a pamphlet in the year following, 1799.

Saint-Martin was now approaching the close of his almost blameless life, and so far as outward circumstances are concerned it was tinged with melancholy. I have said that the condemnation of his first work by the Spanish Inquisition as subversive of true religion and the peace of nations affected him, though it is treated lightly by M. Matter. This took place in 1798. Prior to that date his patrimony had been confiscated, and from means which his modest necessities made him regard as ample he was reduced almost to penury. Add to this that a passing misunderstanding between himself and his cherished friend and correspondent, Baron Kirchberger, had scarcely been set right when the Swiss nobleman died very suddenly, leaving a void which there was no one at hand to fill in the heart of Saint-Martin. His nomination for the short-lived attempt of the Normal School had overruled the proscription which had forbidden Paris to the mystic, and he was now frequently at the capital. He was conscious, considerably in advance, of the likelihood of his end, and it seemed to inspire fresh diligence. Thus in 1800 he published two volumes of detached essays, with, however, something of a central purpose, under the title of "The Spirit of Things." They were followed in 1802 by his first and only formal attempt to conciliate the system he had derived from the school of Martines de Pasqually with the illuminations of Jacob Böhme. This was the "Ministry of Man the Spirit, the most elaborate, and at the same time least diffuse, of all his works. Indeed, in several respects it was the crown of his literary life. Coincidently with each of these works there appeared translations of Böhme's "Aurora" and "Three Principles."

In October 1803 the signs of his approaching end were unmistakably significant. "I feel that I am going," he said to his friend M. Gence: "Providence calls me; I am ready. The germs which I have endeavoured to sow will fructify." He repaired to the country-seat of Count Lenoir la Roche at Aunay, and on the 13th of the same month a stroke of apoplexy put a painless end to his career.

II

In the Occult World

I PROPOSE NOW TO consider in a more particular manner the nature of the initiation conferred upon Saint-Martin in his youth, which involves the important question concerning the sources of his knowledge. The existence of various secret orders which claim to perpetuate and impart, under certain conditions, the understanding of the secret sciences is a fact that is perfectly well known, whatever verdict may be passed on the value of the claim itself or on the rank of the sciences concerned. The literature of Occultism in the West has traces of such orders prior to the fifteenth century; they point to the existence of associations, more or less formally incorporated, for the study of alchemy and the operations which are usually understood by the term Magic. Outside the literature there is the history of the Black Sabbath, which points very plainly to another class of association. The first manifestation in public on the part of an occult body did not occur, however, till the beginning of the seventeenth century, and this was the well-known case of the Rosicrucians, long regarded as a hoax, because the evidence concerning it had been subjected to no adequate examination.* The disappearance of this body was coincident with the obscure transition from operative into speculative

---

* The attempt which I made to collect and appreciate this evidence in "The Real History of the Rosicrucians" (1887), though it requires revision in the light of later knowledge, still constitutes the only available summary of the subject in English.

Masonry, and from that epoch the history of every fraternity which has pretended to dispense initiation into occult knowledge is a part of the history of that great institution, which at the same time neither possesses nor claims such knowledge on its own behalf, and as an institution, at least, has no concern or interest therein. In France, above all, towards the close of the eighteenth century, occult Orders possessing Masonic connections sprang up on every side.* Too frequently they were the consequence of private ambition, inventions of unscrupulous adventurers, or fantastic creations of enthusiasts. In only a very few eases can we trace a serious purpose or discern a genuine claim. To which class must we refer the Order propagated by Martines de Pasqually? The answer must depend, firstly, on the nature of its pretensions, and, secondly, upon the evidence for their foundation in fact. Of the genesis of the Elect Cohens we know little. It was doubtless the institution of its propagator, but it is not explicable by his alleged connection with Swedenborg. So far as we know, its rituals were productions of the period; they bear no traces of antiquity.†
Its catechisms are equally modern.‡ The possibility, however, remains that Martines de Pasqually acted under the direction of an anterior Order, namely, the Rosicrucians, with whom he claimed affiliation. When he first appeared in Paris it was in his capacity as a member of that mysterious brotherhood. Was this an honest claim? We can only decide this question indirectly, for it is unnecessary to observe that documents are not forthcoming to establish it, and might be open to suspicion if they were. We must judge by the character of the man, and by what he did. In other words, we must refer once more to the foundation for the pretensions of his Order. If it really imparted occult knowledge, he, no doubt, derived it from initiation on his own part, whether Rosicrucian or not matters little. What, therefore, did the Elect Cohens pretend to confer upon their disciples? There was

---

* See the concluding chapter of "Devil-Worship in France."

† It is just, however, to say that in one part of his correspondence with Willermoz, Martines de Pasqually states that a portion of the magical ritual had been translated, apparently by himself, out of Latin into French. See Papus, *Martines de Pasqually*, p. 108.

‡ That of the Apprentice Elect Cohen affirms that the Order derives from the Creator, and has subsisted from the days of Adam. Ibid. pp. 225-226

a secret doctrine and a secret practice, by which it may be supposed that the truth of that doctrine was demonstrated. As, however, the theoretical part is scarcely to be found in the catechisms, so the occult operations would probably be wanting in the formal rites designed for use in the lodges. We must look further for our instruction in both cases. The doctrine and the practice, so far as they went, will be found in confidential communications addressed by the master to the more favoured of his disciples, and fortunately still extant.* We find on the one hand a collection of evoking processes, which offer very little to distinguish them from the typical *grimoire* of magic. There are a number of minor variations, but there is no generic difference. There is the observation of astronomical correspondences which characterises the "Key of Solomon" there is the fast which precedes operation, and is enjoined in all rituals from the "Lemegeton" to the latest recension of the "Red Dragon". In so far as there are liturgical portions which are borrowed from the Catholic Church, they are substantially identical with those found in any rite of evocation possessing a Christian complexion, as distinguished from Kabalistic rites. Above all, evocation takes place within a magic circle, accompanied by lights and by perfumes, while the special vestments used by the Elect Cohen are those prescribed by the spurious Agrippa, and the Pentameron of Peter de Abano, a work of similar pretensions and no greater authenticity† There is no occasion to enlarge upon the specific differences, but I may mention the observance of the equinoxes as the only periods for the practice, a peculiar arrangement of the lights, and the entire abrogation of the bloody sacrifice. To put it shortly, the process of Martines de Pasqually is that of the *grimoires* simplified, and I might add that it is civilised and adapted for the use of the higher ranks of society in France of the eighteenth century.

The efficacy of theurgic formulae is a perilous question to investigate, even when there is some presumption that the listeners will be chiefly transcendentalists, but it is sufficient for the present purpose to point out that all theurgic procedure assumes this efficacy, and

---

* They will be found with elaborate analyses in the work of Papus.

† The claims of these works are examined in "The Book of Black Magic," c. iii. secs. 3 and 4.

modifies the formulae in accordance with the occasion, the object, and other determining considerations. While it is possible therefore to class Martines de Pasqually among impostors or maniacs on the common ground of criticism, it is not possible for a critic who is also a mystic to disregard entirely the theurgic claim, though it may not represent a high grade of initiation. Occult orders possessing considerable antiquity exist at the present day expressly for these practices, which have apparently a certain measure of success. The methods differ naturally from those of the *grimoires,* in which everything not actually spurious is garbled, so that the outlines alone remain. It is, therefore, within possibility that Martines de Pasqually obtained his formula not by purgation of worthless printed books, but from some such source as I have indicated, and as may be inferred from his own claim, in which case they may approach, or indeed coincide with, some that are still in use. I must not add that I regard the process as by itself of positive value, for it might as easily induce hallucination as genuine vision.

In either case, the parallel between the theurgic rites followed by the Elect Cohens and the *grimoires* ends with the ceremonial procedure; the purpose differed, because it was not in the ordinary sense concerned with evocation of spirits. It did not deal with the shades of the dead, like necromancy; nor with elementals or elementaries; nor with the planetary orders; nor even with the angelical hierarchy; much less with the so-called angels of magical literature, whose habitations in most cases must be sought with the Klippoth, and in the false sea of Kabalism. The theurgic object seems to have been of a far more exalted order, and was nothing less than an attempt to communicate with the Active and Intelligent Cause* charged with the conduct of the visible universe, as we shall learn later on from Saint-Martin, and apparently in a special manner with the great work of initiation.† By this fact the school of Martines de Pasqually is placed wholly outside the narrow limits and sordid motives of ceremonial magic. Having established this distinction, let us proceed to inquire whether any disciples of the Order believed themselves to have attained its object. The

---

* See Book iv. sec. i.

† Papus, *Martines de Pasqually,* p. 113.

records of a secret society are not usually obtainable, but in this case time has preserved or made known to us some important pieces of evidence in connection with three persons who were initiated by Martines de Pasqually. The first is Jean Baptiste Willermoz, who in 1752 was Venerable of the Lodge Parfaite-Amitié at Lyons, Grand Master of the Grand Lodge of Lyons, 1760, and subsequently President of the Lodge of Elect Cohens in that city. There is abundant documentary proof that this disciple followed the instructions of Pasqually in the practical part, times out of number, with no indication of success, and that he became in consequence extremely dissatisfied with his initiator. But the documents also show that he persevered, that he attained the ends, "obtaining phenomena of the highest importance, which culminated in 1785—that is to say, eleven years after the death of his initiator."*

The second case is that of the Abbé Fournié, for which, however, we are indebted to a narrative published by himself, but now so rare that it is almost unknown in France.† It is an exposition of the doctrine of Pasqually from the standpoint of an ecclesiastic of the period, and the doctrine has no doubt suffered from unconscious substitution. I should infer that Fournié was a man of humble origin, and he confesses that he was uninstructed in human sciences. At an early age he conceived an intense desire for a demonstration of the reality of another life and the truth of the central doctrines of Christianity. After eighteen months of profound agitation, he met, apparently on the banks of the Rhine, an unknown personage who promised a solution of his doubts, and pointing to the throng of a crowded thoroughfare, observed: "They know not whither they are going, but thou shalt know." After this oracular manner the Abbé Fournié made acquaintance with Martines de Pasqually, whom he took at first for a sorcerer or the devil, but consoled himself with the reflection that in the latter case there must at least be a God. He therefore frequented the society of the mysterious stranger, and was admitted among the number of his followers. "His diurnal exhortations were to aspire

---

* Papus, *Martines de Pasqually,* p. 113.

† *Ce que nous avons* éete, *ce que nous sommes et ce que nous viendrons.* London, 1801.

without ceasing towards God, to grow from virtue to virtue, and to labour for the universal good. They resembled precisely those which Christ delivered to His disciples, without forcing anyone to accept them under pain of damnation, without imposing other commandments than those of God, without imputing other sins than those which are expressly opposed to the Divine law, and frequently leaving us in suspense as to whether he himself was true or false, good or bad, angel of light or fiend. This uncertainty kindled so strongly within me, that night and day I cried out on God to help me, if He really existed. But the more I appealed the more I sank into the abyss, and my only interior answer was the desolating feeling—there is no God, there is no life to come, there is only death and nothingness." In this afflicted condition the Abbé did not cease from praying. Sleep left him, but he persevered, continually studying the Scriptures, and never seeking to understand them by his own lights. Other lights came to him after a long time, but only in flashes, and he had moments of vision, apparently of things to come, subsequently fulfilled, which he referred to the occult powers of Martines de Pasqually. In this manner he passed five years, full of agitation and darkness, consumed, as he says, by the desire of God and the contradiction of that desire.

"At length, on a certain day, towards ten o'clock in the evening, I, being prostrated in my chamber, calling on God to assist me, heard suddenly the voice of M. de Pasqually, my director, who had died in the body more than two years previously. I heard him speaking distinctly outside my chamber, the door being closed, and the windows in like manner, the shutters also being secured. I turned in the direction of the voice, being that of the long garden belonging to the house, and thereupon I beheld M. de Pasqually with my eyes, who began speaking, and with him were my father and my mother, both also dead in the body. God knows the terrible night which I passed!"

It is evident from this exclamation that the demonstration so long desired by the Abbé overwhelmed and frightened him in the initial experience. He relates further a very curious sensation as of a hand passing through his body and smiting his soul, leaving an impression of pain which could not be described in words, and seemed to belong rather to eternity than time. After the lapse of twenty-five years he retained the most vivid recollection of his suffering. At the same time he tells us that he held with his director and his parents a conversation that might have passed between men and women under ordinary circumstances. On the same occasion he also saw one of his sisters who had passed away twenty years before. Lastly, he adds these weird words: "There was another being who was not of the nature of men." The integrity of the simple Abbé will be past all question for anyone who makes acquaintance with his narrative. Was he therefore hallucinated, or was he the recipient of visitations from another world as a consequence of the constancy and singleness of his intention? The manifestations in either case were not wonders of a single night. The next time they were of another order, and possess a more direct connection with the grand object of the Elect Cohens. "A few days after I beheld very plainly in front of me, close at hand, our Divine Master Jesus Christ, crucified on the tree of the cross. Again, after another interval, this same Divine Master appeared to me, but this time as He came forth from the tomb wherein His body had been laid. Lastly, after a third interval, our Divine Master Jesus Christ appeared to me, all glorious and triumphant over the world and over Satan with his pomps, passing in front of me with the Blessed Virgin Mary, His mother, and followed by a number of persons." I should add that the vision of Martines de Pasqually and of the Abbé's parents did not occur once only, nor during one week, one month, or one year. "I have beheld them during entire years, and constantly; I have gone to and fro in their company; they have been with me in the house and out of it; in the night and the day; alone and in the society of others; together with another being not of human kind, speaking one with another after the manner of men."

To the divine apparitions the Abbé Fournié ascribes the inspiration which enabled him to write his treatise, he being confessedly illiterate, with extraordinary celerity. The verbal communications he received in his visions he does not, however, report, the reason given being the cynicism and incredulity of the age. There is ground all the same for supposing that they were actually recorded, and formed a second part of his work, which was never published. The first part was written about 1780, the Abbé being then somewhat over forty years of age. It remained in manuscript for the space of five-and-twenty years, when it was at length committed to the press. The author himself was living so late as the year 1819, being then at a very advanced age. It will be seen that his experiences owed nothing to the ceremonial processes of his occult director, but they determine the point of view from which that director was regarded by one of the most spiritual of his disciples, and, hallucinations or not, they indicate the extraordinary influence exercised by Martines de Pasqually, not only while alive in the flesh, but when, as one would say, he was only a sacred memory among those who had followed him.

The third case, which will conclude our inquiry concerning those Elect Cohens who made progress towards the objects of the Order, is that of Saint-Martin himself, the source of information being main-ly his long correspondence with Baron Kirchberger. The date of his admission into the society is not quite clear, but it was probably in the autumn of 1768. He no doubt attached himself to the person of the "director" while they were both at Bordeaux, and, as already seen, he sometimes acted as a kind of informal secretary for Martines, who wrote French imperfectly, and needed help in his correspondence. But the disciple was not at that time his own master; he had peri-ods of enforced absence on military duty, and the date of Pasqually's departure put an end to their intimacy, probably before the forging of its strongest links. On this point we have Saint-Martin's own tes-timony: "We were only beginning to walk together when death took him from us."* At the same time we have sufficient, though not the most ample, material for ascertaining, firstly, the opinion held by Saint-Martin through all his afterlife concerning the initiator of his youth; secondly, the share which he took in the occult experiences of the school to which he was introduced; thirdly, the lesson which he brought away from it. To do justice to all these points we should observe at the outset the disposition of mind which he carried into the Bordeaux college of magic. It must be admitted at once that he did not take either doubt or scepticism. Neither in his formal writings nor in his memorial notes, nor yet in his available letters, do I find any indication that the facts, real or alleged, of occult phenomena came to him with the force of a surprise, but he appreciated them from the beginning at their real worth. "I experienced at all times

---

*   *Correspondance,* Lettre xcii; Penny, "Theosophic Correspondence," p. 318.

so strong an inclination to the intimate secret way that this external one never seduced me further, even in my youth. Amidst much that was to others most attractive, amidst means, formulæ, preparatives of every sort, by which we were trained, I exclaimed more than once to our master: 'Can all this be needed to find God?'"* The student of Abadie, reared strictly in the faith of the Catholic Church, and untinged by philosophy *à la mode,* though not unacquainted therewith, was already an interior mystic when he entered the occult Order of Martines de Pasqually. At the same time he never referred to that early master except with conspicuous reverence. "I will not conceal from you that I walked formerly in this secondary and external way, and thereby the door of the career was opened to me. My leader therein was a man of very active virtues,"† that is to say, he was powerful in occult operations, as Saint-Martin explains elsewhere. Again: "I do not doubt that there have been, and still are, some privileged men who have had, and still have, perceptions of the great work:‡ in other words, the work of reintegration as opposed to the secondary work of the external way, the mystic inward path as opposed to that of occult phenomena. "I do not doubt that my first teacher and several of his disciples enjoyed some of these favours."§ But perhaps the most important reference made by Saint-Martin to his master occurs towards the close of his correspondence with Baron Kirchberger: "I am even inclined to think that M. Pasqualis, whom you name (and who, since it must be said, was our master), had the active key to all that our dear Böhme exposes in his theories, but that he did not think we were able to bear such high truths... I am persuaded that we should have arrived at them at last, if we had kept him longer."‖ To understand the full force of this statement, it must be observed that Saint-Martin at the time when he made it regarded Jacob Böhme as "the greatest human light which had been manifested on earth since One who was the light itself;"¶ and seeing that an acquaintance with the writings of Böhme is obviously not intended, and could not be reasonably sup-

---

*   *Correspondance,* Lettre iv; Penny, "Theosophic Correspondence," pp. 15-16.

†   Ibid.   ‡ Ibid. Lettre xiii; ibid. p. 54.   § Ibid.

‖   Ibid. Lettre xcii; p. 318.   ¶ Ibid. Lettre ii; ibid. p. 7.

posed in Pasqually, it follows that Saint-Martin regarded the Spanish adept as one who had independently attained the same exalted height of illumination as that reached in his opinion by the German theosophist. In other words, he paid to his memory the greatest tribute within his power. It will not be surprising, therefore, that he states also his belief that "there were precious things in our first school," and then adds that "an excellent match may be made by marrying our first school to friend Böhme. At this I am working, and I confess to you candidly that I find the two spouses so well suited to each other that I know nothing more perfect in its way."* The last work of Saint-Martin, on the "Ministry of the Spirit Man," is, in fact, a celebration of the nuptials, in which union there is something superadded to the first of Saint-Martin, but there is nothing lost of the gift.

The personal experiences of Saint-Martin in the order of occult phenomena were decisive to his own mind; but as there was something wanting to his motive, namely, a living interest, so there was something deficient in the result. "I never had much taste or talent for the operations." He mentions two persons, also initiates, whose success was greater than his own; but in the one case, that of M. de Hauterive, Saint-Martin never found anything which could induce him to alter his mind; while in the other, that of Madame de la Croix, he received only "negative proofs."† Again, but this in regard to the later period of his life: "I am very far from having any virtuality of this kind, for my work takes the inward direction altogether."‡ Saint-Martin, however, had seen enough to enable him to formulate an express theory concerning the mode of such super-physical communications. He recognised no such experience as the soul or astral travelling, of which so much was heard in the earlier phenomena of somnambulism and modern spiritualism; no "putting off" of the corporeal envelope. "The soul leaves the body only at death, but during life the faculties may extend beyond it, and communicate with their exterior correspondents without ceasing to be united to their centre, even as our bodily eyes and all our organs correspond with surrounding ob-

---

*   *Correspondance,* Lettre xcii; Penny, "Theosophic Correspondence," pp. 318-319.

†   Ibid. Lettre viii; p. 35.   ‡ Ibid. Lettre xl; p. 133.

jects without ceasing to be connected with their animal principle, the focus of all our physical operations.* It was also his conviction that no physical manifestations connect with the centre, as he terms it, because "this deep centre produces no physical form."† The natural inference which seems to follow hom this statement is that the supreme object of the Elect Cohens was impossible by the external way which was admittedly followed by the Order, but balanced against this we find a no less express assurance concerning the "physical communication" of the Active Intelligent Cause, about which he remarks: "I believe this possible, like all other communications. As for my own testimony, it would not have much weight, since this kind of proof should be personal to obtain the complete effect. Nevertheless, as I believe I speak to a man of moderation, I will not withhold from you that in the school through which I passed, more than twenty-five years ago, communications of all kinds were numerous and frequent, in which I had my share, like many others; and that, in this share, every sign indicative of the Repairer was present. Now, you know that the Repairer and Active Cause are one." He adds, however, a qualification: "As I was introduced by an initiation, and the danger of all initiations is lest we should be delivered over to the violent spirits of the world, I cannot answer that the forms which showed themselves to me may not have been assumed forms, for the door is open to all initiations, and this is what makes these ways so faulty and suspicious. The whole earth is full of these prodigies; but, I repeat, unless things come from the Centre itself I do not give them my confidence. I can assure you I have received by the inward way truths and joys a thousand times higher than those I have received from without."‡ The source of the illusion in question is the astral region; the Centre is the inward Word; and by the development of this Word within us, if I understand Saint-Martin rightly, the powers which surround the centre may be made to produce their forms according to the designs of the Word, and this is the source of the higher class of manifestations. But even then it is not the true form which is exhibited, but a reflex of that

---

*   *Correspondance,* Lettre x; Penny, "Theosophic Correspondence,"p. 44-45.

†   Ibid. Lettre xxiv; ibid. p. 91.

‡   Ibid. Lettre xix; ibid. p. 76-77.

which every spirit produces according to the essence of its thought. I must not say that this is either clear in itself or susceptible of ready elucidation; but the point to be marked is this, that Saint-Martin, ever fascinated by the experiences which he had renounced, regards them always with an indulgent eye. They were much less tainted, he affirms, than those which abounded at the period in other theurgic schools, "or, if they were tainted, there was a fire of life and desire in us all which preserved us, and even took us graciously on our way."*

It remains to point out that, since, after the lapse of a quarter of a century, and after entering another path, Saint-Martin admitted that in his occult experiences there was every sign indicative of the presence of the Repairer, the powers at the disposition of Pasqually were of no ordinary kind. And this said, it may be well to point out that the Spanish theurgist was not an adventurer in any sense of the word: he sought neither fame nor money; and the exalted religious motive with which he appears to have been actuated produced fruit quite outside the sphere of occult operation, as, for example, in the case of Cazotte.†

At the same time, when every allowance has been made for the insufficient nature of the records, there is nothing in the cases which have been here passed under review to show that the experiences consequent on the operations were other than subjective. They possess their importance if regarded from that moderate standpoint, which also justifies abundantly their renunciation by Saint-Martin in favour of another way, also confessedly subjective, but, because it is devoid of results in the sensible order, free from those dangers and follies commonly included by the term "hallucination." With this reservation upon the efficacy of the theurgic processes taught to his disciples by Pasqually, there seems ground for distinguishing in his pretensions a genuine purpose and a claim advanced seriously, while his connection with one or other of the fraternities which from time to time have adopted the name Rosicrucian is not unlikely in itself, and becomes almost plausible if we remember that the occult operations of these bodies, so far as we can glean anything concerning them, are open to the same strictures regarding objective effects as those of the Elect Cohens.

---

* *Correspondance,* Lettre xxiv; Penny, "Theosophic Correspondence," p. 92

† Matter, *Saint-Martin,* pp. 56, 57.

III

In the Inward Man

I SHALL HAVE OCCASION later on to indicate certain points in which the doctrine of Saint-Martin differs from that of other mystics, even of the school to which he approximates. But in himself, his vocation, his interests, he differed conspicuously from most leaders of the Hidden Life. In the first place, he led that life, as we have seen, in the high places of society; he did this truly in view of his mission, but he confesses that he loved the world, that he loved society, though he detested the spirit which imbued it.[*] The professed mystics of the Latin Church were monks and even hermits. Ruysbrœck is a typical instance of the life of complete isolation. The preaching mystic, like Tauler, was a voice heard among men; but it was a voice only, though crowds were drawn by its magic. Of the immediate precursors of Saint-Martin the world was impossible to Böhme, as much by the nature of his gift as by the meanness of his sphere, and Martines de Pasqually was a mere name, an oracle, a formula of magic, giving no account of its origin, and passing quickly to that bourne whence no accounts can come, except also as oracles. The Unknown Philosopher, on the other hand, was always in evidence, a man of many friends, of strong attachments. But, further, the range of mystic interests is usually narrow in the temporal order, because its concerns are in the infinite. Saint-Martin is almost the only mystic

---

[*] *Portrait Historique, Œuvres Posthumes,* vol. i. p. 100.

who was also in his way a politician, with a scheme for the reconstruction of society; an amateur in music; an apprentice in poetry; a connoisseur in *belles lettres;* a critic of his contemporaries; an observer of the times; a physician of souls truly, but in that capacity with his finger always on the pulse of the world. Yet he was not less a true mystic, and as such his disengaged hand was also on his own pulse. As regards the latter, he did what most mystics do not, he registered its variations, and thus it is that he has left us, obviously designed for publication, the precious indices of his memorial notes. To present them as they are found—and these are a selection only at the beginning of his posthumous works—would itself make a small volume, and I must limit myself to those only which seem essential keys to the inward life of the mystic.

Let us observe, first of all, what he has to tell us of the nature of his mission, the fulfilment of which was the governing passion of his life. "My task in this world has been to lead the mind of man by a natural path to the supernatural things which of right belong to him, but of which he has lost all conception, in part by his degradation, in part by the frequently false instruction of his teachers. This task is new but full of difficulty, and it is so slow that its best fruits must be borne after my death. At the same time it is so vast and so certain, that I must be deeply grateful to Providence for having charged me therewith; it is a task which no one has exercised heretofore, because those who have instructed and still instruct us daily exact in doing so either a blind submission or retail only miraculous stories."* It does not follow that Saint-Martin always attained his ideal, but the fact that his intention finds expression in such terms should distinguish at least one mystic from the makers of dark counsel and the purveyors of superstition with whom the mind even of this age identifies them.

The foundation upon which he built was laid at the age of eighteen, when, in the midst of the philosophical confessions offered him in books, he exclaimed: "There is a God, I have a soul, and no more is wanted for wisdom!"† He regarded all the circumstances of his life as the steps of a ladder which God had set beside him to assist his ascent

---

*   *Portrait Historique, Œuvres Posthumes,* vol. i. p. 137.

†   Ibid. p. 5.

towards Him. "He did not will that I should have any consolations, any joys, any lights, any substantial happiness from any hand but His own, and His sole object was that I should abide exclusively with Him."* The consciousness of this election was written, he records, in his destiny from the earliest years; and that there was no presumption in the assurance or the positive terms of the expression is best shown by its abiding presence and development in all the epochs of his life. It is shown further, as in all true mystics, by the no less abiding sense of his own unworthiness, and by the humility which that sense begot. "All that I desire is to defend myself from vicious inclinations, from false pleasures, illusory attachments, unreal sufferings, and ever to be prostrate in humility."† Again: "The greater the work which awaits me, and to which I am called, the more it preserves me from pride, for I am the more conscious that it is impossible for me to accomplish it of myself."‡ To this consciousness may be added the realisation that he possessed no gifts to distinguish him from the rest of men. "I know that they and I are alike the sons of God alone; I am so persuaded of the nobility of this origin that I have striven my best to preserve some shreds of my baptismal certificate."§

Among the faults which he laments he includes sensuality as his characteristic rather than sensibility, and adds his opinion that all men of good faith will make the same confession. Women, on the other hand, are inclined more by nature to sensibility than to sensuality.‖ We should wrong Saint-Martin, however, if we understood the term in its coarser significance, or at least if we conceived him the victim of the passions which it implies. I do not mean that he never had to reproach himself with such errors; there is some evidence to the contrary in the earlier part of his life, but he crushed these inclinations with success; and no one subsequently could boast of purer affections, a higher ideal of love, or a greater horror of impurity. "It is for me a great suffering to listen to light talk concerning that sublime love which is the true and only term of our work. Men do not realise that this beautiful word should never be pronounced by us except in the

---

*   *Portrait Historique, Œuvres Posthumes,* vol. i. p. 7.

†   Ibid. pp. 37-38.   ‡ Ibid. p. 73.   § Ibid. p. 8.

‖   Ibid. pp. 6-7.

same way that it is uttered by God—by living achievements, by living benefits, by living marvels."* I have stated already that Saint-Martin never married, and this is to be accounted for by other reasons than the modest nature of his fortune. The first of these which he records is philosophical rather than spiritual. "I felt that the man who is free has only one problem to resolve, but that he who is married has a twofold problem presented!"† There was, however, a deeper ground, and he confessed to Kirchberger that since God had given Himself to man, he considered that man was not entitled to transfer himself to another except at the command of God.‡ Here the philosopher again passes into the mystic, and as such awaits the direction for which he looked always in matters of real moment, and without which, as in this case, he never acted. Neither reason seems, however, to have satisfied him quite, and his frequent recurrence to this theme seems to indicate that in reality he was looking anxiously for direction. "I feel in the depth of my being a voice which tells me that I come from a country wherein there are no women, and hence it is, no doubt, that all marital designs planned in my regard have been failures."§ He hastens to add that this notwithstanding he honoured and loved women; indeed his lonely life was brightened by many memorable female friendships. At the same time it must be admitted that he had physical and metaphysical views on the subject of woman which are not altogether worthy of so liberal a philosopher and a friend so amiable, though they are not unconsonant with certain acrid notes in other departments of mystic thought. We must pass over these as we can and remember that the eye of the human mind can never be fixed exclusively upon one object, equally remote and exalted, and yet retain its vision unimpaired for those, or some of those, which are at hand. Thus, in things frequent, in matters of daily life, in the interests of the ordinary man, the mystic standpoint is always bizarre for the vulgar, and the solutions offered by the mystic to recurring problems, when not obviously impracticable, are almost always unac-

---

*   *Portrait Historique, Œuvres Posthumes,* vol. i. p. 12.

†   Ibid. p. 29.

‡   *Correspondance,* Lettre lxii; Penny, "Theosophic Correspondence," p. 188.

§   *Portrait Historique, Œuvres Posthumes,* vol. i. 66.

ceptable. The celibacy of Saint-Martin was perhaps the natural state for Saint-Martin, though for persons in the world it is a misfortune when it is not an outrage; with him it was a matter of election, and he gives the clue to it when he says: "I have never loved anything outside God more than I have loved God without experiencing suffering and misfortune. I have never returned to the love of God above all things without the consciousness of rebirth and happiness never failing to come back to me."* And the reason he also gives us: "If I had failed to find God, my spirit would have been unable to fix itself upon anything on earth."† Two results followed naturally, the sense of isolation, by which the mystic, whether in or out of the world, has always the lot of the recluse, and the sense of the necessity of Divine union. "When I have had the joy of perseverance for a time in the path of wisdom, I have become quickly in respect of other men as a nation set apart and speaking a strange language; the attempt to approach them or make myself understood among them is equally labour in vain. It is for this reason that those who are devoted to truth so easily become anchorites.‡ And as regards the second point we have his short summary of all prayer and aspiration, expressing, as he tells us, that which from all time was the real desire of his soul: "My God, be Thou with me so entirely that none save Thyself can be with me!"§

That he did experience a degree of this union is shown by a passage in his correspondence, occasioned by Kirchberger's glowing description of the spiritual nuptials of the German mystic Gichtel: "If I were near you," he says, "I could give you a story of a marriage in which the same way was followed with me, though under different forms, ending in the same result. I have also numerous proofs of the Divine protection over me, especially during our Revolution, of which I was not without indications beforehand. But in all this everything has been done for me as if for a child, whereas our friend Gichtel could attack the enemy in front, in which I should not acquit myself as he did. In a word, for me it is peace, and this is with me wheresoever I am. On the famous 10th of August, when I was shut up in Paris, traversing the streets all the day, amidst the great tumult, I had such signal proofs of

---

*   *Portrait Historique, Œuvres Posthumes,* vol. i. 32.

†   Ibid. p. 37.   ‡ Ibid. p. 27.   § Ibid. p. 21.

what I tell you that I was humbled even to the dust, and this the more because I had absolutely no part in what was doing, and I am not so constituted as to possess what is called physical courage."*

Another passage, in a later letter, describes in mystical language some of the inward experiences of Saint-Martin, and is worth citing, because it proves that he did not deceive himself as to the extent of his spiritual progress: "The person I speak of has known the Crown sensibly for these eighteen years, and not only does he not as yet possess it, but it is exclusively within these last years that he even comprehends it in its true substantial relations, although he understood it numerically from the first acquaintance. Know further, that for nearly twenty-five years he has been acquainted with the voice of anger and the voice of love, but that it is within the last few months alone that he has been able to distinguish between them, either by sound, impression, or direction. He is yet far from the full light on this head, and hopes daily for its increase."†

In the midst of much personal discontent, which made the way of penitence not only the safest road, but also the sweetest and the most fruitful,‡ he seems always to have been sure of his election. "In the order of spiritual things my most lively fear was not that I should fail to be drawn from among the tares by divine mercy, but of leaving so many others among them."§ And again: "My suspensions, my privations, my tribulations alarm me not, though they afflict me. I am conscious in the midst of all this darksome anguish that a secret thread is attached to me for my preservation. I am as a man fallen into the sea, but with a rope bound about his wrist and connecting him with the vessel. He may be the sport of the waves; they will break over him, but they cannot engulph him ; he is held up, and he has a firm hope of being drawn speedily on board."‖

At times his sense of consolation assumed a stronger note: "I have said that God was my passion; I might have said more truly that I was His from the care which He has lavished upon me, by the tenacity

---

*   *Correspondance*, Lettre lx; Penny, "Theosophic Correspondence," pp. 184-185.

†   Ibid. Lettre lxxiv. Ibid. p. 247.

‡   *Portrait Historique, Œuvres Posthumes*, vol. i. p. 9.

§   Ibid. p. 48.   ‖ Ibid. p. 49.

of His goodness, in spite of all my ingratitude. Had He treated me only as I deserved, He would not have cast a glance upon me."* The sense of complete unworthiness is, however, seldom entirely sincere; there is at least a sub-conscious understanding that its presence is to be counted for worth, and Saint-Martin knew well enough that there was pure metal in his interior constitution. We find accordingly one daring aspiration in his notes: "My God, I trust, in spite of all my faults, that Thou still wilt find something within me for Thy consolation."† It has at first sight a verbal touch of impiety, but that which was within Saint-Martin was, according to Saint-Martin, the Divine. With these aspirations and these convictions it does not need to be said that he longed eagerly and longed early for the end of his exile. He tells us that he adored death as much as he hated war,‡ and though without enemies, and denying that he had any real misfortunes in this life, that he felt himself able to pray for release from the burden of the world, not tomorrow, if God willed, but immediately. The sentiment was in harmony with his philosophy and the outcome of his experience. "I have never found peace except in proportion as I ascended towards the world of realities, so that I could compare it with ours, and thus convince myself that this earthly, temporal, social, political world is only as a figure of speech."§ And hence the chief ambition which he possessed while in it was, he says, to be no longer in it, "so much did I feel myself a man misplaced and a stranger here below."‖ At the close of his sixth decade he felt, so to speak, the opening of a new world. "My spiritual hopes grow as they advance. And I also advance, thanks to God, towards the great joys which were proclaimed to me from long ago."¶ When he felt that his end was approaching, he said: "My corporal and spiritual life has been too well cared for by Providence for me to have anything but gratitude to render, and I ask only God's aid to be in readiness."° At the close of the memorial notes, referring again to the end, he summed up his course as follows: "I will not say that I have passed through the world, for, in truth, I have passed only beside it, as in fortune so in honours, as in worldly plea-

---

* *Portrait Historique, Œuvres Posthumes*, vol. i. p. 108.

† Ibid. p. 108.   ‡ Ibid. p. 111.   § Ibid. p. 105-106.

‖ Ibid. p. 115.   ¶ Ibid. p. 129.   ° Ibid. p. 136.

sures so even in those pure and living joys which some are permitted to taste who, not being drawn into the career which I have followed, have been free to yield to the delicious sentiments of the heart. But I will also say that I have passed by the tribulations of the ambitious, the agonies of the covetous, the dreadful blows sustained so often by those souls who have yielded to their tenderness, and to all the motions of their desires. Having been spared, therefore, the misfortunes and distresses of the world, so far from lamenting the privation of its advantages, I will thank God unceasingly that He has granted me far more than all the pleasures of all the ages collective could have ever afforded me."*

I think that we may confess with Saint-Martin that one of the gifts of his spirit was "to desire ardently the manifestation of the Kingdom."

Besides the little history of inward life which has been here gathered up, the memorial notes contain many indications of moment as to the doctrines of the mystic, and many spiritual maxims of great beauty and great acuteness for which a place will be found later on. They also present Saint-Martin in the aspect of a literary man, and we can learn from them that he loved his books, mainly in his capacity as philosopher, for the truths which were contained in them, as apostle for the mission which they represented, but also and certainly, though a little covertly, as author for the children of his talent, dwelling over the circumstances which occasioned them, the places in which they were written, sorrowing occasionally at their imperfections, like a discerning father, and frequently explaining to himself why they were unacceptable to his age, or why rather, since as a fact they were neither unknown nor rejected, they failed to secure that full measure of recognition which his sense of mission required. In this connection we should remember that his writings were the work of a man who neither looked for light in books nor commended that course to others. "The works which I have composed have no other end than to persuade my readers to abandon all books, not excepting my own."† This, however, was in the last degrees only of interior progress.

---

*   *Portrait Historique, Œuvres Posthumes,* vol. i. pp. 137-138.

†   Ibid. p. 7.

"Books," as he says elsewhere, "are the windows of truth, but they are not the door; they point out things to men, but they do not impart them."[*] His own writings he regarded less as an instruction than as a warning and an exhortation.[†] "It is in man himself that we should write, think, and speak, not merely on paper."[‡] At the same time he declares also in his enthusiasm that all the paper of the world would be insufficient for what he alone had to say.[§] Whatsoever he wrote was actuated by tender love for man;[||] while he recognised its obscurity and imperfection, he was convinced also that it rested on a solid and impregnable foundation, which made form of minor importance, though a just criticism would admit that of all spiritual writers his form is the least repellent. "Those having soul," he concludes, "will lend to my work what is wanted, but the soulless will deny it even that which it has."[¶]

---

[*]   *Portrait Historique, Œuvres Posthumes,* vol. i. p. 62.

[†]   Ibid. p. 33.   [‡] Ibid. p. 34-35.   [§] Ibid. p. 13.

[||]   Ibid. p. 42.   [¶] Ibid. p. 129.

IV

Later History of Martinism

S AINT-MARTIN HAS been represented frequently as the founder of a corporate school which, under the name of Martinism, is supposed to have existed for the propagation of his peculiar doctrines. There is some warrant for supposing that, without rites or lodges, he may have attached to himself certain chosen disciples, and that thus a school arose, which has been erroneously represented as a rite of Masonry, affiliated with the German Illuminati of Weishaupt. The question is involved in obscurity, and to elucidate it is as yet scarcely possible; some manifest mistakes which have arisen may, however, be indicated briefly. Unpublished sources of information exist, I believe, in France, and in these may be contained the solution of the difficulties, but they are not likely to be available till those who now hold them have passed them through the literary channel.*

---

* I am much indebted, however, to Dr. Papus for some items of information which he has kindly furnished me, but too late to be incorporated in the text of this study. The most important has reference to certain communications, a list of which is possessed by my correspondent. They were received by the Chevaliars Bienfaisants de la Cité Sainté, working apparently in common. "But," says Dr. Papus, "the *Being* who brought these communications, who also was called by them the Unknown Philosopher (afterwards the pseud-onym of Saint-Martin), appeared one day and burned part of his instruc-tions." Two volumes remain in MS, and are said to have been used largely by Saint-Martin in the composition of his first work.

I write therefore subject to every correction which can be made by more extended knowledge.

The latest historian in England of the Secret Societies, Mr. C. W. Heckethorn* states that Saint-Martin to some extent reformed the rite of Pasqually, dividing it into ten degrees, classed in two temples: "The first temple comprised the degrees of Apprentice, Fellow-Craft, Master, Ancient Master, Elect, Grand Architect and Master of the Secret. The degrees of the second temple were Prince of Jerusalem, Knight of Palestine, and Knight of Kadosh. The Order, as modified by him, extended into the principal cities of France, Germany, and Russia, where the celebrated Prince Repnin (1734-1801) was its chief protector." Mr. Heckethorn also adds that the Order is now extinct. We have here the Unknown Philosopher presented as the secret chief of a vast organisation extended over the great part of Europe. Mr. Heckethorn, however, has entirely disregarded the recent and most reliable sources of information, and his work, laborious though it may be, is very far from representing the existing state of knowledge on the subject of secret societies. For the statement concerning Saint-Martin no authority is cited, but I infer that it has been derived from French sources through Mr. John Yarker, who, so far back as the year 1872, gives substantially the same information,† and at the present day would possibly be open to correct it.

There is good ground for the opinion that subsequent to the death of Pasqually Saint-Martin had a certain connection with the rite which he instituted,‡ for we know by his posthumous works that he read papers on mystic subjects to his fellow-initiates at Lyons. There is no reason, however, for supposing that he had any directing connection, and much less the authority implied in a power to reform the rite.

---

* "Secret Societies of all Ages and Nations," vol. i. pp. 217-218.

† "Notes on the Scientific and Religious Mysteries of Antiquity."

‡ Dr. Papus has since informed me, on the authority of his documents, that Saint-Martin substituted individual initiation for initiation in Lodge, and that in this manner he propagated Martinism in Russia during the reign of Catherine the Great. For the character and method of this initiation consult his own statement, pp. 184-185 of the present work. It should be noted also that the Russian visit referred to is wholly unknown to all Saint-Martin's biographers.

M. Gence tells us[*] that, after the death of its founder, the school of Martines was transferred to Lyons, and the documents published by the French occultist Papus substantiate this statement, because they establish clearly that the acting head of the Order, J. B. Willermoz, was actually located at Lyons at the period of Pasqually's departure for St. Domingo, and there continued. The Order was introduced into Lyons in 1767. In 1774 the death of the Grand Sovereign left his deputy at the head of affairs, in which position I judge that he continued at least till the year 1790. It is not therefore correct that the Elect Cohens ceased to exist in 1778, as stated by M. Gence, nor, as we shall see later on, is the Order entirely extinct at the present day, despite the assertion of Mr. Heckethorn. Nor did it reappear in the society of the Grand Profés and that of the Philalethes, though Papus may be correct in affirming that the latter organisation, together with the Illuminati of Avignon and the Academy of True Masons of Montpellier, "derive directly from Martinism."[†] The statement, however, can be true in the ease of the Illuminati of Avignon only by supposing that this body divided from the Elect Cohens at a very early period, for it was established by the Benedictine alchemist Pernety in 1766. Now, the first apparition of Pasqually is said to have been at Paris in the year 1754.[‡] He was then about forty years of age, but at the beginning only of his Masonic career. As to the Rite of Philalethes, it was invented by Savalette de Langes, keeper of the royal treasury, in 1775, in which year Saint-Martin first published his work, *Des Erreurs et de la Vérité*. The Rite had twelve degrees, of which the ninth was that of "Unknown Philosopher." We have independent evidence for determining that this name was not borrowed from the pseudonym then first adopted by Saint-Martin, as it was applied to a tran-

---

[*]   Cited in the preface to Penny's translation of the "Theosophic Correspondence."

[†]   *Martines de Pasqually,* p. 151

[‡]   The authorities are Matter, who may perhaps have followed Caro, but was usually careful in ascertaining his dates, and Papus (p. 150), who ought to be well informed. But it is right to add that, according to C. A. Thory, *Acta Latomorum,* vol. i. p. 93, the Propaganda of Pasqually did not begin at Paris till 1768. The later date of course embarrasses still further the alleged derivation of the Rite of Avignon.

scendental visitant familiar to the followers of Pasqually. According to M. Gence,* the Order of the Philalethes professed ostensibly the doctrines of Martines and Swedenborg, but pursued in reality "the secret of the philosophical work," and there is independent evidence in abundance for their alchemical enthusiasm. On the same authority, it is said that Saint-Martin was invited in 1784 to the association of the Philalethes, "but he refused to participate in the proceedings of its members, who seemed to him to speak and act only as Freemasons, and not as true initiates, that is, as united to their principle."[†]

It is otherwise perfectly clear from the life and writings of Saint-Martin that he had no Masonic interests.[‡] He loved no mysteries save those of God, Man, and the Universe; and having taken the inward way, he is the last person to connect with schisms and reformations in rites. M. Gence, however, says that he joined meetings cheerfully where the members "occupied themselves sincerely in the exercises of solid virtue." I take this to mean that he kept up some kind of communication with his original centre at Lyons, against which must be placed the much more significant testimony of all his letters, which refer invariably to his theurgic experiences as matters of the far past. In either case, he was in regular correspondence with the existing chief of the Elect Cohens—that is to say, with Willermoz; and Papus states, on the authority of that correspondence, that the theurgic operations of Willermoz frequently drew Saint-Martin to Lyons. But the affairs of the Order, as I have said, were altogether in the hands of its chief, who, in conjunction with Sellonf, the president of the Grand Lodge of Masters, representing the French Rite, and with Jacques Willermoz, his brother, president of the Chapter of Knights of the Black Eagle, representing the Templar Rite, is said to have formed a secret council having the Masonic centres at Lyons in the hollow of its hand.[§] It was owing to the

---

* Penny, "Theosophic Correspondence," p. v.

† In the *Acta Latomorum,* vol. ii. p. 376, Saint-Martin was invited, it is said, to the Convention of Paris, 1785, but refused to attend. Mesmer at the same time acted in the same manner. Ibid. i. 160.

‡ Thory, however, affirms (ibid. i. 223) that he left a ms. entitled *L'Écossime Réformé,* in 2 vols. but does not indicate its whereabouts or mention any authority for the statement.

§ Papus, *Martines de Pasqually* p. 153.

activity of Willermoz that the celebrated Masonic conventions—that of Lyons (1778) and that of Wilhelmsbad (1782)—were organised, at the latter the business being regarded as of such importance that he remained for two years as a deputy.

As a result of this conference a great change seems to have taken place in German Masonry, which passed under the influence of the Elect Cohens. Unfortunately the evidence concerning it is in a state of inextricable confusion, and though I have sifted it with great care, I do not pretend to have placed the result in any sense beyond criticism. Mr. Heckethorn, having mentioned the importance of the Congress, which, under the presidency of the Duke of Brunswick, was attended by Masons from Europe, America, and Asia, informs us that "the result of the Convention of Wilhelmsbad was the retention of the three symbolical degrees, with the addition of a new degree, that of the 'Knights of Beneficence,' which was based on the principles enunciated in Saint-Martin's books, *Des Erreurs et de la Vérité* and the *Tableau Naturel.*"[*] He adds: "Another result was a league between Masonry and the Illuminati, brought about by the exertions of Weishaupt." The grafting of a mystical degree upon the degrees of Craft Masonry, and the amalgamation or junction of both with a society which was revolutionary and infidel, is a heterogeneous and unlikely proceeding, which, if it ever took place, came very speedily to an end, for the Illuminati were forcibly suppressed in 1786. We may picture the feelings of Saint-Martin at his identification with the principles of Nicolai.

Yet he had a closer connection with the mystic grades of Masonry, if we are to accept the evidence of another witness who has recently seceded from modern Martinism—that is to say, from the Order which Mr. Heckethorn affirms to be now extinct. This witness is Jules Doinel,[†] who, since his conversion to Catholicism, has given us a full account of the Knights of Beneficence, more correctly the *Chevaliers Bienfaisants de la Cite Sainte.* The laws regulating this chivalry were, he tells us, definitely framed by a national convention in 1778—that is to say, by the Convention of Lyons, not that of Wilhelmsbad, and

---

[*]   "Secret Societies of all Ages and Nations," vol. p. 62.

[†]   *Lucifer D*émasqué, par Jean Kostka (*i.e,* Jules Doinel), p. 274 *et seq.*

that one of its members was Saint-Martin himself. Cazotte was also a member. When we come, however, to the description of the society, we see that it is not a degree superposed upon Craft Masonry, but an elaborate system subdivided into three classes of knighthood, and its ritual, so far from being based on the works or exhibiting the influence of Saint-Martin, is merely a version of the Templar legend.

The third witness to be cited is Mr. John Yarker,[*] who knows nothing of the Convention of Lyons, and something different from those who have preceded him about that of Wilhelmsbad. What was really established thereat was the "Reformed Rite," consisting of "two degrees above Craft Masonry, namely: IV, Scotch Master; V, Charitable Knight of the Holy City." It passed into Poland under the name of the "Reformed Helvetic Rite." For this witness it has apparently no connection with Martinism; it was a modification of the Rite of Strict Observance, founded in 1754 by Baron Hund, and itself a fusion of the Rite of the Chapter of Clermont with Templar principles and notions. This genealogy accounts well enough for the character of the occult chivalry whose mysteries have been unveiled by Jules Doinel. Unfortunately it accounts for nothing else, for the Convention of Wilhelmsbad, after thirty sittings, rejected the Templar theory of Masonry, and was therefore not at all likely to institute a Templar rite.

If we now have recourse to Papus,[†] we shall find, at first sight, that he seems only to increase the confusion, and that on this important point the archives of the Martinists have failed him. He says: "After the Revolution Willermoz continued single-handed the work of his initiator by amalgamating the Rite of the Elect Cohens with the Illuminism of Baron Hund for the formation of the Eclectic Rite," certain grades of which were, he adds, purely Martinistic. As to the last point, the authority he cites is Mounier[‡] who wrote in refutation of Robison,[§] but there is nothing decisive in the quotation. It is certain that

---

[*] "Notes on the Scientific and Religious Mysteries of Antiquity."

[†] Martines de Pasqually, p. 210.

[‡] *De l'influence attribuée aux Philosophes, aux Franc-Maçons et aux Illuminés sur la Révolution de France.* Paris, 1801.

[§] "Proofs of a Conspiracy against all the Religions and Governments of Europe," &c. Though extremely unreliable, this work is not without importance for the history of Martinism.

Baron Hund was not an Illuminé in the sense that he belonged to the Order founded by Weishaupt, whom he preceded in Masonic activity by many years, nor was his system in the German sense Illuminism. By a curious contradiction, it was both Catholic, Jacobite, and Templar. Now, Papus tells us elsewhere that "it follows from the letters of Pasqually that the Martinists, far from supporting the brethren of the Templar Rite in their political projects, on the contrary were always at war with them." * Finally, the fusion of the Elect Cohens with the Strict Observance could not have produced Eclectic Masonry after the Revolution as its result. The Eclectic Rite appears to have been founded at Frankfurt in 1783 by Baron Knippe, also a member of the Illuminati, to check the spread of the philosophic rites.

Out of this chaos it is possible, however, to develop a certain order, if we compare it with other statements made by Papus, for which he has the authority of the surviving archives of the Martinist Rite. "After the convention of Wilhelmsbad, at which Martinism had played so important a part, an alliance was concluded between the Martinists and the deputies of the Strict Observance.† At this period we must remember that Pasqually had been long dead, that Willermoz was a member of a Templar Rite in France, and that he did not therefore perpetuate the feud of his master. We must remember also that the condemnation of the Templar element in Freemasonry by the Convention resulted in the suspension of the Strict Observance by the Duke of Brunswick. We understand therefore why it may possibly have cast itself on the protection of the Templar Willermoz and on the Order of the Elect Cohens. The Chevaliers Bienfaisants I take to have been in existence prior to the Convention, in which case Jules Doinel is correct up to that point; he is also right in representing them as either a phase of Martinism or affiliated therewith. After the return of Willermoz to France negotiations continued between the two parties, but were interrupted by the Revolution. They were apparently renewed still later, and may have resulted in a fusion with the Eclecticism of Baron Knippe, who had long previously seceded from the Illuminati of Weishaupt. With the doings of the latter personage I

---

* *Martines de Pasqually,* p. 153.

† Ibid. p. 11.

scarcely think there could have been any connection, though a great activity is assigned him among French mystical fraternities including all under notice, in the savage and indiscriminate onslaught of Robison.* Willermoz himself was the very opposite of a revolutionary, and escaped the scaffold to which he had been condemned during the Reign of Terror by the providential expiation of Robespierre on the day prior to that which was fixed for his own execution. In any case, the later connections of Martinism are not altogether of a kind which would have commended itself to the original founder, and we assuredly do not find throughout one trace of the participation of Saint-Martin.

The death of Willermoz occurred about 1815. The archives of the Order passed into the hands of his nephew, whom he named G. M. Profés. His widow, in turn, confided them to M. Cavernier, who restored them a few years ago to the existing Lodge of Martinism at Lyons, which, though in itself of recent origin, has an uninterrupted historical connection with the Elect Cohens through the Italian and German groups.† "In 1887," says Papus, "a strong effort was made for the serious diffusion of the Order, and four years subsequently the results obtained permitted the creation of a Supreme Council comprising twenty-one members and having under its obedience a number of lodges both in France and Europe."‡ As stated in the preface to this work, it is at the present day widely diffused in America.

While anticipating that further evidence may clear up many difficulties in the history of Martinism, it seems fairly certain that by the term itself we are to understand a body of mystic doctrine, and not a Masonic Rite devised by Saint-Martin to replace the Elect Cohens. The distinction between Martinezists and Martinists made by M. Matter has now at least no existence as regards corporate societies, though it is useful to mark off the philosophical disciples of the two

---

* "Proofs of a Conspiracy," c. iv. *passim.*

† Papus, *Martines de Pasqually,* pp. 13-14.

‡ Ibid. p. 212. To this account I may now add the following affiliation of modern Martinism, with which Dr. Papus has supplied me. (1) Saint-Martin. (2) M. de Chaptal (a name previously unknown in the history of the Order). (3) Henri Delaage (a pupil of Éliphas Lévi, and author of *La Science du Vrai,* and other works still in memory among the literati of French occultism).

systems. The sole Masonic activity discoverable in Saint-Martin after the departure of Pasqually is confined to a few mystical papers which he seems to have read before the brethren of the Lodge at Lyons. There is evidence, however, that his books were much in vogue among the lodges of transcendental Masonry, and may have been utilised by his admirers, with or without his own concurrence, in the manufacture of later grades and their rituals. It is in this sense that we may understand and accept the statement of Robison that the book *Des Erreurs et de la Vérité* was "a sort of holy scripture, or at least a Talmud among the Freemasons of France."*

---

*   "Proofs of a Conspiracy," 3rd edition, 1798, pp. 44-45.

Book II

Sources of Martinistic Doctrine

.

I

Reception and Tradition

T HE EVENTUAL RETIREMENT of Saint-Martin from an active
connection with the Elect Cohens did not signify his alien-
ation from its fundamental principles, just as the fusion of
the Order with a form of Templar Masonry which offered nothing
to Mysticism produced no rupture in his amicable relations with
Willermoz, who had brought about this event. From the date of the
departure of Martines de Pasqually to that of the Convention of Wilhelmsbad, the esoteric doctrines of the theurgic school, mainly, but
by no means entirely, apart from its theurgic practices, remained the
ruling principles of Saint-Martin's philosophy. There is no trace whatsoever of such an estrangement between himself and his first master
as his biographer Matter imagines.* There is evidence to show that
Saint-Martin distrusted from the beginning the path of theurgic operation as the direct road to the Divine in the universe. We have it on
his own authority that he confided his doubts to his teacher: "Master,
can all these things be needed to find God?" † And there is something
in the response of his teacher, "We must even be content with what
we have," to indicate that he also regarded them as substitutes, in
which case he was in no real disagreement with his disciple, who, a
quarter of a century later, confessed his belief that the Divine Wis-

---

*   *Saint-Martin,* pp. 66, 72, 73, 270, &c.
†   *Correspondance,* Lettre iv.; Penny, "Theosophic Correspondence," p. 16.

dom made use of intermediary agents to communicate His Word to the interior man.* What he doubted, therefore, was the substitution of the outward communion for the inward illumination. At the same time it is certain that Saint-Martin was engaged for more than two years after the death of Pasqually in practical experiences with his friend the Comte d'Hauterive, which were partly magnetic and partly theurgic in character.

The alleged estrangement between initiator and initiate is based by M. Matter in reality on the fact that after the year 1772 communication did not continue between them, which is perfectly true; but we know what M. Matter had no means of ascertaining at the time, that this was owing to the departure and death of Pasqually, to which considerably later dates were assigned by all authorities prior to the publication of the Martinistic archives by Papus. Finally, as there was separation but not estrangement, so there was no such return to the principles of the master, as M. Matter discovers in the later correspondence of Saint-Martin.† M. Matter, it should be added, did his best, and with admirable results, on the materials that were available at his time. He is the fullest, the most faithful, and, on the whole, most sympathetic of Saint-Martin's biographers, writing from the standpoint of the literary critic, and not at all of the mystic. As a literary performance the memoir of Franck is superior, but it owes nearly all its material to the careful collector who preceded it; whereas M. Matter himself owes nothing, or next to nothing, to the incidental thesis of Moreau, or to the dull if patient digest of M. Caro. There are three epochs in the philosophical career of Saint-Martin which are very clearly denned in his books. In the first, his mystical mind worked almost exclusively on the notions which he derived from the school of Martines de Pasqually. To this we owe his first publication, "Of Errors and of Truth," and its sequel, the "Natural Table of the Correspondences between God, Man, and the Universe." Having regard to his peculiar views and to the period at which they were put forth, I do not see that he could well have made a better beginning than he made in his earliest book. It has many bizarre elements, many strange and

---

*   *Correspondance*, Lettre iv.; Penny, "Theosophic Correspondence," p. 14.

†   *Saint-Martin*, pp. 270-272.

unaccountable views on politics, sociology, and *belles lettres,* which were calculated to challenge opinion; and opinion accepted the challenge, bringing thus into notice a system which, had it been merely mystical, a guide to the devout life, a theosophy without a theocracy, less of a gage thrown down at the door of every fashionable doctrine, would have missed its mark because it would have passed unheeded. In his second work Saint-Martin has less call to impress and startle. It is accordingly more collected, less comprehensive, but more complete in its sphere; it is also far more intelligible, and far better in its literary expression. The second epoch embraces a period which has been referred by some, at least partially, to the influence of Swedenborg. It began with the "Man of Aspiration" and ended with the "New Man." It is a period of inspiration and poetic fervour, of ardent desire after the lost perfection of humanity in its primeval union with the Divine. In a word, the philosopher has passed more definitely into the mystic. There is also an increased literary facility, which, though it never approaches the perfect gift of style, exercises a certain fascination and produces a certain *entrainement.*

The third period includes all the later life of Saint-Martin, and is represented by "The Spirit of Things" and the "Ministry of Man the Spirit." In the first of these Works the author seems to pass in review over much of the ground traversed at the beginning of his literary career, but the essays which comprise it are too detached and occasional in character to produce a homogeneous result. We have, rather, selections from the note-book of a mystic on a variety of subjects, all interesting, all treated unexpectedly, but nothing new that can be regarded as of the first importance. This period is that of the influence of Jacob Böhme, which does not, however, appear specifically except in the "Ministry," the last and most mature work of the author, a further consideration of which must be deferred to the next section.

Through all these works the mind of Saint-Martin predominates; he is at all times an originator rather than a follower; an initiator, not a disciple merely. The influence of his first school also persists throughout, but it is more than modified: it is transfigured. For example, the central doctrine of Reintegration is undoubtedly that of Pasqually, as the MS. Treatise by the latter makes evident; but it has become something "rich and strange" by the illumination of Saint-Martin's gift.

The Martinistic philosophy of numbers is also a special inheritance from the theurgic school, and will help us in its place to determine within certain limits the source of Pasqually's own initiation, and the importance, such as it is, which may be granted to his system from a purely occult standpoint.

That the system expounded by Saint-Martin in his two initial works was in its fundamental elements a reception by tradition will be quite evident to the occultist from the fact that it entailed reticence on several points of importance. In the treatise on "Errors and Truth" there are, however, two kinds of reticence which it is necessary to distinguish. It was the design of Saint-Martin to lead back the mind of his age to Christianity, as understood by himself; but he judged, not altogether incorrectly, that the mind of the age was in no mood to tolerate an explicit defence of Christianity. He "wrote for the rationalists and materialists who had possession of the literary world in France, who made ridicule of the Gospel, and, indeed, were unqualified to hear its acceptable sounds; at least, he wrote for the really thoughtful among them, whose pride of reason had not yet utterly shut up the understanding of the heart."[*] He therefore placed a certain veil over his doctrine, referring, for example, to Christ only under the name of the Active and Intelligent Cause. I am not sure that the device did not serve its purpose, though it looks now a little childish and scarcely calculated to deceive any one, however blinded by the "pride of reason." In any case, this species of reticence is not of any interest to readers at the present day, and it was removed by Saint-Martin himself, as might be expected, when he thought that the time had come. There is another veil, however, which he did not lift even for Baron Kirchberger, and this concerns the precise nature of his knowledge derived from initiation. In the preface to his earliest work he at once reveals the fact that he is the depositary of a secret and exclusive doctrine, and that there is a strung line beyond which he is bound not to pass in regard to it.

"For such an enterprise as that which I have undertaken more than common resources are necessary. Without specifying those which I employ, it will be enough to say that they connect with the essential

---

[*] Penny, Preface to "Theosophic Correspondence," p. xxxi.

nature of man, that they have always been known to some among mankind from the prime beginning of things, and that they will never be withdrawn wholly from the earth while thinking beings exist thereon. Thence have I derived my evidence, and thence my conviction upon truths the search after which engrosses the entire universe. After this avowal, if I am accused of disseminating an unknown doctrine, at least I must not be suspected of being its inventor, for if it connect with the nature of man, not only am I not its inventor, but it would have been impossible for me to establish any other on a solid basis. The principles here expounded are the true key of all the allegories and all the mysterious fables of every people, the primitive source of every kind of institution, and actually the pattern of those laws which direct and govern the universe, constituting all beings. In other words, they serve as a foundation to all that exists and to all that operates, whether in man and by the hand of man, whether outside man and independently of his will. Hence, in the absence of these principles there can be no real science, and it is by reason of having forgotten these principles that the earth has been given over to errors. But although the light is intended for all eyes, it is certain that all eyes are not so constituted as to be able to behold it in its splendour. It is for this reason that the small number of men who are depositaries of the truths which I proclaim are pledged to prudence and discretion by the most formal engagements." *

The claim of initiation and the indication of the bonds which it imposes could not be more clearly expressed. I confess myself unable to comprehend how it is that, in the face of this statement, some previous biographers of Saint-Martin have challenged or depreciated the influence of the theurgic school on their subject, or that his first works are expositions of the system taught in that school.

In accordance with the above indications, Saint-Martin warns his readers with equal explicitness that he has recourse to the veil, and sometimes speaks in reality of things far different from those which he seems to be discussing.† This statement will cover, no doubt, and was intended to cover, both his qualities of reticence, but it has obviously

---

* *Des Erreurs et de la Vérité,* Part I. pp. 5, 6, 7, 8, 10, edition of 1782.

† Ibid. pp. 8-9.

a special application to that which was imposed on him by the pledges to which he refers. There will be no call to extend this section by the laborious collection of cases in which he puts in practice this law of concealment, but I may mention some salient instances to show that what was covered was actually occult doctrine, as distinguished from Christian doctrine in a drapery of evasion. The mysticism of numbers will be admittedly a case in point, and let us take therefore his teaching concerning tetradic progression. It is not readily intelligible as it stands, namely, that the difference between the kinds of corporeal beings is always in tetradic geometric proportion. The progression is apparently from man to animals, from animals to vegetables, from vegetables to minerals, which are the final term of the progression of created things, as man is the second, thus inverting the alleged order of material evolution, though the instruction should perhaps be understood only of the archetypal world. This progression applies also to the beings who transcend matter, but Saint-Martin states that here his obligation prevents him from speaking clearly.[*]

For other instances we may pass from numbers and their hidden properties to the nature of man himself. Here the reserve of the adept is exercised concerning the bond which subsists between the interior act of the will and the sensible manifestation which follows it in the outward act. This, says Saint-Martin, constitutes the true royalty of man, and cannot be enlarged upon without indiscretion and danger.[†] He promises to refer to it again, but never without reserve. So also when it is affirmed that the life of man's intellectual productions is not from man himself, it is added that this is a mystery which can never be entombed sufficiently.[‡] Even the familiar doctrine concerning actives and passives, superior and inferior, is considered too exalted to be fully exposed to the eyes of the multitude,[§] while the Martinistic doctrine as to the origin of religion is sealed to the casual reader in the vase of a clumsy parable[||] The same considerations render Saint-Martin inexplicit on the subject of suffering in the animal kingdom. Why are animals so often deprived of that sensible felicity

---

[*] *Des Erreurs et de la Vérité,* Part I. pp. 60-62.

[†] Ibid. p. 152.   [‡] Ibid. p. 98.   [§] Ibid. p. 132.

[||] Ibid. p. 219 *et seq.*

which would make them happy after their own manner? "I could explain this difficulty were it permitted me to enlarge upon the bond which subsists between things, and to show how far evil has extended through the errors of man; but this is a point which I can never do more than indicate; for the moment it will be enough to say that earth is no longer virgin, which exposes both itself and its fruits to all the evils entailed by the loss of virginity." *

To quote a last instance, it is affirmed that those who have understanding may infer from the adultery of the flesh some clear indices as to the adultery of the spirit committed by man before he became subject to the law of the elements; but the obligations of Saint-Martin interdict him from any explanations on this point, and, moreover, for his own weal, he prefers to blush at the crime of man rather than to discourse of it." †

I must be excused from debating whether this law of concealment has ever guarded anything which was worth despoiling, and if so, whether it can be justified morally, and is therefore really binding on the conscience of those who subscribe to it. These are matters which will be approached differently by those who accept or reject the claims of the secret sciences, and by those, I may add, who, like M. Jules Doinel, experience a change in the substance of their honour collaterally with that of their convictions in matters of religion. I have only sought to demonstrate that Saint-Martin received by tradition some things which he believed to be of value, and that he spoke of them as he best could. ‡ I must not add that I should regard anything which he has withheld in his wisdom as fit to be compared with all

---

*   *Des Erreurs et de la Vérité*, Part I. p. 73. He justifies subsequently the sufferings of the animal world on the ground that the animals are instruments of Wisdom, and further, that the fall of man has involved both things above and things below in its consequences. *Tableau Naturel*, i. 126-131.

†   Ibid. Part II. p. 50.

‡   For other instances of reticence see *Des Erreurs et de la Vérité*, Part II. 119, 131, 149, 172, 173, 175, 186, 196, 214, 229, 230. Also *Tableau Naturel*, i. 167, which seems to refer in mysterious terms to the existence of special emissaries of darkness operating on earth and in the flesh. I have omitted further reference to the alleged transcendental origin of part of Saint-Martin's first work as beyond the scope of literary criticism.

that he has made known in his goodness, and chiefly by gifts of illumination, which are particular to no association, and do not need the technical training of an occultist to understand or profit by them. But I will add that many occult secrets—whether in the last analysis they did not exceed revelation, or the gravity of responsibility sat lighter as years went on, or time and the death of Pasqually had cancelled the considerations of concealment, or yet more probably because the missing half of revelations generally slips out by an accident—which Saint-Martin once reserved somehow escaped him afterwards. In the present examination of his philosophy it has been purged of all arbitrary oracles. I must confess that some of it continues oracular, but that is through the obscurity of the mystic and not the reservations of the adept.

II

Swedenborg and Böhme

A T THE PRESENT DAY the name of Swedenborg scarcely possesses a place in the history of occult philosophy. In the annals of occult experience it is remembered assuredly, but it connects with a quality of experience which has come to be regarded as nearly devoid of consequence. It was otherwise in France towards the close of the eighteenth century. The Swedish illuminé died in the very year that Pasqually departed to St. Domingo, but prior to both events his transcendental doctrines had become the subject and occasion of more than one Masonic Rite, and are said to have exercised an influence on that of Pasqually. The Illuminati of Avignon, founded, as we have seen, in 1766, and described doubtfully as an offshoot of Martinism, connected alchemy with the extra-mundane revelations of Swedenborg. This rite was transplanted to Paris, with certain modifications, and appeared as the Illuminated Theosophists. It had branches all over the country, and enjoyed a brief success in London. The Rite of the Philalethes, a modification of that of the United Friends, had the same inspiration. Finally, in 1783, the Rite of Swedenborg was founded by the Marquis de Thorne, and survives to this day. The English Grand Master is Mr. John Yarker. Swedenborg died in London, where he produced an immense impression for a moment, and out of his teachings there arose, both here and in his own country, an institution which has assumed the title of the Church of the New Jerusalem, but it has few followers. Swedenborg may be said in a sense to have prepared the way for Spiritualism. No man of visions and illuminations has done more than he to commonise the world of spirits. He is the one great prophet of the extra-natural world to the mediocrity of intelligence yearning for tidings there from; he brought it precisely the kind of tidings which it could understand and welcome. Other prophets and other methods of communication have now superseded him, and his ministry is therefore of the past.

There can be no doubt, of course, that for a time he was an interesting figure to the occultist, for a few on account of his visions, for more in spite of them. He had affinities with Kabalistic tradition by his law of correspondences and his doctrine of the grand man. Astrologers deciphered his horoscope; alchemists, to their own satisfaction, proved that he was a Hermetic philosopher.* This has also passed away, and the sect which represents him in England is without light, leading, or literature. It is better for a prophet to be forgotten entirely than to leave so pitiful a testimony behind him, and Swedenborg deserved assuredly a better fortune in his following. In his way he was the most gracious, most approachable, and the clearest of natural seers. He was also a man of culture, and his personal good taste is reflected in the tone of his illumination—an element which is conspicuously wanting in some revelations, supplementary to his own, which we hear of, let us say, in America.

It would be *à priori* exceedingly improbable that the mystic whose inward predilections made him avoid theurgic manifestations should be attracted by the profuse and bourgeois visions of Swedenborg. On this ground only we might be justified in dismissing the view which makes such an attraction predominate for several years in the life of Saint-Martin, and find a definite expression in some of his most important books. An examination of these will show that there was no such influence. The "New Man" was written, as we have seen, at the suggestion of the nephew of Swedenborg, but this did not mean that Saint-Martin became indoctrinated with the shallow illuminism of Swedenborg, nor that he was in any sense a recorder for Silferhielm, Saint-Martin was personally much attached to Silverhielm, and the

---

* On this point see especially an interesting piece of pleading by the late E. A. Hitchcock, published anonymously in America under the title of "Swedenborg a Hermetic Philosopher."

book represents the development of his own philosophy in the conversations which took place between them. The sole resemblance between the doctrines of the New Jerusalem and the poetic aspirations of the "New Man" is that the work of regeneration is there represented by Saint-Martin as an inward parallel of the outward life of Christ in the Gospel history; and although it is a fascinating, it is at the same time a fragile artifice, which compares a little indifferently with the masculine strength and boldness in the allegories of Pope Gregory the Great, arbitrary and strained as are these for the most part.

Fortunately, however, we possess Saint-Martin's own opinion, expressed in the "Man of Aspiration," after certain strictures on the threefold sense of Scripture according to Swedenborgian tenets.

"There are a thousand proofs in his works that he was often and highly favoured, a thousand proofs that he was often and deeply deceived, a thousand proofs that he beheld only the middle of the work, and knew neither its commencement nor its end. For the vulgar man these proofs are, however, less than nothing, for he does not suspect their existence. He is ever ready to believe everything when he finds that one thing is true; he is ever ready to deny everything upon the warrant of a single error. But what, furthermore, are the credentials of Swedenborg? He offers no proof beyond his own visions and Holy Scripture. Now, what credit will these witnesses find with the man who has not been prepared beforehand by healthy reason? Prove facts by their confirmations. Prove the principle by logic and reasoning. Never say to anyone: 'Believe in us.' Say rather: 'Believe in thyself; believe in the grandeur of thy nature, which entitles thee to expect everything and to verify everything, provided thou dost ask all from Him who giveth all.' O illustrious and estimable man! Thy writings may confer, notwithstanding, a great good, by imparting to humanity a galvanic shock in its lethargy! If they cannot provide man with a complete plan of the spiritual region, they help him to discern that it exists, and this is no slight service to render him in the abyss where the systems have plunged him." [*]

In his correspondence Saint-Martin refused to express any other opinion of Swedenborg and his writings than that which he had re-

---

[*] *L'Homme de Désir,* No. 184.

corded above, but in his memorial notes we find a single paragraph containing his final judgment: "While re-reading some extracts from Swedenborg I have been impressed that he had more of what is termed the science of souls than the science of spirits; and, in this connection, though unworthy to be compared with Böhme as regards true knowledge, it is possible that he may be suited to a greater number of people; for Böhme is intended only for men who have been regenerated wholly, or at least for those who have a great desire to be so." * In other words, Böhme's light came from the centre of that circle of which the centre, according to Hermes Trismegistus, St. Bonaventure, and Pascal, is everywhere and the circumference nowhere; but the illumination of Swedenborg came from the circumference of the same circle, namely, the astral region, which is that of illusion, and has therefore no place in reality.

To dismiss the influence of Swedenborg after appreciating it at its true extent is not a matter of difficulty, but I have now to approach a question of another order, and to show that the undoubted and real influence exercised on Saint-Martin by the writings of Jacob Böhme has also been greatly exaggerated, and by no one more than the man who has confessed to it himself. Saint-Martin, in the last analysis, was at all times *sui generis;* he did not belong to another who was able to belong to himself. † I do not mean to dispute that on the inward life of the French mystic the German theosophist did not exercise a great power and diffuse a strong light. I do not mean that the correspondence of Saint-Martin is not full of testimony to this effect. It is vivid with it; his admiration and exaltation of Böhme appear on every page. He is "not worthy to untie the shoe-strings of that wonderful man." ‡ He regards him as "the greatest light that has appeared on the earth since One who is the Light itself" § Böhme is "the abyss of knowledge and profound truths." ‖ He has a "solidity that cannot be shaken;" ¶ an "elevation and a nourishment so full and so unfailing that I confess I should think it lost time to seek elsewhere, so I

---

* *Portrait Historique, Œuvres Posthumes,* vol. i.

† The motto of Paracelsus, *"Alterius non sit qui suus esse potest."*

‡ *Correspondance,* Lettre ii; Penny, "Theoeophic Correspondence," p. 7.

§ Ibid.   ‖ Ibid.   ¶ Ibid. Lettre viii; ibid, p. 33.

have given up all other readings." * He, in fact, is the "divine writer;" †
Saint-Martin is but a stammerer compared with him. ‡ He is supreme
over all his brethren;" I find in all grandeurs of the highest order, but
he only seems to me to be really born in the thing. The others look
sometimes as if they were greater than their affair, but with him the
affair always looks greater than he." § This admiration, as he tells us,
did nothing but increase; "I feel that a prodigy like this, carefully
weighed and meditated, is all that is wanted to put oneself into the
mould naturally." To sum all, in the "grounds and developments"
which Böhme opens up may be found "the keys of every universe and
the principle of every key."

Now, I mean that this immeasurable enthusiasm does exaggerate
the influence which it represents, because it creates an indiscriminate impression concerning it. On collecting such encomiums our
legitimate inference might be that Saint-Martin, his life and his doctrines, had been merged soul and body in Böhme; that henceforth we
should find the French mystic merely giving Böhme to his country
by translation, as in fact he did, and expounding Böhme's doctrine in
substitution of his own. The inference is strengthened when we find
Saint-Martin stating that he would have written some of his books
differently had he been acquainted at the time with those of his "beloved author." ‖ But so far from this being the case, we find that the
two works which he did produce—outside his political pamphlets
and the nondescript "Crocodile"—present no fundamental differences. Apart from the revelations of his correspondence on this subject,
and apart from several references in the "Ministry of Man the Spirit,"
I do not know that it would have occurred to anyone to connect
Saint-Martin with Böhme in any very close manner. M. Gence says
that the object of the "Ministry" is to show how man, conceived as
exercising a spiritual mission, "may improve and regenerate himself
and others, by restoring the Logos to man and nature. It is from this
Word that Saint-Martin, full of the doctrine and sentiments of Jacob
Böhme, draws the life with which he here inspires his reasoning and

---

*   *Correspondance,* Lettre viii; Penny, "Theoeophic Correspondence," p. 33.

†   Ibid. Lettxe xiii; ibid. p. 57.   ‡ Ibid. Lettre xx; ibid. p. 80.

§   Ibid. Lettre lv; ibid. p. 163.   ‖ Ibid. Lettre ii; ibid. p. 7.

style."* Again, "the amelioration consists in the radical development of our inmost essence."† But this was the doctrine taught by the French mystic from the beginning; what differs is the terminology alone. We have the recurrence of the term Logos more frequently, though that is not new in Saint-Martin. In fact, M. Gence himself ends by confessing that "all his writings rest more or less on this ground."

The true key to Saint-Martin's admiration for Böhme is that he believed him to have penetrated more deeply into the same ground, and that therefore he himself had nothing to unlearn when he added the *mysterium magnum* to the *grand œuvre* of Pasqually; for he had been prepared by the one for the other, as he expressly says, during "twenty-five years of wonders, both in acts and intellectually."‡ I have quoted elsewhere the passage in which he announces his intention to marry the doctrines of Böhme with those of his early school, in which, like a shrewd observer, he laid a finger on some points which were either unknown by the German mystic or of which Böhme would not speak, even as he observed in the latter one point about which he felt constrained to watch him.§ We have indications more than once in the correspondence of his satisfaction over the union which he projected; it was not the satisfaction of an explorer keeping close upon the track of another in a strange country, but of one in an unknown region, approaching the end of his journey, meeting unexpectedly with another who has travelled the road. In the very book which is most supposed to exhibit the influence of Böhme we find Saint-Martin building on his own foundation, referring his reader point by point to his earlier books, that he might be excused from returning to the "first elements."‖

I conclude, therefore, that the mystic philosophy of Saint-Martin is Saint-Martin's own philosophy, but that he derived part of his materials from a school of Mysticism to which he was attached in early life, which will always have a claim on those who love Saint-Martin, because it was loved by him discerningly even to the end. He did not

---

* Penny, Preface to "Theosophic Correspondence." † Ibid.

‡ *Correspondance,* Lettre lxxiv; Penny, "Theoeophic Correspondence," p. 57.

§ Ibid. Lettre xiii; ibid. p. 57.

‖ *Le Ministère de l'Homme-Esprit,* pp. 21-28

reject, as became him, anything that seemed to him true and good in Swedenborg, and he accepted with a whole heart of joy and gratitude the great good and the great truth which came to him in Jacob Böhme.

As an appendix to this section, I now add a little summary of the "Teutonic Theosophy" in the words of Saint-Martin, because, in the first place, it seems to me that it will help us to understand the correspondences between the two writers, and, in the second place, because it also seems to me to in a manner that is perfectly admirable the pith and essence of the thirty treatises of Böhme by a few master-strokes.

"This German author, who has been dead for nearly two centuries, has left in his numerous writings some astonishing and extraordinary developments concerning our primitive nature; the source of evil; the essence and laws of the universe; the origin of weight; the seven powers of nature; the origin of water (confirmed by chemistry); the prevarication of the fallen angels; that also of man; and the method of rehabilitation employed by Eternal Love to reintegrate the human species in its rights. The reader will find therein that the present physical and elementary nature is only a residue and alteration of an anterior nature, called eternal by the author, and that in its entire circle it constituted formerly the empire and throne of one of the angelic princes, named Lucifer; that this prince, seeking only to reign by the power of fire and wrath, setting aside that of love and the Divine Light, which should have been his sole enlightenment, stirred up conflagration through its whole extent; that the Divine Wisdom opposed to this incendiarism a temperating and refrigerating power which circumscribed without extinguishing it, and hence comes the mixture of good and evil which we find in nature as it is; that man, formed of the principle of fire, the principle of light, and the quintessential principle of physical or elementary nature, was placed in this world to repress the guilty and dethroned king; that the quintessential principle of elementary nature should have been kept absorbed by man in the pure element which then composed his corporeal form, but that he allowed himself to be attracted by this temporal principle more than by the two others, and was dominated and put to sleep thereby; that overcome thus by the material region of this world, his pure part has been absorbed in the grosser form which now envelops him, so that he has become the subject and victim of his enemy; that the Divine Love which contemplates itself eternally in the mirror of the Divine Wisdom, termed the Virgin Sophia, perceived in this mirror, which comprises all forms, the model and spiritual form of man; that it clothed itself with this spiritual form, and afterwards with the elementary form, in order to present to man the image of what he had become and the model of that which he should be; that the actual end of man on earth is to recover physically and morally his likeness to his primitive model; that his greatest obstacle is the astral and elementary power which engenders and constitutes the world, and for which man was never made; that the actual generation of man is a speaking witness of this truth in the pain of child-bearing; that the aqueous and igneous tinctures which should be joined in man and identified with wisdom or Sophia, but are now divided, seek each other with great yearning, looking in one another for the Sophia, but finding the astral only, which oppresses and opposes them; that we are as free to restore by our efforts the original divine image to our spiritual being as to allow it to assume images which are inferior and disordered, and that whatsoever likeness we impart to it will be the mode of our being—in other words, our glory or our shame, in the state which is to come."*

I do not know that any mystic at the present day would care to accept the system thus delineated in its literal sense, but those who are able to discern, so to speak, its essence and spirit, stripped of the bizarre form and reclothed in a possible language, will have, as a Frenchman would say, *à peu prés* the mystical doctrine of Saint-Martin long years before he made acquaintance with Böhme. I do not offer the system of Saint-Martin as an adequate measure of the providence of God in respect of the destinies of man: I know of no adequate measure, mystic or non-mystic; but I could not be a transcendentalist without holding that man has come forth from God, that he has erred somehow in the way, and that he has to return. Saint-Martin has something to teach us as to the way of that return; and if even in the last analysis we could accept nothing that he tells us, he is still an object of imperishable interest because he is actively occupied, as

---

*   *Le Ministère de l'Homme-Esprit*, pp. 29-31.

we also should be with him, in the one pursuit which, to quote his own words, "engrosses the entire universe." But I think also that in that last analysis there is light in Saint-Martin, and that where he is not directly helpful he is invariably consoling. To again quote his own words, but this time in another sense, for he was speaking of the French Revolution, we hope with him, and he can and does help us also to believe each one of us with him, "that one day the star of truth and justice will rise on my country and on my life."

III

Saint-Martin and the Occult Sciences

SAINT-MARTIN PROBABLY HAD very little first-hand acquaintance with the occult sciences, though as regards theurgic practice he had once walked in "this secondary external way." Of their literatures he knew next to nothing; but then, as he frankly confesses, "I seldom frequent the libraries." * With the mystical writers of his own nation, and even his own time, he was very imperfectly acquainted. When approaching the age of fifty years he confessed that he had not read the works of Madame Guyon; and when he came to know something of them in a very slight and derived manner, he was dissatisfied, as might perhaps be expected; they made him feel "how feeble and vague feminine inspiration is compared with the masculine, as, for example, with that of Jacob Böhme. I find in the former a groping in the dark, morals, mysticism, instead of light; some happy interpretations, but many which are constrained; in short, more sentiment and affection than demonstration and proof; a measure which may be more profitable for the salvation of the author, but is less serviceable for the true instruction of the reader." †

With German mystics he had no familiarity whatever, always excepting Böhme. I do not think that he had ever heard of Gichtel till Kirchberger presented him, and then he knew only so much as Kirch-

---

* *Des Erreurs et de la Vérité*, Part I. p.9

† *Correspondance,* Lettre viii; Penny, "Theosophic Correspondence," p. 33

berger informed him—namely, the strange and somewhat weird history of Gichtel's mystic marriage with the divine Sophia. He accepted that story with his whole heart, and found, as we have seen, a parallel in his own experience, though one can scarcely help feeling that sober mysticism, well as it may appreciate the sincerity of Gichtel, will admit a certain doubt as to the nature and quality of the alliance which took place in the "third principle."

Arnold's "History of the Church and of Heretics" gave Saint-Martin a slight introduction to Joachim Greulich, but Engelbrecht was known to him by name only, Ruysbrœck perhaps as much, Tauler not at all. Returning to French writers, he sought earnestly for the works of Antoinette de Bourignon, but never met with them except in the National Library, where at one time he went daily to read them.* He also derived profound consolation from the Life of Blessed Margaret of the Holy Sacrament,† and at one time found much light in the writings of Jane Lead. On account of his devotion to Böhme, he was, on the whole, better acquainted with the English school of William Law than with any on the Continent; but the books which really influenced him and entered into the life of his heart would make only a small collection.

Returning to the occult sciences, as distinguished from the science of the soul, it must be repeated that he shows no substantial connection with any, though he sometimes used their terminology in a fantastic or transliteral sense. In his earlier books we find references to the three principles of the alchemists—salt, sulphur, and mercury‡ and he took these experimental philosophers sufficiently seriously to deny the fiery quality which they attributed to mineral mercury. § On the other hand, he agreed with them, though he does not seem aware of the agreement, as he had not read the alchemists, in reducing the four official elements of ancient physics to three.‖ His conception

---

* *Correspondance,* Lettre c; Penny, "Theosophic Correspondence," p. 347.

† Ibid., Lettre liii; ibid. p. 156 *et seq.*

‡ *Des Erreurs et de la Vérité,* Part I. pp. 131, 139, 142, 143.

§ Ibid. p 63.

‖ Ibid. p. 124. He agrees with them also when he observes that there is no substance which will not yield by extraction the principles which serve for the production of all bodies in the three kingdoms. *Tableau Naturel,* i. 156.

of the Great Work was, however, entirely different from that which has been usually referred to the Hermetic philosophy; it approached more nearly the transcendental interpretations of alchemy which have become current within recent years, but it was not in itself an alchemical interpretation, and owes nothing in reality to the occult science from which its name was derived.[*] There is a passage in Saint-Martin's correspondence which seems to indicate that the door by which the Great Work is approached is such an extension of the faculties as is supposed to occur sometimes in mesmerism. We know that he made prolonged experiments in that art, and in phenomena connected with it, at Lyons, in conjunction with another initiate, M. de Hauterive, who had peculiar gifts in this order. This was during the three years ending in 1776. Sixteen years later, referring to the of his associate, he observed: "It is not, however, the less true that if this experience of M. de Hauterive belongs to the secondary order, it is only figurative of the Great Work which occupies us; and if it is of the higher order, it is the Great Work itself."[†] That is a little oracular, but yet significant, and we must remember that Saint-Martin was writing to a non-initiate, to whom he consistently refused precise information as to sensible experiences. The mesmeric basis of the magnum opus was first broached definitely in a work published in the year 1850[‡] by a writer who had no opportunity of being acquainted with the letters of the French mystic, then, and till long after, unpublished and in private hands.

So far as I am aware, the possibility of transmuting metals into gold is scarcely mentioned, and certainly not discussed, by Saint-Martin.[§]

---

[*]   In one place he defines it as the conversion of the will. *Tableau Naturel.* i. 156

[†]   *Correspondance,* Lettre x; Penny, "Theosophic Correspondence," p. 45.

[‡]   "A Suggestive Inquiry into the Hermetic Mystery and Alchemy."

[§]   He discusses in a general manner the claims of the HermeticArt. He denies that its secrets are veiled by classical mythology, as his contemporary Pernety maintained. He condemns it on the broad ground of its material concerns and on the particular ground that such concerns do not justify its enigmatic language and its assumption of mystery. He was also wholly opposed to the contra-natural way of operation taught by some alchemists. He heaps ridicule on the supposed dangers attaching to the publication of its pretended secrets, while as to that class of its professors who claim to achieve the Great Work without any material substance, though their road is more distinguished, it is not more honourable or lawful. *Tableau Naturel,* i. 209-219.

He says expressly that "the Great Work is very different from the philosophical stone,"* and he denies no less expressly "the possibility affirmed by the alchemists of a continued revivification which might place them and all beings beyond the danger of dissolution;" that is to say, he denied the doctrine concerning the universal medicine on the ground that "the existence of bodies has only a limited duration, and that their destruction cannot be retarded without the infusion of a new principle in place of that which is preparing to depart."† Such an infusion he considered to be outside the natural order of things. It is, of course, the foundation of the old conception concerning the elixir of life.

But if, physically speaking, Saint-Martin rejected the doctrine of the universal medicine, in accordance with the practice already mentioned, he borrows the name, making use of it frequently enough in the spiritual order. "As the love of the Eternal Wisdom for its production is infinite, so that love could not fail to provide man in his condition of privation with a universal medicine to assist his recovery from that condition."‡ It is in conformity with the law which governs physical medicaments, that is to say, it is more active than the evil which it combats, and also, like those, it occasions more pain at the moment than does the evil itself. It is the peculiar suffering which awaits every man who puts his hand to the Great Work. It is the participation of the human in the divine sorrow of the universal charity, and the gates of this participation are the spiritual sufferings and oppositions which we encounter daily on earth, whether from the chief enemy, our individual astral laws, or from the rest of mankind.§ It is perhaps to be regretted that the issues of occult science and the mysteries of the inmost life are confused thus by a fantastic transposition of terms. Hermetic philosophy recognises, of course, an analogy between physical and spiritual processes, but this does not justify—rather it forbids more clearly—the expression of the one process in the symbolism of the other.

---

* *Des Erreurs et de la Vérité*, vol. ii. p. 25.

† Ibid. Part I. p. 111

‡ *L'Esprit des Choses,* vol ii. p. 319

§ Ibid. pp. 320-321

It must be understood, however, and this in a distinct manner, that Saint-Martin was an occult philosopher, though he was neither alchemist nor kabalist.* He was this after a fashion of his own, for his uncommon mind regarded everything from a peculiar standpoint; he understood nothing conventionally, and is almost invariably unexpected, frequently bizarre, in his views. He regarded occultism as a theurgist who had proved the efficacy of theurgic formulae but had abandoned operation because it is "in near neighbourhood to the spirit of this world, and especially to the astral region in which that spirit dwells;"† he distinguished with Jacob Böhme between *magus* and *magia*,‡ and with him the divine magic was an operation far different from anything of an external kind.§ He admitted, however, that there were many points of departure for different travellers. "I think the matter itself has acted variously on the elect, giving to some inward communications only but nothing outward; to others the outward simply and not the inward; to yet others both. I believe that the traditions or initiations called second-sight may have misled some men and proved useful to others, because, with upright beginnings and a well-intentioned heart, God sometimes leads us to the light, even over precipices."‖ He adds at the same time that no tradition or initiation of man can lead surely to pure communica-

---

* And subject also to the reservations instituted by his judgment on all sciences, which are based on conventional secrets and formulae, or depend exclusively on inanimate materials, amulets, pentacles, and talismans. Among these he includes expressly Geomancy, Chiromancy, Magic, and Astrology. He mentions also a fifth class, "which is that of abomination itself," but he describes it in obscure terms, so that it is difficult to determine the reference. I think he means the Black Magic of debased Kabalism; but the point is not of importance. See *Tableau Naturel,* ii. xxx, 113.

† *Correspondance,* Lettre viii; Penny: "Theosophic Correspondence," p. 37.

‡ Ibid. Lettre xxiv; ibid. p. 93.

§ So also he appears to distinguish by implication two orders of astrology—one, which may be called transcendental, which is really the discernment of divine truth in the heavens which are the work of the Divine and declare His glory; the other that judicial art which, like the rest of conventional occultism, "by subordinating the Principle to secondary causes, leaves man in ignorance of the true cause." *Tableau Naturel,* i. 148; ibid. p. 111.

‖ *Correspondance,* Lettre xxxii; ibid. p. 111.

tions, which are the gift of God alone. Those who are called to the work from on high will have also the criterion of judgment. "They are a universal couple which purifies everything and itself suffers no corrosion.* The theurgic path may therefore lead into truth, but it is beset by difficulties, and it needs the conduct of "pure, enlightened, and potent masters." † Since the death of Martines de Pasqually, Saint-Martin seems to have been acquainted with no one possessing such qualities.

The dangers offered by the astral region to theurgic experiment have been treated at large by occult writers within recent years. Saint-Martin, I think, was the first to expose them clearly, and to account for them mystically, by the help of a doctrine which we shall have to consider at some length in its proper place. I refer to the Fall of Man, esoterically understood, by which event he became subject to the elementary region, and consequently to the astral or sidereal rule, which is the pivot of that region, to which rule he was originally superior. The science of this region has two chief branches, one passive and one active. "The passive branch is that which engenders somnambulism and an infinitude of false communications of every order; but as this branch has a twofold or composite sap, like the tree, it is evident that its fruits are blended of true and false, clear and obscure, apparent and real, ordered and unordered. The active branch is that which concerns the entire domain of theurgy; it includes also simple magnetic power in activity, the results of which belong to the passive branch. So long as it has no point of union with that fixed source which should ordain and govern all, it is permeated, like the passive branch, with a double sap, and is thus uncertain in its action, good or evil, according to the sap which predominates. Acting, moreover, only on the composite properties of the passive branch, it is chance acting on chance, darkness on darkness.‡ All this, however, is only the elementary science of the astral. There is one of a superior kind, but more dangerous and fatal, for it operates extensively on what is evil in the region below it.§ I infer that Black Magic is intended, but Saint-Martin refuses to speak of it in a definite manner. He says

---

*   *Correspondance,* Lettre xl; ibid. pp. 132-133.   † Ibid.

‡   *De l'Esprit des Choses,* vol. i. p. 192.   § Ibid. p. 193.

merely that it was the criminal occupation of several peoples; that it is even represented in astrology, because all things are interlinked, and that man will always find "false actions ready to respond to his false thoughts, so as to achieve an ascendency over him after appearing to favour and serve him." The bulk of humanity is divided practically into two sections, "one of which is continually in astral passivity, or in a servile and baleful somnambulism, while the other is in astral activity more unfortunate still, for after it has attained its term it relapses into the most severe and terrible of slaveries." * Above these there is a salvage of humanity which has transcended the astral region and is directed by the pure spirit. "These are men who have entered truly into the lineal way; they have separated the metals within them, and are united to the tested gold. †

It is, in like manner, from the sidereal source that all enchantments derive. ‡ For Saint-Martin, as for Eliphas Lévi, it is in itself apparently a negative region, open equally to the activity of good and evil. By its physical properties it influences bodies, and it exercises bewitchment over our mind" by the potent and virtual pictures which it offers to us, which also, however alluring, distract us far from our true destination. They do not actually plunge us into the abyss, but holding the middle place between the abyss and the divine region, they expose us no less to error than to truth, to accepting the fruits of the abyss for fruits purely astral, and astral fruits for divine. Finally, they tend to make us hesitate continually between all kinds of complications. §

With modern occultism Saint-Martin not only the individualisation of the astral in man, but the danger and the frequency of its predominance. Less or more it preserves its empire during the whole of our elementary life, with a fortitude so imposing that it threatens to efface within us the recollection of that reign of freedom for which we were made. "The astral dominates our terrestrial part, for it sustains this; the astral itself is dominated by the spirit of the universe which stimulates it; the source of iniquity insinuates itself through all these regions so that it may reach us; at least it increases our yoke to delay

---

* *De l'Esprit des Choses,* vol. i. p. 194.   † Ibid.

‡ Ibid. p. 199.   § Ibid. p. 200

as much as possible the day of our emancipation. In such dreadful bondage is the poor soul held far from its native country, and exposed even to forget that it has one. Yet if our temporal destiny is interlinked with the astral, it disappears before the divine, for this is the eternal unity which man has the power to rejoin. Hence our present sidereal subjection does not exclude our ascent."[*]

Not only man in his normal material state, but also all Nature is said suggestively by Saint-Martin to be in somnambulism. "A dense cloud seems to envelop the totality of things, spreading either the darkness of death or a life so blind, so narrow, that all things exhibit a kind of distraction, an unquiet stupor which resembles dementia. In fine, we are forced to regard Nature as plunged in somnambulistic sleep. When man allows himself to be subjugated exclusively to its regimen, he shares this condition, to which must be attributed all that state of incertitude and all those gropings in the dark which are observable in human doctrines and in the minds of all those who come forward to instruct us before awaking from their state of somnambulism, that is to say, before being instructed themselves by those simple and natural lights which our source has preserved for us, in spite of our lapse, to assist us in assuring our progress."[†]

Between the permanent somnambulism of Nature and that induced magnetically there is this difference, according to Saint-Martin. On awaking from the artificial trance, the subject remembers nothing; but in the other and greater awakening, he will remember all. The distinction was made, however, at an early epoch of magnetic experiences, and would not obtain now, when it is well known that memory in the patient depends sometimes on the suggestion of the operator.[‡]

Saint-Martin also distinguishes both these forms of somnambulism from that which he understands by magism. The latter is the veil of things; it manifests their beauty without surrendering their principle, and it is of two kinds. There is a universal magism of Nature which covers with its glamour the infected region in which we now abide; there is also the divine magism of real Nature which unveils

---

[*]   *De l'Esprit des Choses,* vol. i. p. 197.   [†] Ibid. p. 125.

[‡]   Ibid. p. 126.

the reflections of the eternal magnificence. As to magnetic somnambulism, it lays bare the root of the soul before the time and in the absence of suitable preparations.[*] It is not the warder who opens the gate of the city, but the thief who unfastens the window or enters by a breach in the wall.[†]

---

[*] Ibid. pp. 128-129.

[†] There will be no difficulty in reconciling the standpoint of this section with the statement of Papus in his latest brochure, namely, that Saint-Martin, at the beginning of his literary career, made experiments in alchemy, and set up a laboratory at Lyons for this purpose. Like most seekers, he tried many ways before finding what was for him the true path.

Book III

The Nature and State of Man

I

Introductory

THE MESSAGE OF Saint-Martin may be fitly termed the Counsel of the Exile. It is concerned with man only, with the glorious intention of his creation, with his fall, his subsequent bondage, the means of his liberation, and his return to the purpose of his being. It is in most respects a concrete, practical message, and there is not much evidence in Saint-Martin of any concern or any specific illumination as to merely abstract problems. He speculates, indeed, upon many matters which have at first sight the air of abstractions, but, later or sooner, they all refer to that which is for him the great, the exclusive subject—namely, man and his destiny. This consideration will help us to account for the meagre references which can alone be gathered from his works upon a subject that is seemingly of such transcendent importance in a mystic and theosophic system as the Divine Nature considered in itself that Nature with which the true mystic must ever seek to conform, that First Principle with which fallen and deviated humanity must strive to recover correspondence. It is not the only consideration that is needed, for there are others belonging in a more formal manner to the domain of philosophy, but it expresses the force of these; and it is herein that Saint-Martin differs somewhat conspicuously from other transcendental teachers, whether those of the Latin Church, or those, for example, who connect with the higher school of Kabalism. The Divine Nature and the modes of its manifestation are the chief theme of mystic literature, and all its departments seem tacitly in agreement that it is only by an intense dwelling upon the attributes of God that the soul of man is sanctified and drawn back towards its source. The return is, in either case, the one end, and what Saint-Martin tells us concerning it harmonises in two chief points with the teachings of other mystics:—It can be immediate, and there is one only instrument. It is not a union which must be looked for after this mortal has put on immortality; it can be accomplished here and now.* It has nothing to do with the exercise of the faculties commonly called transcendental; the possession of a so-called sixth sense does not bring man nearer to God. By his occult experiences Saint-Martin must have been well aware that we possess transcendental faculties, and that it is possible, when these have been developed, to communicate with fields of existence which are beyond the knowledge of our normal state; but at an early age he abandoned all such methods in favour of the inward way, and there is little trace in his writings that he regarded the operations called magical, theurgic, and so forth, as instrumental to the attainment of Divine Vision. Conceivably they were perhaps instrumental, for all may help, and nothing that is not absolutely evil can be rejected absolutely, more especially at the beginning of the supernatural life; but, on the whole, they were redundant rather than necessary, to be avoided rather than pursued.

"Ordinary men, when they hear of living and spiritual works, conceive no other idea than that of beholding spirits, termed ghost-seeing by the benighted world. For those who believe in the possibility of spirit-return, this idea occasions frequently nothing but terror; for those who are in doubt as to the possibility, it inspires curiosity alone; for those who deny it altogether, it inspires contempt and disdain—firstly, for the opinions themselves, and secondly, for those who advance them. I feel it necessary, therefore, to state that man can make enormous advances in the career of living spiritual works, and can even attain an exalted rank among the labourers of the Lord, without beholding spirits. He who seeks in the spiritual career chiefly communication with spirits, does not, if he attain it, fulfil the main object of the work, and may still be far from ranking among the workers for the

---

*   *Correspondance,* Lettre cx; Penny, "Theosophic Correspondence," p. 337.

Lord. The possibility of communicating with spirits involves that of communicating with the bad as well as the good. Hence the communication in itself is not enough; discernment is required to determine whence they come and whether their purpose is lawful. We must also, and before all, ascertain whether we ourselves, supposing that they are of the highest and purest class, are in a condition to accomplish the mission with which they may charge us for the true service of their Master. The privilege and satisfaction of beholding spirits can never be more than accessory to the true end of man in the career of divine works and in enrolment among the labourers of the Lord. He who aspires to this sublime ministry would be unworthy thereof if actuated by the feeble motive or puerile curiosity of beholding spirits, more especially if to obtain these secondary evidences he trusts to the uncertain offices of other men, those, above all, who possess but partial powers, or possibly powers that are corrupted." *

The true transcendental instrument is the will, and the true way is its conformity. "Let me affirm that divine union is a work which can be accomplished only by the strong and constant resolution of those who desire it; that there is no other means to this end but the persevering use of a pure will, aided by the works and practice of every virtue, fertilised by prayer, that divine grace may come to help our weakness and lead us to the term of our regeneration." †

We shall see in another section by what manner of mediation this union of the will with God may be and alone is attained. Apart from such mediation there is, according to Saint-Martin, no knowledge of God possible, either for men or angels. ‡ At the same time, and by an extension, or as a result, of this mediation, Nature is for humanity a means of discovering the eternal marvels of the Father. § Natural theology is, however, only a stepping-stone to higher knowledge, and I do not know that Saint-Martin has left us any instruction of real or original moment concerning it. There is nothing in his later writings that takes us appreciably farther than the little summary which occurs in *Des Erreurs et de la Vérité*. "Since we discern so much regularity

---

* *Le Ministère de l'Homme-Esprit,* pp. 43-44

† *Correspondance,* Lettre cx; Penny, "Theosophic Correspondence," p. 377.

‡ *Le Ministère de l'Homme-Esprit,* p. 51. § Ibid.

in the progress and in all the operations of Nature, since we are also aware that the corporeal beings which constitute it are not capable of intelligence, it follows that in the temporal order there is for them a powerful and enlightened hand which directs, an active hand set over them by a principle true as itself, hence indestructible and self-existent, and that the law which emanates from both is the rule and the measure of all the laws which operate in corporeal nature." *

If this will not carry us farther than the first conclusions of the teleologist, the reason must probably be sought less in the limitations of Saint-Martin's mind than in its peculiar attitude. He did not really regard Nature as the chief mirror of Divinity.[†] It was man, and not his environment, which proved the Supreme Agent.[‡] "Man has been set amidst the darkness of created things only to demonstrate by his individual light the existence of their Supreme Agent, to convince all who misconstrue it." Nature herself seems to be presented rather as the term or point at which the voice of God expires, and she offers serious obstacles to the reverberation of that voice. [§] "All things should speak, since the spirit and the voice of God should fill all, and yet is all mute about us." For this reason, while esteeming the intention of natural theology, Saint-Martin discountenances the methods of those writers who endeavour to prove that there is a God by considerations borrowed from the external order. The attempt was characteristic of his period, and enlisted some of its strongest minds, but, as he well observes, in spite of all such testimonies, atheism had never so much vogue, and never so diffused an empire. [‖] For him, however, the failure of natural theology was a source of consolation and not of dismay. It was by no means a discomfiture for his faith, but rather an aid thereto; in a sense, it was even its victory. "It is a sign of the glory of our humanity, as it is an instance of the signal wisdom of Providence,

---

* Part I. p. 137.

† "It is in vain that we seek in matter for real and permanent images of that principle of life from which we are separated unhappily." —*Tableu Naturel,* i. 152.

‡ *Les Voies de la Sagesse, Œuvres Posthumes,* vol. ii. p. 68.

§ *Esprit des Choses,* vol. i. p. 73.

‖ *Le Ministère de l'Homme-Esprit,* p. 2.

that all such proofs adduced from the external order are thus deceptive in their last analysis... The entire universe, notwithstanding all the splendours which it displays before our eyes, can never of itself manifest the truly divine treasures."* The teleology which is based upon Nature apart from man, the so called arguments from design, the fantasia of the watchcraft of Paley, make only a weak appeal; but the evidences which are drawn from man himself speak the language of our own nature, and are for Saint-Martin not only welcome, but also irresistible. "I except neither the geometrical demonstrations put forward by Leibnitz, nor the fundamental axiom of Newton's mathematics, nor the considerations of Nieuwentzt on that axiom, nor the superb observations of other distinguished authors, whether upon the combination of chances to infinity which still effects nothing, or upon motion, which, tending to spread in all directions, is urged in a definite direction by a superior force."† Nor would Saint-Martin have excepted the last stand made by teleology in those more recent days, when for a moment the hypothesis of material evolution seemed about to seize the strongholds of official religion, namely, the necessity of a force impressed from without for the production of a change in the nature of the primal homogeneous ether. Proceeding with his argument, he observes: "From this world we borrow suppositions so as to arrive at a fixed being in whom all is true; we borrow abstract and figurative truths to establish a real and absolutely positive being; we attempt through unintelligible substances to ascend unto a being who is intelligence itself—substances void of love to demonstrate Him who is love alone—substances bound and limited to make known Him who is free. Finally, substances which die to explain Him who is life."‡ These considerations lead Saint-Martin for a moment into the fascinating regions of paradox. "If man be a sure and direct means of demonstrating the Divine essence; if the proofs which we derive from the external order are defective and incomplete; if the suppositions and abstract truths which we infer from this world belong to the metaphysical order and have no existence in Nature, it results evidently that we understand nothing in this world wherein we are save by

---

*   *Le Ministère de l'Homme-Esprit,* p. 2.

†   Ibid. p. 4.   ‡   Ibid. p. 7.

the lights of that world wherein we are not; that it is far more easy for us to attain the lights and certitudes which shine in the world wherein we are not, than to naturalise ourselves in the obscurity and the darkness of the world wherein we are. Finally, since it must be said, we are far nearer to that which we term the other world than to this. It is not indeed difficult to admit that it is by an abuse of words that we term the world wherein we are not the other world, and that it is this which is for us in reality another world. If we are to distinguish two given things as the one and the other, that which is first, and therefore without points of comparison prior to itself, is truly the one, and that which is second, subsequent, possessing points of comparison preceding it, is the other. Now, this is the case with the two worlds which are in question, and I leave it to the reader to compare the lights and certitudes which we find in the transcendental order, or in that which we call the other world, with the obscurities, approximations, and uncertainties of that in which we dwell, and thence to decide whether the world wherein we are not possesses no rights of priority over that wherein we are, as much by the perfection and knowledge which it offers us as by the right of age which it seems to possess over this world wherein we are now imprisoned. In this case it is truly this world wherein we are which is the other, while that which we call the other is the one, or the first, an archetypal and not another world." *

The essential nature of Divinity, if not actually unknowable by man, is at least described by Saint-Martin as an impenetrable sanctuary, in which there is neither succession of action nor diversity of function, and all that can be conceived of it by the mind of man is a unity so indivisible that it would be impossible without danger and without crime to contemplate its faculties separately, since they act in concert always, and represent in all their operations that sacred unity which constitutes their eternal essence. †

"As all things in God are united by a universal communication, there is nothing separable in His nature. Each faculty is the univer-

---

* *Le Ministère de l'Homme-Esprit,* pp. 7-9.

† *Traité des Bénedictions, Œuvres Posthumes,* ii. 203. Cf. *Tableu Naturel,* i. 162. "In God nothing is superior and nothing inferior; all is one in the indivisible, all similar, all equal in unity."

sality of His faculties, and the universality of His faculties is found in each." The Martinistic unity of the Divine Nature contains, however, the implicit notion of the triad, and hence the fundamental doctrine of this mystic system is identical with that of Christianity.*

Having established these few points, I may say at once that we have exhausted all that Saint-Martin has expressed in the course of many volumes as to the essential nature of the Deity in the eternity which preceded manifestation.† There is, therefore, properly speaking, no theology in his system, or rather there is only the great theology of the one Mediator by whom we know God, of the Divine Providence manifested to man in Him, and of the eternal union which we can effect through Him with God. At the same time, we shall find, in developing this system, that the accepted Christian doctrine has undergone a strange and wonderful transfiguration; it has lost in rigidity of outline, but it has gained in depth; there is a fuller office and a sweeter ministry; it has removed nothing and displaced nothing; but there is added I know not what—since in a way it exceeds expression—of light and satisfaction.

---

* *Des Erreurs et de la Vérité,* Part I. p. 126; *Traité des Bénedictions, Œuvres Posthumes,* ii. 155.

† The school from which he derived his first theosophical knowledge had no doubt a fuller instruction on the subject than appears in the books of its disciple, and that instruction was veiled in numerical mysticism, as appears by the following passage from the *Tableu Naturel,*—'I shall not attempt to render more sensible the nature of this Being, or to penetrate into the sanctuary of the Divine faculties. To reach that sanctuary it would be needful to know some of those numbers which constitute the Divine faculties. But how should it be possible for man to subject Divinity to his calculations, and to fix its prime number? To know a prime number it is necessary to have at least one of its aliquots. In attempting to represent the immensity of the Divine Power, suppose that we filled a book, even the whole universe, with numerical signs, we should not then have attained the first aliquot, since we could always add fresh numbers, *i.e.* find ever new virtues in this Being."— Part I. p. 17.

II

The Inward Way

T HAT LIFE OF interior illumination which is the subject of continual reference in the formal writings of Saint-Martin, which
his private memoranda and his correspondence show that he
cultivated assiduously, making such an advance therein that he is entitled to be included, not merely among mystical philosophers, but
among the disciples of the mystic life, must be distinguished, like the
rest of his doctrine, and like all his practice, from that hidden path of
contemplation, usually termed quietism, in which most of the mystics
walked. It is not less mystical, nor does it less lead direct to the centre,
but it is to some extent an individual and peculiar way, more healthful, and, if the term must be used, in a manner more sane—I should
rather say, more reasoned—than we find in St. John of the Cross or
in Ruysbrœck. It depends chiefly on the analysis of the constitution
of man. The concentration of the mind in spiritual contemplation
is most certainly an active work, and in one sense it may well be the
most strenuous and difficult of intellectual labours; but as it develops
it approximates more and more towards a passive condition. Thus, St.
John of the Cross explains that the soul is set free from infernal temptation in this hiding-place of absorption because the gift of contemplation is infused passively and secretly, and the illuminations which
come to it are awaited rather than sought. And Ruysbrœck describes
the soul in contemplation as a glass receiving the rays of the eternal
splendour of God; it is without modes or phases, and independent of

any operation of the reason. This was not the way of Saint-Martin, though no mystic recognised more than he the limitation of the rational faculty. He sought to establish the correspondence of the soul with the Divine by the active path of works, and to strive after the recovery of its law, the one path for the attainment of true science.

"At the first glance which man directs upon himself, he will perceive without difficulty that there must be a science or an evident law for his own nature, since there is one for all beings, though it is not universally in all, and since even in the midst of our weakness, our ignorance, and humiliation, we are employed only in the search after truth and light. Albeit, therefore, the efforts which man makes daily to attain the end of his researches are so rarely successful, it must not be considered on this account that the end is imaginary, but only that man is deceived as to the road which leads thereto, and is hence in the greatest of privations, since he does not even know the way in which he should walk. The overwhelming misfortune of man is not that he is ignorant of the existence of truth, but that he misconstrues its nature. What errors and what sufferings would have been spared us if, far from seeking truth in the phenomena of material nature, we had resolved to descend into ourselves, and had sought to explain material things by man, and not man by material things; if, fortified by courage and patience, we had preserved in the calm of our imagination the discovery of this light which we desire all of us with so much ardour." [*]

I have placed this point at the head of the Martinistic doctrine of human nature because it is the keynote of the whole; it explains Saint-Martin's abandonment of the beaten track of natural theology; it is the justification of his idealism, the reason why he regards the external world as illusive in the last analysis, though not in the crude sense that it is without objective existence and physical reality. [†]

1 *Des Erreurs et de la Vérité,* Part I. pp. 15, 19.

2 *Tableau Naturel,* Part I. pp. 82-83.

III

Good and Evil

THE ATTAINMENT OF light and truth being the object not only of the inward way, but of all human research, the first condition of attainment is a proper appreciation of the obstacles which hinder us. Man and Nature are alike in disorder, or, as Saint-Martin terms it, in extralignment. We are in darkness since we seek for the light, in delusion since we yearn for reality; but the fact that we desire both shows that we were made for both, and that in our present environment we are remote from the purpose of our being.* I must not say that this reasoning is entirely superior to criticism, but that in a general sense desire indicates capacity, and capacity supposes the possibility of achieving the end of desire, seems to be a strong and sound position. It is, of course, a postulate of optimism, and its foundation is in the veracity of God, who does not deceive His creatures by implanting in them the highest aspirations without also providing the means of their fulfilment. But before all things man must gauge accurately his present position; he must understand the precise nature of the disorder that is about and within him; he must learn if possible how it came about, in order that he may escape there from. If light, if truth, if order are good and desirable above all things; if darkness, falsehood, confusion are evils, we must at the outset obtain a certain criterion of judgment as to good and evil, and this was the first task

---

* *Des Erreurs et de la Vérité,* Part I. pp. 38-40.

to which Saint-Martin applied himself. It is the incessant confusion of these, the confusion of light and shadow, of harmony and disorder, which man perceives in the universe and in himself, that obscures so often the rays of the true light.*

"This universal contrast disquiets him, causing an entanglement in his ideas which it is difficult to unravel. The most signal service which can be rendered him is therefore to convince him that he can become acquainted with the source and origin of the disorder which astonishes him; it is, above all, to dissuade him from concluding, on account of it, anything opposed to that truth which he confesses, which he cannot dispense with, and cannot cease to love."†

Before considering the promised explanation of the disorder, let us see how Saint-Martin defines good and evil. "Good is for every being the fulfilment of His proper law, and evil is that which is opposed thereto."‡ The definition is inclusive, and therefore philosophical; it makes the attainment by man of the aspirations which he is compelled to cherish the express end of his nature, and thus raises them into the absolute and real order. There is no doubt that he was formed to enjoy the light and to possess the truth, since he is not otherwise in his law, and he has at once an unfailing criterion for distinguishing the evil from the good, since evil is all which hinders him from the attainment of light and truth.

"Since all beings have but a single law, for all derive from a first law, which is one in like manner, good, as the fulfilment of this law must be one also, single and exclusively true, though it embraces the infinity of existence. On the contrary, evil can have no correspondence with this law of being, because it is at war with the same; it cannot, therefore, be comprised in unity, since it tends to degrade it by seeking to form a rival unity. In a word, it is false, since it cannot exist alone;" that is to say, it is a derangement, and a derangement supposes an order which preceded it; "and since, despite itself, the true law of beings co-exists with it, which law it can never destroy, though it can disturb it and retard its fulfilment."§

---

*   *Des Erreurs et de la Vérité,* Part I. p. 16.

†   Ibid. p. 17.   ‡   Ibid. p. 20.

§   *Des Erreurs et de la Vérité,* Part I. pp. 20-21.

In accordance with the practical nature of his doctrine, Saint-Martin does not long delay over the question in its metaphysical aspect, but hastens to account for the existence of evil* in the universe and man according to the doctrine of the duality of principles.

---

* "The proportion of evil to good here below is numerically as 9 to 1; in intensity as 0 to 1; and in duration as 7 to 1." *Tableau Naturel,* Part I. p. 36.

IV

The Two Principles

WHEN M. JULES DOINEL, whom I have had occasion to mention previously, seceded from modern Martinism in the year 1894, he came forth to disseminate I know not what charges against its founder.* The fundamental accusation was, however, that the Martinistic doctrine was Manichæan, and that its good principle was Lucifer. The calumny has been repeated in England by a few writers, who had no qualification to judge the question, as they were unacquainted with the works of Saint-Martin. He was no Manichæan, and his doctrine concerning the evil principle, as to its origin and the part assigned to it in the material universe, does not even depart in any serious sense from the view accepted by orthodox Christian teaching. If, in regard to the ultimate destiny of that principle, he shows signs of such a departure by an approximation towards Origen, it must be said, firstly, that this is accessory and not essential to his system;† secondly, that he did not insist on it;‡ and,

---

* See *Lucifer Démasqué* published under the pseudonym of Jean Kostka, a contribution to the history of Satanism in France. The work in itself is worthless, but it is useful to the student of Martinism, because it publishes an abstract of the modern ritual of the order.

† It enters, as will be seen later on, into the hypothesis of the primal mission of man.

‡ That is to say, not dogmatically; there is no doubt that he held the view of universal resipiscence at the beginning of his literary life, and it appears plainly

thirdly, that, orthodoxy notwithstanding, in so far as Saint-Martin held or tolerated what he termed the resipiscence of the evil principle, he connects with rational eschatology. Indeed, one defect of his system is that of Jacob Böhme's, though not in the same degree, that it does not provide a sufficient ground for hope in the world to come.

The revolutions and contrarieties experienced by all natural beings, says Saint-Martin, have compelled man to recognise the existence of two opposed Principles,[*] and this inference from the facts of the external order has been strengthened still further by his inward experience. When he has succeeded in surmounting the opposition that is set up within himself, he finds himself at peace with Nature. But should he grow weary in the warfare, still more if he should neglect it altogether, or, to use his mystic symbolism, if he should permit a fire foreign to his essence to obtain an entrance within him, he suffers and languishes until he is entirely delivered there from.[†] In a word, he finds happiness and peace with the good which is consanguineous with himself, while the evil is invariably accompanied by weariness and torment.[‡]

"There is nothing better founded than this observation, and nothing more exact than the consequence which he has drawn from it."[§] But in attempting to explain the nature of the two principles he has adopted too narrow foundations, and even in the act of admitting them has failed to distinguish their difference. "Sometimes he has attributed to them an equality of power and antiquity, which has presented them in the light of rivals. Sometimes he has, indeed, represented evil as in every sense inferior to good, but has fallen into contradiction over its nature and origin.

"He has had occasionally the temerity to place good and evil in one and the same principle, thinking to honour this principle by ascribing to it an exclusive power as the author of all things. In the end, weary

---

(Continued...)
in the papers which he read before the Lodge of his fellow-initiates at Lyons. In his later life he ceased to speak of it, but his sympathy with the general view appears to have remained.

[*] *Des Erreurs et de la Vérité,* Part I. p. 17.   [†] Ibid. p. 20.
[‡] Ibid. p. 21.   [§] Ibid. p. 17.

of drifting longer over a sea of incertitude where no solid conception could be reached, some have undertaken to deny both principles; in a word, having failed to account for evil and good, they have said that there was neither good nor evil." *

The explanation and the distinction are both sought by Saint-Martin by a recurrence to man's own experience under the dominion of each.

"I have said that in approximating to the good principle, man is overwhelmed with delights and is consequently superior to all evils. He has no longer the perception or conception of any other being, and hence nothing which derives from the evil principle can intermix with his joy, which proves that man is then in his true element, and that his law is fulfilling itself. But if he seek another support than this law, his joy is at first disquieted and timid; he cannot partake of it without self-reproach; divided between the evil which allures him and the good which he has deserted, he experiences sensibly the effect of two laws, and is taught by the suffering coming from their opposition that he has swerved from his true law. It is true that this unstable enjoyment soon strengthens, and may even possess him entirely, but far from approaching harmony, it produces in the faculties of man a disorder which is the more deplorable, because the action of evil being sterile and limited, the felicity of him who gives way to it sends him quickly to the abyss and to inevitable despair. Here then is the infinite difference which is found between the two principles; all its power and all its value is derived by the good from itself, while evil is nothingness wheresoever good reigns. The presence of the one destroys every vestige of the other, which even in its most conspicuous triumphs is opposed invariably by the proximity of the good. Evil by itself is without force or capacity, while the powers of good are universal; they are in like manner independent and extend over evil itself. It is thus evident that no equality of power or antiquity can be ascribed to these two principles; we must recognise in that which is good an immeasurable superiority, unity and indivisibility, with which it has pre-existed of necessity before all. To establish in this way the inferiority of the evil principle is to prove that it did not, nor will

---

* *Des Erreurs et de la Vérité,* Part I. pp. 17-18.

ever, possess the least alliance with good, to which it is opposed diametrically in its very essence. However powerful it may be, the good can never cooperate in the birth or consequences of evil, nor can any germ or faculty thereof have been present in the good principle prior to the origin of the evil." [*]

But if the genesis of evil occurred independently of the good, how are we to account for its existence? Could we look to Saint-Martin for an entirely original explanation of this world-old problem of philosophy, it would be so much the less likely that we should find it useful or adequate. No solution has ever done more than remove the mystery one step or so back into the darkness. The answer of the mystic is not new; it is that which has always been given by Christianity, namely, that it came through a free act of the will of an intelligent agent. We have known long that this is no real answer, and that in the ultimate it has to be admitted, if evil be posterior to good, that it must have originated within the sphere of the higher order. We have most of us been contented to conclude that there are some questions which man has the capacity to ask, but that he cannot answer. The solution of Saint-Martin is not worse than are most, and it is better than are some; it is better than the somewhat nebulous metaphysics which present evil as the mere negation of good, whereas it is its active and virulent opponent. [†]

There is no need to follow Saint-Martin at the moment in his doctrine of the free intelligence as it is developed more fully in the case of human liberty; he does not reach the root of the matter, for he makes no attempt to explain how, in the midst of universal goodness and eternal order, there could arise intelligence possessing the capacity for error, in other words, the capacity for evil; or, conversely, how the liberty of choice between good and evil could be offered to any being without presupposing evil.

---

[*]   *Des Erreurs et de la Vérité,* Part I. pp. 21-24.

[†]   I must add, however, that Saint-Martin does himself occasionally offer considerations suggesting the negative view, but it is either by a confusion of terms, or by an attempt to regard evil as apart from the intelligence which embodies it according to his system. The fact that he regards an intelligence as the author and embodiment of evil gives it, of course, a positive aspect.

The origin of evil is, notwithstanding, for Saint-Martin exclusively in the degeneration of the will;* we must accept it provisionally for the same reason that Martines de Pasqually required the satisfaction of his disciple in the intercourse with intermediate agents when he had asked for God: "We must even be content with what we can get." It is from human sin that the analogy is, of course, borrowed.

"When man by aspiration towards the good contracts the habit of attachment thereto, he loses the very notion of sin. Had he but will and courage never to descend from this height for which he is born, evil would be nothingness for him; he experiences its influences only as he lapses from the good principle."† The punishment entailed thereby supposes that his action is free; a being devoid of liberty cannot diverge of itself from the law imposed on it; it is therefore impossible that it should be guilty or liable to suffer in consequence—an argument which presupposes morality in universal law, but that has been already granted to a system based on the pre-eminence of the good principle.

"Since power and all other virtues are the essence of this principle, our sufferings are proof palpable of our errors, and hence of our freedom. If, therefore, the evil principle be opposed evidently to the fulfilment of the law of the unity of beings, whether in the sensible or the intellectual, it follows that it is of itself in a disordered situation;"‡ and if its sufferings be inseparable from disorder, they also are a punishment, because justice being universal must act thereon, even as it acts on man. "But if it be thus under punishment, it must have diverged freely from the law which would have ensured its felicity, and must have become evil by its own will. Had the author of evil made proper use of his liberty, never would he have broken from the good principle; and could he at this day direct his will to his advantage—namely, in the direction of return—he would cease from his wickedness and evil would exist no more. But we see that it is daily riveted by its works to its criminal will, not a single act of which has any other object than the perpetuation of confusion and disorder."§

---

‡ *Des Erreurs et de la Vérité,* Part I. pp 14-27

† Ibid. p. 25.   ‡ Ibid. pp. 25-26.   § Ibid. pp. 26-36.

But if the source of evil must be sought in a depravation of the will inherent in that which is now the evil principle, this is equivalent to saying that it was good in its first estate.* Was it then on an equality with the good principle which preceded it? Saint-Martin answers in the negative. " It was good, but not equal; it was inferior, but not evil; it was derived, and therefore subordinate." † At this point it becomes somewhat difficult to follow the line of reasoning, though I do not know that the mystic is herein more confused than the theologian, or, I might add, the soul itself when it attempts to penetrate this dark night of mystery which lies behind all human experience, but with which human experience notwithstanding has a living connection. We must remember that the absolute independence and self-existence of the good principle is founded by Saint-Martin on the nothingness of evil when compared with it.‡ I have already indicated that this view of evil is not satisfactory, and furthermore it is not quite in harmony with the origin of evil in the liberty of intelligent action; but if we attach to the self-existent principle the connected notions of omnipotence and infinity, we shall clear up the difficulty, and the mystic will be at one with the theologian. In a word, God is postulated, with whom nothing co-existed from the beginning, and from whom all proceeds. But He being goodness itself, that which He has created must be good also but inferior.§ Equality with its source is impossible, "because its law was not derived from itself" But possessed of free will, "it had the power to follow or not that which it had received by its origin; it was therefore exposed to deviation from its law and to becoming evil; while the superior principle, deriving its law from itself, must of necessity remain in the goodness which constitutes it, and can never deviate towards another end." ‖

Such being the state of the two principles, the question will arise as to why the author of evil makes no attempt at reconciliation with the good, which Saint-Martin answers as follows:—"When we descend into ourselves, we perceive clearly that one of the first laws of universal justice is an exact proportion between the nature of the penalty and the offence, and this is accomplished by the subjugation

---

* *Des Erreurs et de la Vérité,* Part I.p. 35. † Ibid.

‡ Ibid. p. 22. § Ibid. p. 35. ‖ Ibid. p. 36.

of the offender to acts parallel with those which he has produced criminally, and hence opposed to that law which he has abandoned."[*] This is put somewhat obscurely, but seems to mean that the punishment of injustice is that which would itself be unjust except when exercised upon injustice. It means also, and more pertinently, that the punishment of crime is in the crime itself. "This is why the author of evil, corrupted by the guilty use which he has made of his liberty, perseveres in the wickedness of his will, and does not cease from opposing the acts and will of the good principle, in which vain efforts he undergoes a continuity of the same suffering."[†] But he has cut off correspondence with goodness, and there is on this account no way of his return. "If the good principle be essential unity, if it be purity and perfection itself, it can suffer in itself no division, no contradiction, no defilement; and it is clear that the author of evil must be separated and rejected by the one act of opposing his will to the will of the good principle, so that henceforth an evil power and an evil will alone remain to him, without any participation in goodness, or any communication therewith. The willing enemy of the good principle, and of the one eternal, invariable law, what law could he possess within him outside of this rule? He can no longer know or produce anything that is good, nor can anything follow from his will but acts without rule or order, and an absolute opposition to goodness and to truth. Being thus plunged in his proper darkness, he is not susceptible of any light or of a return to the good principle; for in order to direct his aspirations towards this true light, he must first have knowledge thereof; it must be possible first of all that he should conceive a good thought; and how could these enter into him if his will and faculties be wholly corrupted and infirm?"[‡]

Saint-Martin adds that the law of justice is fulfilled equally upon humanity, though not by the same means; and we shall learn in another place upon what grounds the depravation of the will in man has not been visited by the same penalty.

It must be confessed that he appears at the moment like those heroes of romance who, according to all the laws of probability, could

---

[*]   *Des Erreurs et de la Vérité,* Part I. p. 37.

[†]   Ibid. p. 37.   [‡]   Ibid. pp. 37-38.

not have escaped alive, but are yet brought through all dangers to a happy estate and a long life afterwards. The two principles have been so far considered only on the intellectual side of their opposition; the interference of evil with the harmony of the material universe is a part of human history, and its consideration must be subsequent to that of the origin and first estate of man.

Let us now sum up the entire position of Saint-Martin in a few words of his own: "If there are only three classes of existence—God, intellectual beings, and physical nature; if the origin of evil cannot be sought in the first, which is the source of good exclusively, nor in the last, which is neither free nor thinking, and if, notwithstanding, the existence of evil be incontestable, we are compelled to attribute it either to man, or to some other being holding, like him, an interme-diate rank." * But while the fact and its beginning are thus accounted for, "we may strive in vain to know the nature of evil in itself. For evil to comprehend itself it must be true, and then it would cease to be evil, since the true and the good are identical. To comprehend is to perceive the correspondences of an object with that order and harmo-ny the rule of which is within us. But if evil has no correspondence with this order, but is wholly opposed to it, how can we perceive any analogy between them, and, consequently, how can we understand them?" †

---

* *Tableau Naturel des Rapports qui Existen entre Dieu, l'Homme et l'Universe*, Part I. p. 35.

† Ibid. pp. 35-36.

V

Of Liberty in Man

MAN, ACCORDING TO Saint-Martin, is an exotic plant of the material universe. In his true nature he does not belong to the earth, and the depreciation of his type is the cost of his naturalisation. He is not precisely an exile, for he came here under a high commission, which, as we shall see, he failed to fulfill, but he is the inhabitant of a far country; the earth is the place of his encampment, but it is not his home; it is at his peril that he rests therein as in a true abiding-place. The aspiration after his true home, the home-sickness of Stilling,[*] is the most saving sentiment that he can cherish; yet this sentiment is in most cases exceedingly vague, and, obscured by the multiplicity of desires, is too generally lost, even as the recollection of his origin and the consciousness of his first mission. This is equivalent to saying that he has passed under the dominion of evil; he has acquired, and daily persists in acquiring, more fully a fatal science which plunges him deeper in the darkness, whereas he was born for goodness and light.[†] Such domination and its attendant suffering can be explained, as we have seen, by Saint-Martin only on the principle of man's liberty; he does suffer, hence he has committed wrong, and wrong-doing is possible only to the possessors of free intelligence.

---

[*] *Correspondance,* Lettre xcvi.; Penny, "Theosophic Correspondence," p. 331.

[†] *Des Erreurs et de la Vérité,* Part I. p. 27.

The false views which prevail on the subject of human liberty are referred by Saint-Martin to want of correct observation on the correspondence between liberty and will.* Will is the sole agent by which liberty can be conserved or destroyed. No faculty independent of the will is conceivable in man, for herein is his fundamental essence. He defines liberty as consisting not in the power to perform opposite and mutually exclusive actions at the same moment, but in the power to do so alternately.† Man is "the sole being in the natural order who is not compelled to pursue the same road invariably."‡ But before a contradiction in action can prove liberty, it must be shown that it is done freely and not from external impulsion. What, therefore, do we understand not merely by the idea of liberty in the abstract, but by a free being? "One who can maintain himself of his own accord in the law prescribed for him, preserving his power and independence by the voluntary resistance of those obstacles and objects which tend to prevent him from acting in conformity with that law; whence follows, of necessity, the tendency to succumb to those obstacles,"§ the failure of the desire to oppose them being all that is required herein.

Saint-Martin also lays down that the principle of the will is in the will itself, which is not to be explained by reference to external causes. It is a being operating by itself without assistance from another, having the privilege of determining itself alone according to its own motive; otherwise, it would not deserve the name of will. The philosophy which ignores this truth has not the first notion of volition, for if this were dependent on causes operating from without, we should not be its masters, and, in a word, we should not have liberty. We are made to act by ourselves, and the action of external causes is precisely what hinders and oppresses us.‖ After what manner the will determines of itself, independently of foreign motives and objects, is, however, an impenetrable mystery for man, and is indeed a dangerous subject of inquiry, because it exhausts his faculties to no purpose. "The wise man

---

*   *Des Erreurs et de la Vérité*, Part I. p 27.

†   Observe that the Divine Liberty is said to be like the Divine Essence; its existence and its *raison d'être* are identical. *Tableau Naturel*, i. 167.

‡   *Des Erreurs et de la Vérité*, Part I. p. 29.

§   Ibid. p. 30.   ‖   Ibid. pp. 31-32.

inquires into the cause of those things which possess a cause, but is too prudent and too illuminated to seek for what does not exist. Now, the cause of the will which is native to humanity is of this kind, for it is itself a cause."[*]

This is language which makes for confusion, because it seems to arrogate to human intelligence an almost divine attribute. It is not, however, intended that the will of man is uncaused in the sense that it is self-existent and therefore eternal. The man who says "I will" does so in virtue of a power within him which is imparted from the source of all power, and not through an impulsion from without. The inquiry however pursued, and its result however expressed, are certain to terminate in contradiction, for on the one hand we can conceive of nothing which is independent of God as He is understood by Christian theology and by Saint-Martin, while, on the other, the will of man can signify an apparent independence by contradicting and opposing Him. We must not, therefore, deceive ourselves by imagining that, in virtue of some mystic illumination, Saint-Martin can provide us with a doctrine of human liberty which is beyond criticism, or demonstrate even that we possess it in the sense which he argues; it must be enough that his view is the best which could be expected from a mystic at his period, and that others which have since arisen are not more free from difficulty.

Saint-Martin makes haste to add that it is not for the blind, trivial, and undesiring man that he exposes his teaching; he appeals from those who judge things as they are to those who discern what they were, transcending the conclusion of the senses and of the dead, unintelligent law.[†] "The innate will," he continues, "is the only remaining faculty of the active principle in man. This he enjoyed in his glory, and he enjoys it still in his fall. By it he went astray; by it alone can he hope to be reestablished in his primeval rights;[‡] it is this only which preserves him from the abyss. He cannot prevent good and evil from

[*]   *Des Erreurs et de la Vérité,* Part I. p. 33.

[†]   Ibid. pp. 32-33.

[‡]   "Will is the agent by which alone man and every free being can efface in them and round them the traces of error and crime. The revivification of the will is therefore the chief work of all fallen creatures."—*Tableau Naturel,* Part I. p. 118.

communicating with him, but he can choose, and he can also choose the good; so also he is responsible for the use which he makes of his will, and he is punished when he chooses badly." *

Finally, the comprehension of the higher truths depends on our confidence in the grandeur and power of this faculty. † "After the first temporal cause nothing in time is more powerful than the will of man, which, in its impure and criminal state, still has capacities similar to that of the principle which originally became evil." ‡

---

* *Des Erreurs et de la Vérité,* Part I. pp. 65-66. † Ibid. p. 166.

‡ Ibid. Part II. p. 55.

VI

Man in His First Estate

1 – Spiritual Generation

I F THE EXISTENCE of sin among men be the consequence of a rebellion or misdirection of the will, it follows that their existing state of disorder is neither their true nor their first estate. When man came forth originally from the bosom of the Divine Goodness, he was pure like the rest of its productions; he was devoid of any motive towards evil; his will must have turned instinctively towards good alone. It follows also from the principles laid down by Saint-Martin that evil must have been nothingness for him. I do not know whether the mystic had developed by his own speculations, or had derived from his occult tradition, any adequate or intelligible doctrine of this primeval condition; we are aware only that he did not speak his whole mind; and I must add that he has given us in consequence nothing that is really consistent or intelligible. Having regard to the inscrutable nature of the subject, it is impossible that his unreserved explanation should have been adequate, at least for all the issues. Let us take one point only, and inquire what is the operation of free will in a perfect being who has no conception of evil? It cannot be the choice between a lesser and a greater good, because it would cleave by its nature invariably to whatsoever was most excellent, and that nature would therefore make it impossible to choose otherwise, while in the absolute order of the good principle it is difficult to conceive how there can be a lesser good. The operation of free will in the choice between good and evil must suppose the knowledge of evil, and more than this, a privation of the felicity in goodness to make evil a possible temptation. We shall see that the system of Saint-Martin is silent on this point. At the same time he has much that is suggestive to tell us concerning the first estate, and something also concerning the original mission of man, from which we may infer that he was not subjected to an arbitrary ordeal, but was exposed to temptation for an end which justifies the designs of the Eternal Providence. It is well, therefore, that at this point he should speak at sufficient length in his own person, and first as to whether primeval man is to be understood individually or collectively. It is certain that he is to be regarded spiritually at the beginning of his emanation, though in the second stage of his history he entered into connection with the physical world. It must be observed first of all that the hierarchy of Saint-Martin is no doubt identical with that of Christian angelology, though he refers very seldom to the angelic orders under their familiar names; they are the Intermediate Agents of Pasqually, the subjects of continual mention in the earlier writings of the disciple, and at a later period must be also those "primitive spiritual chiefs" whose generation is said to have been instantaneous—that is, collective, "because it took place in a region wherein there was no time, and was a kind of generation which could not have been operated temporally."[*] On the other hand, the generation of the spiritual circle of the first man could only occur successively, because time had then been created, and it was necessary that it should be effected in time.[†] Man did not, therefore, descend into generation, as some occult doctrines suppose, but his generation descended with him from purity into defilement.

The spiritual generation of the circle of man takes place in the material region not only in succession, but with division and danger, because he has devoted all his posterity to the peril and disasters of this infected region, as the first spiritual chief entrained all his own in his fall. The difference is, therefore, that the entrainment of the circle of man takes place successively because his generation is successive. This in itself is sufficient to silence those who cry out at their share in the punishment for a fault which they have in nowise committed—"firstly, because the solidarity of a family destroys the ground for the re-

---

[*] *Del'Esprit des Choses*, t. i. p. 265.   [†] Ibid. p. 265.

proach; and, secondly, because we are in any case better off than the posterity of the first spiritual chief The entrainment of man's posterity is inevitable, but its consequences can be escaped; in the other it is equally inevitable, and there is no escape from its consequences." *

As to the mode of generation, souls reproduce one another; they are not created by God at the moment of corporisation, which I take to be the view of Christian theology. There is therefore no pre-existence in the sense of Glanvil the Platonist, nor, it may be added, is there any reincarnation. In that estate which is now about to be described, primeval man was therefore one and alone; but he had apparently a dual aspect, for man and woman are said to be one spirit divided into two bodies.

The Martinistic doctrine of the first estate is based on the aspirations of humanity towards a perfect order in the midst of his privation and misery.

2 – Union With the Good Principle †

No person possessed of good faith or an unbiassed and unobscured reason will deny that the corporal life of man is an almost incessant suffering and privation. In pursuance of the conceptions which we have formed of justice, it is not without ground that we regard this life as a period of chastisement and expiation, but we cannot do so without concluding immediately that there must have been an anterior state for man, to be preferred before his actual state, and that in proportion as the latter is restricted, painful, and abounding in things distasteful, so was the former illimitable and replete with delights. Each one of man's sufferings is the index of a felicity which fails him, each of his privations proves that he was made for enjoyment, each of his enslavements proclaims his ancient authority; in a word, the realisation that today he has nothing is a secret proof that once he possessed all. By the sad consciousness of our present frightful situation we can therefore form some conception of that bright estate in which

---

* Ibid. pp. 265-266.

† Adapted from *Des Erreurs et de la Vérité*, Part I. pp. 38-40, 44-46.

man existed formerly. He is not now the real master of his thoughts, he is tortured in awaiting those which he desires and expelling those which he fears. From this we realise that he was made to dispose of thoughts and to produce them at his pleasure. He obtains now a certain slender peace and tranquillity only after infinite efforts and many painful sacrifices, from which we conclude that he was designed to participate everlastingly in a calm and fortunate estate, and that the house of peace was his only true abode. Having the capacity to behold all and to know all, he trembles notwithstanding in the darkness, and shudders at his ignorance and blindness; does this not show that the light is his proper element? Lastly, his body has been made subject to destruction, of which alone of all beings in nature he possesses a conception, and this is the most terrible step in his physical career, the act of all most humbling and held the most in horror. But does not this severe and frightful law lead us to conceive that man's body was once under a more glorious obedience, and that he was intended to enjoy all the privileges of immortality?

Now, whence could this sublime estate derive, if not from the intimate knowledge and continual presence of the good principle, that sole source of all power and all felicity? Why does man languish here in ignorance, weakness, and wretchedness, if not because he is separated from this same principle, which is the sole light and the one support of all beings? As the principle of evil must still endure the punishments inherent in his rebellious will, so also the present sufferings of man are but the natural consequences of a first error; so also this error could issue only from the liberty of man conceiving a thought opposed to the supreme law and adhering thereto by his will. But albeit the crime of man and that of the evil principle are equally the fruit of their perverted will, the nature of these crimes is very different. They cannot be subjected to the same penalties or possess the same consequences. Justice takes into account the difference of the places wherein these crimes occurred. Man and the evil principle have therefore their sin ever before their eyes, but both have not the same succours or the same consolations. Man, despite his condemnation, can appease justice; he can reconcile himself with truth; he can taste at times its sweetness as if he were in some sort still undivided therefrom. It is true, however, to say that the crime of both is not punished otherwise than by privation, and that there is a difference only in the measure of the chastisement. It is still more certain that this privation is the most terrible of all penalties, and the only one which can really subdue man. It is a grave error to pretend that we can be led to wisdom by a frightful portrayal of physical sufferings in a life to come; such a picture is of no effect when it is not experienced, and the blind masters who have recourse to it, unable to make us realise, save in idea, the torments which they fancy, possess of necessity but little influence. Had they taken the same pains to depict the remorse which man must feel for his wickedness, they might have reached him more easily, because this suffering is possible here below. But how much more happy would they have made us, and how much more worthy a conception would they have imparted concerning our principle, if only they had been so sublime as to proclaim before man that the good principle, being love itself, punishes man only by love, but also, being love, when it deprives us thereof it no longer leaves us anything! So would they have enlightened, so sustained men, bringing home to them that nothing need dismay them save to cease having the love of this principle, without which they are in the abyss, and certes the conception of the abyss which man may experience at every instant would be for him more efficacious and salutary than that of eternal tortures, to which, despite these ministers of blood, man always sees an end and never a beginning.

The succours accorded to man for his rehabilitation, however precious they may be, are contingent all the same upon very rigorous conditions. And surely, the more glorious the rights which he has lost, the more should he endure to recover them. In fine, being subjected by his sin to the law of time, he cannot avoid experiencing its painful effects, because having opposed to himself all the obstacles which time comprises, the law wills that he should gain nothing but in the measure that he passes through and overcomes them.

3 – Man the Organ of Divine Order[*]

The diurnal occupation of man, his endeavours to introduce order and regularity everywhere, his faculty for adding to regularity and order the charm of taste and the creations of a magical imagination, proclaim that, in his most perfect primitive condition, it was still his task to increase the perfection of all about him, and to embellish more and more the abode which he inhabited. A uniform law, which admits of no varieties save in its mode of execution, is inherent in being, and accompanies it even in the alienations to which it may become abandoned. Furthermore, by distinguishing in the earthly task of man those more gross and material cares which seem a sentence passed upon the whole race, from the taste for ordering and perfecting which also occupies the species, and seems rather a privilege than a punishment, we may be sure that the end of man's primal existence was the embellishment of his abode, and that the means were derived from that higher source whence he himself descended. He follows the same course at the present day when he has plans to conceive and works to produce. He concentrates and withdraws into himself, seeming to await from some source distinct from himself that light which he seeks, that ray of instruction which he needs. His works are more or less regular according to the patience of his search and the fidelity with which he follows the light. So, also, the more obedient man was to that order which joined him to his principle, the more successfully he fulfilled the task of culture imposed on him; and, reciprocally, the more he laboured with zeal and success therein, the more did he increase for himself the advantages of the superior order whence he derived his essence, because all was interlinked for man in this supreme work, as it would be still at this day did not the grosser material cares contract his capacities, and did not the inferior powers, civil or religious, which rule the social man, altogether destroy or ab-

---

[*] Adapted from *L'Esprit des Choses,* sec. *État Primitif de l'Homme.* See vol. i. pp. 45-50.

sorb them. Through man as an organ that luminous and divine order would then have passed, with infinite diversities, forming through them and by them the most delicious harmonies, as he still may observe at this day when he enters into himself and directs his inner sight towards the source of his being. He experiences then the descent of this superior order, and he is made naturally thereby the friend and brother of all men, having neither the desire to be their master nor the need to be their subject or disciple.

If, therefore, the faculties of man are simply more contracted than they were when he was in his true measure, we can form a correct notion of his original privileges—the production of harmony, the multiplication of marvels, the ascent in all regions from altar to principle, the cultivation of all the treasures of nature, their harvest, the increase of their perfection by their passage through his own channel, for the extension of the kingdom of truth. We may read the proof of this primal law in all the inventions, all the arts to which man applies himself successfully, although after a material manner. Does he not purify by his operations the substances of this inferior world? Does he not produce by his skill the notes of harmony with his fingers? Does he not heal by the counsel transmitted through his speech? Does not the strength of his arm overthrow armies? Does not he multiply by painting the image of all things in nature? And if in this mournful state, when he can accomplish nothing save in the inferior order, his works are still so wondrous, what therefore would they be if he were reintegrated in realities?

4 – The First Envelope of Man

By his origin man enjoyed all the privileges of an intelligent being, although he possessed an envelope, for in the temporal region no existence can dispense with one. The first envelope of man was an impenetrable armour, because it was unified and simple, while owing to the superiority of its nature it was not subject to decomposition, the law of mixed bodies having no power over it. Since his fall man finds himself clothed with a corruptible envelope, because, being composite, it is subject to the different actions of the sensible, which operate successively, and consequently destroy one another. But by this subjugation to the sensible, man has in nowise lost his quality and rank as an intelligent being, so that he is at once great and little, mortal and immortal, ever free in the intellectual, but bound in the physical by laws outside his will; in a word, being a combination of two natures diametrically opposed, he demonstrates their effects alternately in a manner so distinct that it is impossible to be deceived thereon.

5 - The Book of Man *

The inexpressible advantages enjoyed by man in his first estate were attached to the possession and comprehension of a book without price which was included among the gifts of his birthright. While this book consists only of ten leaves, it comprises all illuminations and all sciences, past, present, and to come; and, moreover, the power of man was at that time so much extended that he had the faculty of reading the ten leaves at once and of embracing them by a single glance. After his prevarication this book was indeed left him, but he was deprived of his ability to read it with that former facility; henceforth he could only master its leaves successively. He will never be re-established entirely in his rights until he has acquired them all, for though each of these ten leaves contains a particular branch of knowledge proper to itself, they are yet so connected one with another that it is impossible to be acquainted perfectly with one of them till familiarity has been acquired with all; and though I have said that man can now read them only in succession, he will never be established in his path until he has acquired them collectively, the fourth above all, which is the focus of all the others. Upon this truth men have seldom fixed their attention, but it is one notwithstanding which it is infinitely necessary to learn, for all are born with the book in their hand; and if its study and comprehension are precisely the task for their fulfilment, we may judge how important it is that they should not despise it. Their neglect on this point has been carried, however, to an extreme; scarcely one among them has remarked the essential union between the ten leaves

---

* *Des Erreurs et de la Vérité*, Part I. pp. 221-230, condensed.

by which they are made absolutely inseparable. Some have broken off in the middle, some at the third leaf, others again at the first, thus producing atheists, materialists, and deists. A few indeed have perceived the bond between the ten, but have failed to recognise the important distinction which must be established between each, regarding them as equal and of the same nature. What has ensued? Limited by the point of the book which they have not had the courage to pass, and yet resting on the fact that they spoke only by its authority, they have pretended to its complete possession, whence believing themselves infallible in their doctrine, they have exerted all their efforts to promote it. But the isolated truths, receiving no nourishment, have perished speedily in the hands of those who have divided them, and with these imprudent men there has rested only a vain phantom of science which they could not present as a solid body or substantial being without having recourse to imposture. It is hence precisely that those errors which we contest have issued—namely, as to the nature and laws of corporeal beings, the several faculties of man, and the principles and origin of his religion and worship.

We must complete, however, the conception of this incomparable book by specifying the different sciences and properties referable to each leaf. The first treats of the universal principle or centre, from which all centres emanate continually. The second treats of the intermediate cause of the universe; of the dual intellectual law operating in time; of the twofold nature of man; and, generally, of that which is constituted by two actions. The third treats of the basis of bodies; of all resultants and all products, whatsoever the kind; and here also is found the number of those immaterial beings which are not endowed with thought. The fourth treats of whatsoever is active; of the principle of all tongues, temporal and extra-temporal; of the religion and worship of man; and here also is found the number of immaterial thinking entities. The fifth treats of idolatry and putrefaction. The sixth treats of the laws governing the formation of the temporal world and the natural division of the circle by the radius. The seventh treats of the cause of winds and tides; of the geographical scale of man; of his true science; and of the source of his productions, both intellectual and sensible. The eighth treats of the temporal number of Him who is the sole support, the single force, and the one hope of man, that is to say, of that real and physical being who has two names and four numbers, because he is both active and intelligent, while his action extends over four worlds. It treats also of justice and all legislative powers, including the rights of sovereigns and the authority of generals and judges. The ninth treats of the formation of corporal man in the womb of woman, and the decomposition of the universal and particular triangle. Lastly, the tenth is the part and the complement of the preceding nine; it is the most essential of all; failing this the others cannot be known, because by arranging all the ten circumferentially, according to their numeric order, it is found to have most affinity with the first, whence all emanate; while, if we would judge further of its importance, let it be known that in virtue of this is the Author of things invincible, because it is a barrier which defends Him on all sides, and there is no being that can pass it.

As in this enumeration are contained not only all the knowledge to which man can aspire, but all the laws imposed on him, it is clear that he will never possess any science, nor fulfil any of his true duties, until he draws from this source. We know also what hand should lead him thereto, and that if of himself he can make no progress towards this fruitful source, he is still sure of attaining it by forgetting his own will and giving place to that of the Active Cause, which should alone operate for him.

Although this book possesses only ten leaves, as it still includes all things, nothing can exist without belonging by its nature to one of them, and there is no being which does not itself indicate its class and to which of the leaves it belongs. Thereby does each offer us the means of instruction about everything that concerns it; but in order to direct ourselves in these studies, we must know how to distinguish the true and simple laws which constitute the nature of beings from those which men imagine and substitute daily in place of them.

Let us turn now to that portion of the book which I have said was the most misused, that fourth leaf, the most in correspondence with man, for therein are inscribed his duties and the true laws of his thinking part, as also the precepts of his religion and worship. By following exactly, with constancy and a pure intention, all the points clearly enunciated therein, he might obtain the help of the very hand which punished him, and so transcend this corrupted region wherein he is relegated by his condemnation, recovering the vestiges of that ancient authority in virtue of which he determined formerly the latitudes and longitudes for the maintenance of universal order. But as such powerful resources were attached to this fourth leaf, error in regard to it assumed proportional importance; indeed, had not man neglected its advantages, all would still be blissful and at peace on earth. The first of these errors has been the transposition of the fourth and substitution of the fifth page, or that which treats of idolatry; the second is the conception of gross notions attaching to the properties of this leaf, and the attempt to apply those properties to all; the third is the belief, on only a slight presumption, that man is in possession of the sacred advantages belonging to this fourth leaf.

VII

Primeval Mission of Man

WE HAVE SEEN in an earlier section that the intellectual liberty of man, so far as it consists in the ability to choose between good and evil, is one of those fundamental problems about which Saint-Martin fails to enlighten us. On the one hand, he conceals doctrine, and, on the other, what he does tell us is inadequate. It was indicated, however, that in the account of man's primal mission we should find an unusual warrant for the ordeal to which man was made subject. It is not an account which can be derived from any one place in the writings of the mystic, and it is the subject of many obscure references. We may take as the keynote the statement that "the function of man differs from that of other physical beings, for it is the reparation of the disorders in the universe."[*] Though dogmatic in form, this affirmation, like most which are made by Saint-Martin, is a conclusion based upon facts which he discovered in humanity as it now is. "Man possesses innumerable vestiges of the faculties resident in that Agent which produced him; he is the sign or visible expression of the Divinity."[†] Again: "Man has been placed in the midst of the darkness of creation only to demonstrate by his native light the existence of a Supreme Agent, and for the conviction in this respect of all those who disbelieve it."[‡] For this

---

[*] *Tableau Naturel,* Part I. p. 55.   [†] Ibid. pp. 57-58.

[‡] *Les Voies de la Sagesse, Œuvres Posthumes,* i. 68.

purpose he came forth strong and well equipped from his source; he was vested with "immense powers" to effect this manifestation, for he could not proclaim the grandeur of that Being whom he represented in the universe unless he were great himself, nor would those whom he was intended to subdue confess the might of the sovereign unless the delegate could convince them in his own person that it was real and invincible.[*] Here we are not dealing with a picture of the perfect man sent to confound the wicked of his own order; the doubters, the rebels, the enemies are of another class; in a word, they are the generations of the evil principle, and even in his fallen state he is ever surrounded by this cloud of witnesses, and can still testify to them the splendour and power of his master.

"The saintly race of man, engendered from the fount of wonder and the fount of desire and intelligence, was established in the region of the temporal immensity like a brilliant star for the diffusion of a heavenly light."[†] He was placed "between Divinity and the old prevaricator, and could produce at will in the realm of the spirit the majesty of storm and lightning, or the serenity of the mildest zone; he could load the guilty with chains and plunge them in darkness, or erect in peaceful regions the banners of love and consolation." He was not, therefore, assigned a mission only of wrath and judgment. He was "chosen by Supreme Wisdom to be the sign of his justice and his power," to "confine evil within its limits," but also to "give peace to the universe."

We must understand here the archetypal world, pure, calm, and beautiful in itself, the domain of perfect human sovereignty; in a word, the unfallen world, threatened with invasion by the powers of darkness which encompassed it. Or perhaps we should understand rather, for it is not clear in Saint-Martin, that world as it is pictured by Böhme, the kingdom of the unfallen Lucifer, devastated by his crime.

But the mission of man was more even than ensuring peace to what was already at peace in the universe; it was the production of harmony in disorder. And here we touch upon an instruction which was derived by Saint-Martin from his first school of initiation, and we

---

[*] *Les Voies de la Sagesse, Œuvres Posthumes,* i. p. 69.

[†] *Le Ministère de l'Homme Esprit,* p. 162.

shall not be surprised that it was developed most completely by the mystic in a lecture for a lodge of initiates.

"The first enemies of the Creator were not called after the same manner as men; they were not required to lead into the right way those who had departed therefrom, for prior to their own crime there was no creature which had turned aside from its proper law, and all were consequently in union with the divine universal law. Their vocation was to honour unceasingly that Principle from which they had emanated, to confess the ineffable majesty of its powers, and to partake of the beatitude derived from the inexhaustible influences of life. Now, if the eternal laws can never fail to be accomplished, these same beings, despite the darkness and corruption in which they lie, will doubtless one day acknowledge the authority of the hand which has chastised them. Then will this simple act of resipiscence prove the immutability of their law—a law inherent in the divine essence itself, which cannot tolerate the success of criminal assaults in any being whatsoever. As to that which may follow this act of resipiscence, the Divine Wisdom alone knows, and it is unlawful for man to judge of it.[*]

It follows, notwithstanding, from this derived teaching of Saint-Martin that man's original mission was to recall those to life who, by an improper use of its liberty, had forfeited its essence. Now, the evil principle and the generations thereof were the only lost virtues of the universe at that epoch. Man therefore had two purposes in his existence, whereas the children of the first emanation had one only, for the divine worship was also his duty, and it is by reason of this twofold vocation that he is always regarded by Saint-Martin as superior to the angels, and hence more fitted to represent the universal agent. "By the universality of the powers imparted to him, he approached nearer to the likeness of his author."[†]

In another instruction delivered under similar circumstances, the mission of man in regard to the evil principle is even more clearly expressed. "He had only one crime to avenge, and the punishments to which he should have had recourse were rather upbraidings and instructions than scourges and torments; he would have sought rath-

---

[*] *Les Voies de la Sagesse, Œuvres Posthumes,* i. 71-72.

[†] Ibid. p. 73.

er to soften the perverse being than to chastise it, would have been rather his good angel than his destroyer. We have a proof of this at the present day in the office of our good intelligence towards ourselves, which is to lead rather than to punish; to give us light, not to plunge us in darkness; to inspire us with consolations, not afflictions. Such should have been our duty towards him whom we were charged to restore to order and to the obedience of the Creator. But as when we ignore that saving guide set over us to communicate all good things to us, he sets hostile laws in motion, changes gentleness into wrath and wrath into ve1'itable torments ; so the perverse being, having tempt- ed and seduced the son of the second emanation sent to effect his reconciliation, has obliged the divine justice to turn the law against him, to delay the term of his spiritual regeneration, and to change the favourable ways offered him into ways of severity entailing acute sufferings."[*]

The spiritual sign of the alliance[†] is interpreted by Saint-Martin along lines which lead him to the same conclusion as to man's pur- pose in the universe, but it must be taken in connection with doc- trines developed elsewhere in his writings. Saint-Martin distinguish- es three universal creative powers[‡]—the Divine Thought, to which correspond the eternal spiritual natures; the Divine Will, to which correspond the temporal spiritual natures; and the Divine Activity, to which corporeal existences correspond. But in proportion as things which are produced are more remote from the productive principle, the more numerous are the intermediate agents. Thus the agents of the material universe are to be distinguished from the universal agents, and both in Martinistic doctrine are seven in number. "There are thus two classes of spiritual beings operating unceasingly in the circle of temporal immensity. The one are the special custodians of the different regions of the corporeal universe,"[§] which they preserve from confusion on the part of the evil principle by his continual re- striction. The others preserve the children of the second emanation, in like manner, from the assaults of the perverse being, assist them

---

[*] *Traité des Bénédictions, ŒuvresPosthumes,* ii. pp. 194-195.

[†] *Rapports Spirituels et Temprorels de l'Arc-en-ciel,* Ibid. pp. 247-251.

[‡] *Traité des Bénédictions.* Ibid. p. 158.   [§] Ibid. p. 172.

during their term of probation, and communicate those graces which the divine mercy can conciliate with the divine justice.[*] The physical agents are described in symbolical language as the seven pillars of the universe, the keys of the seven arches on which the temple of Solomon is based; they are also the seven angels whose trumpets sound in the Apocalypse. "The combination of their actions produces the incessant variety of elemental influences and changes experienced by physical beings, less or more favourable to these according to the preponderance of one or other of the agents, and subject to all the derangement which may be occasioned by the interference of the evil principle warring continually with the restricting powers. In fine, these agents are the realisers of the creative word which produces and preserves matter."[†] According to Saint-Martin, man in his first estate directed the action of these seven agents, which action is symbolised by the seven colours displayed in the sign of the alliance.[‡] That is to say, he effected through them the restriction of the evil principle, and was thus the universal mediator of the supreme power,[§] disposing of his subordinate agents as he now disposes materially of elementary creatures, emanated and emancipated to manifest the glory and justice of the Creator, retaining direct correspondence with the Divine and Eternal Son, occupying the middle place between that divinity and the temporal spirits submitted to his power.

[*] *Traité des Bénédictions, ŒuvresPosthumes,* ii. p. 175.

[†] Ibid. pp. 173-174.

[‡] *Rapports Spirituels et Temprorels de l'Arc-en-ciel.* Ibid. p. 250.

[§] *Rapports Spirituels,* p. 263.

VIII

The Fall of Man

THE MARTINISTIC DOCTRINE of the Fall of Man is, put shortly, that the evil principle which he was created to constrain and to reconcile succeeded in seducing him. As in regard to the origin of evil, so here we must not expect to find a complete or wholly intelligible teaching, and, in this as in the other case, the failure of Saint-Martin is, broadly speaking, the failure of Christian theology. By the latter there is attributed to unfallen man a nature and a knowledge which make it absurd to suppose that he could sin, as it also says that he did upon a trivial pretext. And Saint-Martin has given us a picture of man in his first estate which sets him higher than the angels, ruling the agents of material creation, enjoying the full powers of the divine messenger in the universe, manifesting to that universe the majesty of his Master, and guarded and guided apparently by the supreme chiefs of the first emanation. With all these endowments we shall find that the fall of man is attributed by the mystic to weakness and the facility of seduction. His doctrine on the subject does not differ materially at any period of his literary life. I cannot trace that it underwent any conspicuous change which can be attributed to Jacob Böhme. He was merely more explicit at the end than he was at the beginning, but he was never clear. In his first published work the reticence of the adept caused him to take refuge in a figurative picture which represents primeval man as deviating from his assigned post at an inaccessible

---

* *Des Erreurs et de la Vérité,* Part I. pp. 41-44.

centre,* but it offers nothing to the faculty of interpretation. In the "Natural Table" he drops allegory and attempts a concise statement: "The crime of man was the abuse of the knowledge he possessed as to the union of the principle of the universe with the universe. The privation of this knowledge was his punishment; he knew no longer the intellectual light."* Now, we know that the union of the universe with God is, according to Saint- Martin, by means of intermediate agents, and that a subordinate class of these agents was at the disposition of primeval man.† He therefore abused the power which had been delegated to him in this respect, whence it would seem to follow that his sin was not one of weakness but of strength; that he did not yield to seduction, but committed outrage. With this view we may connect an enigmatical statement in the earlier work, that the crime of the first man was adultery, though before he committed it there were no women. He adds: "Since then the vortex which drew him to this original sin has subsisted ever since, and furthermore men are now exposed to the adultery of the flesh, which was made possible by his first adultery."‡ He recurred to this aspect of the fall of man after an interval of sixteen years, but the section of the "Spirit of Things"§

---

*   *Tableau Naturel,* Part I. pp. 94-96.

†   Compare *Tableau Naturel,* Part I. pp. 60-62:—"Before temporal things could possess the existence which makes them sensible, there were necessary primitive and intermediate elements between them and the creative faculties whence they descend, because temporal things and the faculties from which they descend differ too much in their nature to coexist without intermediary. These elements, unknown to the senses, but of which intelligence attests the necessity and the existence, are determined and fixed in their essence and number, like all laws and means used by Wisdom for the accomplishment of its designs. They may be regarded as the first signs of the supreme faculties, to which they hold immediately. Everything in corporeal nature is a combination or division of the primitive signs, in which all sensible things are written. Man in his material works is also bound to these primitive signs. He would be otherwise the creature of another nature and another order of things. All his works are varied combinations of the fundamental elements which are the primitive indices of the creative faculties of Divinity. He and his productions are in a secondary sense the expression of the universal creative action."

‡   *Des Erreurs et de la Vérité,* Part II. p. 49.   §   Vol. i. pp. 61-65.

devoted ostensibly to this subject tells us nothing concerning the nature of the crime so characterised, though it deals at some length with the dual nature which, we have already seen, was inherent in the first man, and with the spiritual generation involved therein.

"Had man remained in his glory, his reproduction would have been the most important of his acts, and the one which would have increased most the lustre of his sublime destiny, because he abode in the unity of all his essences, and, being joined with his source, his generations would have participated in the advantages of this union, which they would have perpetuated in their turn."[*] Further, "This primitive spiritual and hermaphroditic state which is inherent in our true nature is the distinctive mark of the Divinity, which possesses in itself all that is necessary to its eternal and universal generation, whilst it can experience no alteration and no foreign admixture."[†]

It will be seen that this presentation of the original sin has no apparent connection with the definition which describes it as the abuse of man's knowledge concerning the union of the principle of the universe with the universe. At the same time it does not represent a changed standpoint, for we meet with both views about the same period, and it can only be concluded that the whole mind of Saint-Martin was not expressed on the subject. If we recur to the "Natural Table," we shall find the doctrine of the Fall depicted under yet another aspect.

"Liberty was necessary in order for the primal man to manifest the Supreme Principle—liberty to behold the real, fixed, and positive rights which are therein. A title was needed for his entrance into his Temple, to enjoy the spectacle in all its grandeur. But, as a free being, it was possible also for man to cease coming into the Temple with the humility of a Levite, to put the victim in place of the sacrifice, the priest in place of God. The entrance of the Temple was then closed to him. He introduced and looked for another light than that which filled its immensity; he sought that light outside the Being who is its sanctuary and source; he sought real, fixed, positive faculties in two beings at once. This error plunged man in an abyss of confusion and darkness, without, however, any exercise of its powers on the part of

---

[*] *Des Erreurs et de la Vérité,* Vol. i. p. 61. [†] Ibid. p. 65.

the Eternal Principle of Life to add to this disaster. Being felicity by essence and the one source of beatitude to all beings, God would act in opposition to his own law did he separate any from a condition adapted to ensure their happiness; and being also by his nature good and peace alone, he could not of himself afflict them with evils, disorders, or privations without producing that which the perfect being can in nowise know; which demonstrates that he is not and cannot be the author of our sufferings. None of the power which resides in this beneficent hand has been employed except to comfort us, and if the virtues of this Supreme Agent were unfailing from the beginning, they were for us and not against us."*

However we may interpret this temple to which man had to earn his title before he could be inducted therein, we here lose sight of that mission by which he was deputed to restore order in a place of confusion, and to reconcile the leader and institutor of that disorder. There is substituted in place of it the more usual and arbitrary conception that he had to do something for himself, that his task was concerned with his own interest rather than with the fundamental issue of the universe. In a word, he was a being in probation, not the ambassador of God. If I may put it somewhat crassly, he seems even to have gone over to the allegiance of the evil principle, to have committed that crime of Satanism which, in a sense, is imputed to him by orthodoxy. "So soon as man sought fixed and positive faculties in another being than the Divine, he lost sight of them altogether, and he now knows only the simulacra of those virtues."†

The view last presented comports far better with the original weakness of man than with his transcendent strength and glory. Thus, in 1782, Saint-Martin said that man was strong, glorious, unsurpassed, but exhibited by an alternative hypothesis that he was weak and easily led away. In 1800 he expressly admits and develops the latter point, without, however, being conscious that his instructions exclude one another. His thesis in the "Spirit of Things" is that the first source of our degradation was not pride. "It was rather the feebleness and facility with which man allowed himself to be seduced by the attraction of this physical world, wherein he had been placed as moderator

---

* Part i. pp. 77-79.   † Ibid. p. 80.

and had been designed for its government; it was rather for gazing on its wonders with an eagerness which surpassed his essential and obligatory affection, whereas they should have been only of secondary importance in comparison with the divine wonders which he was entitled to contemplate still more intimately, for in his capacity as the first mirror he came immediately after God.* Pride could have no place in man till his weakness had opened the door to that insolent error; it could be only the consequence of a prior corrupting cause distinct from himself. The truth on this point is shown naturally by children. They have no pride in their earlier years, but they are weak and easily led away by the sensible objects which encompass them. When their mind has advanced sufficiently to receive impressions of a higher order, they exhibit the signs of their ruling passion, and even of an imperious and uncurbed will, but not the usurping pride which would seize on superior and unknown powers. But the company and example of a person possessing this vice to which they are strangers will soon communicate it to their hearts. Following this simple analogy, we shall find in proximity to the primitive man, and anterior to him, a source of pride which opened the path to this sin, in the absence of which he would either have never known it, or it would not have been the beginning of his fall. Hence the traditions which tell of a rebellious angel prior to humanity are borne out by a simple revelation in the natural order, while the key of their rebellion is found, like all keys, in the same simple path of observation. If the existence of these haughty and insubordinate beings can be demonstrated by the facts of our childhood, reason tells us that, to have an adequate occasion for such pride, they must have abode in a region still more alluring than that of the first man; they must have inhabited a decorated, garnished, and splendid region, whilst man had to repair his own, or rather that which was defiled by the fallen angels when their mirror became tarnished. The more splendid this angelic region, the closer were the angels in contact with the unveiled principles of beauty, and there was also the more room for the temptation to possess them. But before their haughty cupidity could be imputed to them for crime,

---

*   On this point, and generally concerning the divine, spiritual, and natural mirrors, see *De l'Esprit des Choses,* i. 50-53. The conception is a little fantastic, at least verbally, and does not require development.

the power to have suppressed it must be assumed, and there was adequate cause for this suppression, because at the back of the wonders which they beheld there was an impenetrable centre. They were thus themselves the source of this ambition, and their fall was greater than that of man, because the former began by a crime and the latter by a seducing deception; for the knowledge of man was not at first so extensive as the angelic knowledge, though if it had come to maturity it would have exceeded theirs because it would have comprised the two. These natural considerations explain to us why the traditions of the whole earth represent primitive man passing through a period of trial in a garden of delight, which was, however, but the beginning of a perfection and embellishment which should have extended over all the earth; they offer us also the key to the two original prevarications without having recourse only to revelations for proof on these points, as they are demonstrated sufficiently by what passes daily before our eyes." *

It would be unjust to an influence, the existence of which I have admitted, to say that there is here no trace of Jacob Böhme; it would be unjust to Saint-Martin to say that what traces there are do not confuse his system. I not only see what he has borrowed, but l can understand why he borrowed it. We have found the germ already in the "Natural Table," but side by side with a doctrine which assigned such powers and splendour of vocation to primeval man that it left him no room for weakness, and hence no occasion for fall. Under the light derived from Böhme he developed this germ, and the one instruction, so to speak, checks the other without being intended to supplant it. It does not need to be said that there is no real elucidation, and if the dilemma is not sharpened, it is because the doctrine developed in the "Spirit of Things "stultifies itself, much after the fashion of orthodox Latin theology. If man in his Hrst estate had the privilege of contemplating the divine wonders, as it is said, from a nearer point of view than the wonders of the physical world, there is no hypothesis upon which we can suppose that the tarnished kingdom of the dethroned Lucifer could have seemed the more attractive; nor can we suppose that a being thus in correspondence with Divinity partly unveiled

---

* *De l'Esprit des Choses,* pp. 56-61.

could in such light, and under such favours, have been either weak or easily seduced. The same may be said as to the original estate of the fallen angels, which was much too close, by the hypothesis, to the centre and the heart of God for them to cease from being drawn by that centre.

If we have recourse, in the midst of this confusion, to those papers already cited, which were written for and read apparently to a body of initiates, we shall find that Saint-Martin expressly passes over the problem of the Fall on the ground that his audiences had already more ample instructions than he could provide independently. So far as those instructions are identical with the doctrine of man's primeval mission, they offer a dazzling conception, worthy, as I have said at the beginning, of the designs of Providence, if we can admit these materials; but they leave man's lapse insoluble. The alternative instructions, which he did not derive from initiation, which are referable for their development, but not their conception, to the German mystic, are not only inadequate and arbitrary, but are inconsistent with themselves, and would almost justify us in regarding Saint-Martin's admiration for Böhme as the mistake of his advancing years.

IX

General Consequences of the Fall

IN THE DOCTRINE of the first estate and in that of man's lapse there from, we find in Saint-Martin, amidst considerable agreement, a certain extra-lignment, to make use of his own terminology. He was in possession of a system which, though it has its Gnostic correspondences, may be said to have been unknown in mysticism, and he sought to marry it, as he tells us,* with that of Jacob Böhme, whose vast glass of vision reflected the depth and height of the entire universe, but was, I think, full of scoriæ and blemishes. The nuptials were celebrated after a somewhat forced fashion, and the union was not a happy one. Saint-Martin, moreover, had done most of his best work. In the "Spirit of Things" we find him on a lower level of illumination, approaching at times even a commonplace philosophy, and though the "Ministry of Man the Spirit" did much to redeem the defects of that work, and well deserves the encomium already passed thereon, it cannot be compared with the "Natural Table," either for its philosophical profundity or as a literary performance, nor with the "Man of Desire" for the gifts of inspiration and insight. We have now finished for the moment with the metaphysical part of Martinism; in considering the consequences of the traditionary fall of man, there is no longer extra-lignment in Saint-Martin; he is at one with all mysticism; he is on the solid ground of actual human experience; he is not

---

* *Correspondance,* Lettre xcii; Penny, "Theosophic Correspondence" p. 319.

endeavouring to dovetail hypotheses or to effect marriages without the consent of the parties, who end by defrauding one another. We are face to face, of course, with a doctrine which is the antithesis of materialistic evolution, though it does not exclude evolution; but it is, in any case, the catholic doctrine of the mystics, common both to East and West.

Man, by the fact of his fall, has "entered into a region of illusions and nothingness, which, by the multiplicity of its laws and actions, presents in appearance another unity than that of the Simple Being, and other truths than His."[*] This statement is the common ground of transcendentalism. It receives, however, the peculiar aspect of Martinism when man is represented as passing under the dominion of the physical agents whom he once directed. "Uniting himself as a consequence of the corruption of his will to the mixed substances of the apparent and relative region, he is subjected to the action of the different principles which constitute them, and that of the different agents set over to sustain them and to preside over the defence of their law. These mixed substances produce only temporal phenomena in their assemblage, hence time is the chief instrument of the sufferings of man, and that obstacle which keeps him remote from his Principle."[†] In symbolical language, "the chains of the first fallen man were composed of the extract of all parts of the great world."[‡] That is to say, "Man received being to exercise his power in the universality of temporal things, and he has willed to exercise it only on a part. He should act for the intellectual against the sensible, and he has chosen to act for the sensible against the intellectual. Finally, he should reign over the universe, but instead of guarding the integrity of his empire, he has himself degraded it, and the universe has collapsed upon the powerful being who should administer and sustain it. As a consequence of this fall, all the sensible virtues of the universe, which should act in subordination to man within the temporal circumference, have acted in confusion upon him, and have compressed him with all their force. On the contrary, all the intellectual virtues with which he should work in concert, which should present him a unity

---

[*]   *Tableau Naturel,* Part I. p. 80.

[†]   Ibid. p. 101.   [‡]   Ibid. p. 114.

of operation, are now divided for him and now separated from him. What was simple and one has for him become multiple; what was multiple has become conglomerated, and has crushed him with its weight. The sensible has taken the place of the intellectual, and the intellectual of the sensible."[*]

The chief organ of our sufferings is the material body, which constitutes a gross barrier to our faculties, and thus keeps us in privation. "I must not conceal that this crass envelope is the actual penalty to which the crime of man has made him subject in the temporal region. Thereby begin and thereby are perpetuated the trials without which he cannot recover his former correspondence with the light."[†] It is not, therefore, as we shall see more fully later on, an arbitrary penalty, but rather the narrow way of our salvation. The sufferings connected with it begin, however, at the very moment of our corporeal birth. "It thus exhibits all the signs of the most shameful reprobation; it originates, like some vile insect, amidst corruption and mire; it is born amidst the sufferings and cries of its mother, as though it came forth to her disgrace; its breath is first drawn amidst tears and in acute discomfort; its earliest steps in life show that it has come to suffer, and that it is truly the son of crime and woe. On the contrary, had man remained guiltless, his birth would have been the first experience of felicity and peace; he would have greeted the light with transport and with hymns to the principle of his beatitude. Undisturbed as to the legitimacy of his origin, at peace as to the stability of his lot, he would have partaken of all delights, because he would have known sensibly their advantages. But now, from the earliest years of his elementary course, the disquietude of his situation increases. He suffers at first in the body; he is destined to suffer in the mind. He has been the butt of the elements before he had any power to defend himself, and he is now hunted in his thought before he can exert himself in the will, whence he is an easy prey to error, which wins entrance by a thousand avenues, and corrupts his tree to its roots. At this period assuredly man begins a career so painful and so perilous that he would succumb infallibly if help did not accompany his course. But

---

[*] *Tableau Naturel,* Part I. pp. 112-113.

[†] *Des Erreurs et de la Vérité,* Part I. p. 48.

the hand from which he came spares nothing for his preservation; as difficulties multiply with his age, opposing the exercise of his faculties, so his corporeal envelope requires consistence; in a word, his new armour hardens, so that it can resist the assaults of his enemies, until the intellectual temple being at length built up, the scaffolding is required no longer, and its removal discovers the edifice complete and impregnable."*

I do not know that this picture has less force at this day than it would have possessed at the period of Ruysbrœck, who might well have been its author, who has, in fact, written many pages which make it read like a transcript from the Flemish mystic; but I do not quote it as specially illuminating; like all half-truths, it is perhaps more disconcerting than helpful, but it shows the connection of Martinism with ascetic Christianity; and it is otherwise suggestive to find in a book which was indexed by the Spanish Inquisition a passage, and one out of many, which might have been signed by the author of the "Imitation." I will connect with it one other which will show the later reflections of Saint-Martin on this subject.

"Observe what occurs in those accidents which take place daily before our eyes. A man who falls into the water, the slough, or the ditch, comes out drenched, defiled, disfigured by the substances with which he has come in contact, and he is sometimes past recognition. It is worse still if he be cast into the crater of a volcano or on sharp rocks, for he is then burnt, or bruised and broken. Recall now the ancient beauty of man, the superior essences of his original form as compared with his actual form. Think of the corrosive elements which now constitute Nature, so far removed from the harmonial and vivific essences amidst which he first originated, and in which he might have fixed his abode. Remember also those proud and rebellious agents who preceded man, and we shall then have those pointed rocks, that water, that slime, those ditches, that volcanic gulf—in fine, all those heterogeneous and hurtful actions with which the human soul has been connected in its fall, which have so disfigured and polluted its primitive and corporeal form that all its members are broken, so to speak, and it offers no means of recognition. For if we confess that

---

* *Des Erreurs et de la Vérité,* Part I. pp. 47-48.

man's primitive object was the embellishment and perfecting of the earth, and the manifestation of the splendour of his principle therein, then that of the perverse power, since it passed into corruption, was, on the contrary, the degradation of all earthly forms, and especially of man, who was sent to restore order, to check the efforts of the evil principle, a task which, in the moral order and that of the spirit, is, we feel, still ours. We are conscious, furthermore, that this human form which is now so soiled, so alloyed with contemptible elements, is in no way analogous with ourselves, and that after its use has ceased it cannot be concealed too soon. Hence man is the sole animal who inters his dead, a custom which also indicates the pre-eminence of the primitive human form and the respect which was due to it."[*]

The indication here given that man, in spite of his fall, has not forfeited his mission, was developed many years earlier by Saint-Martin when addressing his fellow-initiates. "Notwithstanding his terrible degradation, the nature of man has not changed; his essence, his rights are the same, and hence his actual destination must be, as it first was, to prove before all that environs him the existence, unity, and divinity of one Supreme Agent; in a word, to represent here below all His acts and virtues. The first law given to man must be accomplished inevitably, and no snares to which we are liable will ever destroy it. We may evade it for a time; we may depart from it by our vicious habits and our false, corrupted desires, but in the midst of all our errors still that law follows us, and we can never escape it.[†] The double law of our origin still possesses jurisdiction; in our punishment, as in our prime, we have still to honour the Supreme Being and to perform his temporal work, the restoration of unity. Herein is the true object of wisdom, the real, solid, satisfying, fruitful end, towards which the soul of man must strive unceasingly, as to the sole nourishing sustenance and the sole fruit wherein he need fear no bitterness.[‡] There is nothing more important than the duties imposed by this twofold law. The first of the objects with which it is concerned explains itself. To honour the Supreme Being is to regard Him as the one and universal

---

[*]   *De l'Esprit des Choses,* i. pp. 71-73.

[†]   *Les Voies de la Sagesse, Œuvres Posthumes,* i. pp. 70-71.

[‡]   Ibid. pp. 73-74.

chief, to believe in no power but His and that which derives from Him, to tremble at our own nothingness compared with that infinite immensity, which in the essence and in the fruits of its essence suffers neither defects nor darkness, but creates and maintains order and life everywhere. This object, being love in the last analysis, is the attitude of pure spirit; it is that which has preceded all things and whereby all shall finish, but in our existing condition we have only its evanescent lights, which yet are priceless, for they exhibit the delights of that principle from which we derive and the inexhaustible blessings which it showers on us; it binds us thereto by the indissoluble ties of our essence, and helps us to pass without shipwreck through the floods which inundate our terrestrial abode. Hence we must never lose sight of it, and though our homage cannot be compared with that which was rendered in our origin, it is so indispensable that it cannot be withheld without denying the Divine Nature and our own, or without plunging us in the abyss of evil and sorrow.[*]

"The second object, or the manifestation of the Supreme Being before the eyes of our kindred and those of the enemies of truth, is a confirmation and extension of the first. By Himself must we manifest Him, by His grandeur make Him known, recognising His power in all, seeking in all things His true law, and extending His honour by that which we ourselves bear Him. This second object has therefore two branches, to make us in His own image and to lead His enemies to render Him due homage.[†] Herein His own power supplements our weakness, or rather it is His own love which we represent when united therewith, that living charity which makes us merciful to each other in our miseries; in a word, that true earth which Wisdom, when it finds it prepared, sows broadcast with all its gifts, and it becomes thus that vast field where germinate those virtues of the Divine Principle which we are all of us here to manifest."[‡]

---

[*] *Les Voies de la Sagesse, Œuvres Posthumes,* vol. i. pp. 76-78.

[†] Ibid. pp. 79-80.   [‡] Ibid. pp. 83-84.

X

Man and Nature

THE VOCATION OF the mystic is pre-eminently to announce that there is an inward secret way by which the soul of man can return to its Divine Source. It is only in a secondary sense that his vocation is concerned at all with the external world. It follows from that fundamental axiom of all mystic science which tells us that truth and reality are to be sought within, that the things which are without are in some sense illusory. The sense in which they are illusory is the outward sense, beneath which we infer from the veracity of God that there is a concealed principle; they are therefore not false testimony, but parable, and Saint-Martin observes finely: "There is not a people, and I may say there is not a man in possession of his true self, for whom the temporal universe is not a great allegory or fable which must give place to a grand morality."* But the idealism of the mystic must be distinguished from the false idealism of the Berkeley school and its connections, which derives its considerations from the phenomena of the material world and breaks down at every step. For example, it is no "argument against the existence of matter" that colour is not a quality which is inherent in objects. The communication of the physical world through the senses to the mind is performed by a variety of artifices. To say that there is no truth in the artifices is merely crass, because it is understood that they are vehicles; they are

---

* *Tableau Naturel,* Part II. p. 207.

128

commensurate to the extent of the communication which man is at present capable of receiving; to say that there is no principle communicating is to talk distraction; to say that the communicating principle, the vehicles, and the mind which receives the messages are bound up inseparably one with another, so that the mind can receive no testimony except through the senses, and can have no being when the senses cease to transmit, is to be what is called a materialist—that is to say, one who denies that the inner man is to be distinguished from the man without, or is other than the product of his environment. To say that the communicating principle and the recipient principle are realities having veiled intercourse, is to establish a true doctrine as to the correspondence between man and the universe. To say that there is another mode of communication, and that with a higher principle, possible to the man within, is to establish the mystic correspondence between man and God. It is in virtue of this correspondence that Saint-Martin terms humanity the exotic plant of the universe, and it is in this general sense that we must understand him when he says that "sensible things, though void and apparent only for the mind of man, have reality analogous to his sensible and material being. Wisdom is so fruitful that it establishes proportions in virtues and realities relatively to each class of its productions. This is Why there is a conformity, and even an insurmountable law attached to the course of sensible things, without which their action would be of no effect. Thus, it is true altogether for bodies that bodies exist and intercommunicate, and that there is an indispensable commerce between all substances of material nature. But it is true only for bodies, since all material actions, operating nothing analogous to the veritable nature of man, are in some sort, or may be, foreign to him, when he wills to make use of his forces and to draw near to his natural element. Matter is true for matter, and never for spirit."* And this leads up to his more explicit doctrine of the natural world." When God has recourse to such visible signs as the universe to communicate his thought, it is to employ them in favour of beings separated from him. Had all

---

* *Tableau Naturel,* Part I. pp. 82-83. And elsewhere it is classed as one of those substances which present in the sensible order all the signs of reality while they have none at all for man's thinking part (ii. 173).

beings remained in his unity, they would not have needed this means to draw towards him. The universe is therefore a sign of God's love for corrupted creatures separated voluntarily from the First Cause and submitted to the laws of justice in the womb of the visible universe. God operates unceasingly to remove the separation so contrary to their felicity." *

The doctrine of Saint-Martin as to the connections between man and Nature is far too many-sided to be represented by a mere definition. We know that, according to his teaching, the physical universe was the splendid habitation of the evil principle in its first estate; and that when it was destroyed by the rebellion of the chief of the first emanation, it became part of man's mission to restore it. Whether he attempted this mission does not appear, but material things became or remained sufficiently beautiful and wonderful to prove, in connection with the evil principle, a source of seduction to himself. By his fall he either failed to remove the curse in which it was involved or it was made subject to it for a second time. In any case, as it looked to him at first, so it now looks to him for its release and repose. There is no doubt that in a certain sense the sin of man is the pain of Nature, and we have high authority for the belief that even the whole creation is groaning for the manifestation of the sons of God. It is also mystically true that the transfiguration of man's environment must proceed side by side with the transfiguration of man, and even at this day the curse is lifted from the world for every soul who ceases from evil. † But it is almost impossible to pass, as Saint-Martin does, from these general considerations to their particular development without entering a fantastic region. The first step towards our assuagement of Nature must be, he says, to cease from tormenting it; the first step towards healing it is to cease from infecting it further, as we now do, not only by our corrupt corporeal exhalations, but still more by the disease of our thoughts. "The earth whereon we walk offers us all its pores like so many mouths crying for consoling balm to cure the wounds which

---

*   *Tableau Naturel,* Part I. p. 40.

†   "The wisdom and bounty of the Divine Being are manifested by the birth of man into terrestrial life. He is thus placed in a position to soothe by his labour and striving s part of the evils which the first crime has caused on the earth."—Ibid. p. 100.

devour it, and, instead of giving it rest and life, we would appease its thirst with the blood of men spilt in fanatical and warlike furies, even as the atmosphere which surrounds us is filled with our dead and death-bearing speach."* These are poetic exaggerations which have no place in philosophy, mystical or otherwise, but they may be tolerated poetically for their suggestion. At times, moreover, through the glamour, symbolism, and high colouring of such fantastic pictures, we find something which is at least conformable to more sane and serious doctrine.

"The universe is on its bed of suffering, and it is for us, O men, to console it! The universe is on its bed of suffering because, since the Fall, a foreign substance has entered into its veins, and torments unceasingly the principle of its life; it is for us to bring it words of consolation which may encourage it to bear up under its evils; it is for us to proclaim the promise of its deliverance and of the alliance which the Eternal Wisdom shall yet make with it. It is a duty and a justice on our part, for the head of our family is the first cause of its sorrow, and we must confess that it is we who have widowed it. Is it not expecting ever the restoration of its spouse? Ah! sacred sun, we indeed are the first cause of thy disquiet and solicitude. Thine eager eye turns successively upon all the zones of Nature; thou dost rise in joy each day, expecting that men will restore thee that cherished bride, that eternal Sophia, of whom thou art deprived; thou fulfillest thy daily course, imploring the whole earth, with ardent words painting thy consuming desires. Thou retirest to thy rest in the evening, afflicted and weeping, for thou hast sought in vain; thou hast asked in vain of man, who still leaves thee to sojourn in barren places and in houses of prostitution.

"Man, the woe is still greater! Say no more that the universe is on its bed of suffering; say, rather, it is on its dying bed, and it is thine to fulfil the final duties; it is thine to reconcile it with that pure source from whence it came, purging it from all false substances with which it is now impregnated continually, and cleansing it from having passed all the days of its life in vanity. Not thus would its time have been misspent hadst thou remained on the throne of thy first splendour,

---

*   *Le Ministère de l'Homme-Esprit,* pp. 131-132.

whence thou shouldst have anointed it daily with an oil of joy which would have preserved it from infirmity and sorrow, performing for it what now it performs for thee in the daily produce of the light and fruits of those elements to which thou art subject. Draw nigh to it, therefore; seek forgiveness for its death; it is thou who hast caused it.

"Man, the woe is still greater! Say no more that the universe is on its bed of death ; say, rather, that it is in its sepulchre, that putrefaction has claimed it, and thou art answerable. Except for thee it would not have been brought to the tomb, it would not have seen corruption. Thou art the tomb thereof. In place of being the cradle of its perpetual youth and beauty, thou hast buried it within thee as in a grave, and hast clothed it with thine own putrefaction. Inject quickly, by all its channels, the incorruptible elixir; it is for thee to resuscitate it." *

Fantastic as this picture must seem, if we accept the system of Saint-Martin it has a side of truth, † and assuredly never poet or mystic has been haunted before or since by such images in his ecstasy. So also amidst all the voices of Nature, this thinker of things unexpected, and yet too deep to be wholly false, was oppressed by its dumbness, and speaks of that privation as the chief source of its suffering. It is in that state, he says, which men of the spirit have termed vanity, because, being void and speechless, it could mean nothing for them. "God alone is full, God alone signifies everything, and that which does not participate in the plenitude of his divine being can show only the opposite of his universal properties. They know, these men, that we cannot pray without preparation—that is, until our atmosphere is filled with speech, or, in its full sense, till speech be restored to the universe. Deprived of this, it cannot take part in prayer; it is even an obstacle thereto, since we can pray only in the midst of our brethren. ‡ Before we can pray freely we must lead back Nature into joy by participating in her sufferings and coordinating our actions

---

*   *Le Ministère de l'Homme-Esprit,* pp. 55-57.

†   The philosophical idea which underlies it had been expressed many years previously. "Intellectual man, voluntarily reduced to an inferior and limited class, must generate all his being and extend all its virtues to the extremities of his particular environment, if he would return to that universal and sacred environment from which he is banished."

‡   *Le Ministère de l'Homme-Esprit,* pp. 73-74.

with these. "Man finds commonly a solemnity and majesty in solitary places, clad with forests or watered by some vast river, and these imposing pictures extend their empire upon him when he contemplates them in the silence and darkness of the night. But amidst such surroundings he may receive other impressions, showing the true cause of that which we have designated by the name of vanity. In effect, all Nature is like a dumb being who depicts by motions, as best it can, the principal wants which consume it, but, void of speech, ever leaves its expression far below its desires, and blends even with its gaiety some serious and melancholy characteristics which are a check on our own joy. Thus, amidst so many sublime objects we feel that Nature is dejected at her enforced silence, and a languor which is deeper than melancholy succeeds our enthusiasm when this painful thought possesses us. We comprehend intuitively that all should speak, and the same intuition instructs us that all should be fluid and diaphanous, that opacity and stagnation are the radical causes of the silence and weariness of Nature. For us it has, however, its consolation, for us that silence is eloquent; it is the silence of sorrow, not of insensibility. The more we observe Nature, the better we shall recognise that if it have its times of sadness, it has also its times of joy, and we only can discover and appreciate them. It is conscious of a secret life circulating through all its veins, and through us as an organ it waits the accents of that speech which sustains it, and offers to the enemy an insurmountable barrier. It seeks in us the living Ere which radiates from that speech, and brings it through our mediation a saving balm for all its wounds. It is even true that in a sense it is only the terrestrial man who finds Nature silent and weariful; for the man of desire everything sings in her, everything prophesies her deliverance in sublime canticles. We must be therefore advised that all must sing within man to cooperate in that emancipation, so that all men on earth may be able to say with us that everything sings in Nature." *

Inconsistency is the common error of enthusiasm, but it will not disconcert the reader seriously when he finds that the mystical silence of Nature is represented as the discovery first of the spiritual and afterwards the mistake of the earthly mind. It is not less true that Nature

* *Le Ministère de l'Homme-Esprit,* pp. 75-77.

in the last analysis is dumb for the soul of man, though, in a sense, it has music for the soul; it is also true that she is full of noise and voices for the man of earth, and yet in the last analysis she never speaks really to the earthly man. The confusion of Saint-Martin is therefore in the form only, and as this failing is frequent, he lends himself seldom only to a literal presentation. I observe that in one line of the "Ministry" he has said all that needs saying from the mystic standpoint when he described Nature as "the portrait of an absent person," [*] and he has put us in possession of the key to all her phases when he says that she is in somnambulism, [†] and this explains why her aspect is invariably what is termed magical, for the state of somnambulism is the state of mediumship, and Saint-Martin and Böhme both describe Nature in her visible manifestation as the medium for her invisible and fundamental properties. It is in this state of trance that she is at once eloquent and silent; she speaks if man can interpret; she is silent unless he prophesies; her voices are oracles, as becomes her somnambulism, and for the explanation of the words of the pythoness the presence of her priest is needed.

Having said something of the mystical aspect of Nature as it was presented to the mind of Saint-Martin, it is necessary to add that he regarded her also scientifically, and that he had a system of natural philosophy which depended from his metaphysical system, but is at the same time so far extrinsic thereto that I shall not derogate from the present value of his metaphysics when I say that his physics were absurd even for his period. I do not mean that he has no clear sight and no just observations on these matters, but he was not a man of any considerable scientific attainments, and his views upon elementary substances, [‡] upon composite bodies, [§] upon the cause of thunder and lightning, [||] of the flux and reflux of the sea, [¶] upon generation, [°] destruction, [**] and so forth, are of the period of Robert Fludd rather than of Laplace, Newton, and Buifon. Upon speculative points he was

---

[*] *Le Ministère de l'Homme-Esprit,* p. 82.

[†] *De l'Esprit des Choses,* i. 125, *et seq.*

[‡] *Des Erreurs et de la Vérité,* Part I. pp. 62, 127, and elsewhere.

[§] Ibid. pp. 82, 101, 135, and elsewhere.   [||] Ibid. p. 140, *et seq.*

[¶] Ibid. p. 136.   [°] Ibid. p. 88 *et seq.*   [**] Ibid. p. 92 *et seq.*

sometimes shrewder than his period, as, for example, about the divisibility of matter to infinity,* and sometimes it must be added that he was narrower, as, for example, about the plurality of worlds.† Speaking generally, his natural philosophy was based on *à priori* considerations of a kind more or less arbitrary, and it would serve no useful purpose to notice it in any detail, much less to present it critically, for it does not now deserve any serious consideration. When he attacks the materialism of his age, he is, of course, on surer ground, for he is then dealing with fundamental principles, and what he says, when it does not convince, is at least consistent with his transcendentalism; and I am not sure that some of the points which he scores against those who "explain matter by matter, man by the senses, and the Author of all things by elementary Nature," ‡ are not as pointed now as when they were first sharpened on the eve of the French Revolution. But we are concerned here with the natural world only so far as the essential doctrines of his metaphysical system affect it. We know that according to those doctrines the evil principle has an active and continuous communication with the universe, because he is responsible for its disorder, and I infer also that it is the place of his punishment or expiation. Outside the class of temporal things evil cannot coexist with the Good Principle, and as it is impotent in relation therewith, it cannot affect the essence of the material universe, but all things comprised "within the darksome sphere where it is confined" are exposed to its action, and it can and does "war with the agents of the First Cause, creates obstacles to their action, and introduces its rebellious operation into the minor derangements of particular beings to augment the disorder further." § The opposition of the two principles is, however, "purely intellectual," and has its source in their conflicting wills, though its effect is felt in the sensible and corporeal. ‖ Following there from, Saint-Martin traces a law of dual action in all created beings, "one side of which is fixed and imperishable while the other is transitory, and hence unreal for intelligence, though not for the

---

*   *Des Erreurs et de la Vérité,* Part I. pp. 79-80.

†   *Le Ministère de l'Homme-Esprit,* i. 212-225; *Œuvres Posthumes,* ii. 116 *et seq.*

‡   *Des Erreurs et de la Vérité,* Part I. pp. 70-71.

§   *Tableau Naturel,* Part I. p. 27.   ‖   Ibid. p. 75.

bodily eyes."* To recognise the action of this double law in temporal things will, it is said, "assist us to distinguish it in ourselves, because he who is most discerning in the judgment of bodies will soon arrive at discernment in judging man."† The nature of the sequence remains, however, in obscurity, but the double action is described as attached to beings of the corporeal order for their reproduction and nourishment.‡

This obscurity, however, involves nothing of importance, and need not delay us. There is indeed only one more point in the physical system of Saint-Martin which deserves to be noticed for its intrinsic value. It is his distinction of the principle of matter from matter itself, which recalls the old postulates of the scholastic philosophy. This principle "cannot be subjected to the measurement of bodily eyes." § Were it matter, it must possess extension, and so forth. "But it is acknowledged universally that a principle is indivisible, incommensurable, absolutely different from matter as presented to our senses. It is, in a word, a simple being, while matter, which is divisible and measurable, is not simple." ‖ To the confusion existing on the subject of the principle of matter Saint-Martin refers the false conclusions, already noticed, as to the infinite divisibility of matter, "which, as regards its essence, cannot be divided at all." ❡ The form of matter is variable unceasingly; that of the principle remains always the same,° a statement which includes apparently the distinction between material and substantial form. "Matter itself may perish, but its principle remains unalterable and indestructible. It existed before bodies, and can remain after them. The principle of bodies may therefore be conceived apart from every form of matter, no particle of which can at the same time be conceived or exist unsustained or unanimated by its principle." **

---

* *Des Erreurs et de la Vérité*, Part I. pp. 74-75.   † Ibid. p. 76.

‡ Ibid. p. 75.   § *Des Erreurs et de la Vérité*, Part I. p. 78.

‖ Ibid. p. 79.   ❡ Ibid. p. 81.   ° Ibid. p. 83.

** Ibid. p. 85.

XI

The Privation of Man

ROM THE CONSIDERATION of the general consequences of the Fall, sketched in the eighth section, we have learned already that the present state of man is one of extreme privation. The Martinistic significance of the term is exceedingly comprehensive; it involves much more than the loss of his original felicity, his powers, his knowledge, his exalted place in the divine economy; it involves more than the limitations, the narrowness, of our physical being, more than the humiliation of lapse, the misery of degradation, the woe of the darkness; it involves the idea of a defenceless, or at least a feeble state, the proximity of enemies, the danger and dread of their assaults. "Our thinking part is no sooner united to its form than it is assailed and tormented."[*] In that union there is comprised above all, as we have seen, the idea of imprisonment. At the same time, our durance constitutes our opportunity; we are not within dead walls so much as within a living fortress."[†] Still more, the body is not merely our rampart, it is the channel of our knowledge, and hence also the way of our salvation. This is a point of great importance in the system of Saint-Martin, because it leads to his central doctrine concerning the Active and Intelligent Cause—in other words, the doctrine of the Repairer, which will be the study of the next book. For a mo-

---

[*] *La Source de nos Connaissances et de nos Idées,* Œuvres *Posthumes,* i. 357
[†] *Des Erreurs et de la Vérité,* Part I. p. 48.

ment only it seems to identify one of the most spiritual of the mystics with a view which has in a special manner been connected with the history of Materialism, for, in common with Locke and his school, Saint-Martin virtually denied the existence of innate ideas. At this day Materialism and Spiritualism have far other issues for contention than were dreamed of in the "Essay on the Human Understanding," and the source of our knowledge and ideas is a question of academic rather than real interest. But there are issues raised by the standpoint of Saint-Martin which are not academic for the mystic, and the field of its observation begins on the skyline of Locke's horizon. The ideas of man, he says, are derived to him from without by the way of his material envelope, and the physical senses are their first organs.[*] He confesses that in this sense our very thoughts are not our own; they are suggested to us, but do not arise within us. The suggestion occasions, however, an interior act, and the sentiment of thought is within and independent of the senses.[†] But to understand the peculiar manner in which Saint-Martin refers the origin of our ideas to sensations, we must glance at his doctrine of the two natures in man; we shall see that he recognises the existence of an intellectual sensibility, a twofold channel of communication, and that the origin of our intellectual ideas is in reality not material. "There is a sensible faculty relative to the intellectual nature, and a sensible faculty relative to the corporeal nature;"[‡] in other words, man has two beings. "He was not at the beginning made subject to this assemblage; he enjoyed the prerogatives of a simple being, possessing all in himself, by reason of the precious which he derived from his principle. When the overwhelming sentence was pronounced against him, of all these gifts there remained only that shadow of liberty which resides in his will, but this will is usually without force or empire. By his union with a sensible being he was reduced to an assemblage of two inferior causes, like those which rule all bodies."[§] The similitude does not, however, indicate equality, "for the object of the two natures in man is more noble, and their properties are far different, but in regard to the act and exercise of their faculties both are absolutely subject to the same law, and the

---

[*] *Des Erreurs et de la Vérité,* Part I. p. 49. [†] Ibid. p. 151.

[‡] *Des Erreurs et de la Vérité,* PartI. p. 65. [§] Ibid. pp. 177-178.

two inferior causes which now compose man have no more inherent strength than the inferior corporeal causes. Man, it is true, as an intellectual being, has an advantage over the animals because he is conscious of needs that are unknown to them, but, like them, he is unable of himself to minister to his needs, for as they cannot give life to their own natures, so he cannot enliven his intellectual faculties, and thus cannot dispense with that Active and Intelligent Cause without which nothing temporal can operate efficaciously. His works of themselves have no value apart from the support which can alone sustain them, and his two natures are in perpetual yet ineffective struggle. They may be compared to the two lines of any angle which move in contrary directions, approach and even coincide with one another, but can never produce an enclosed figure without the junction of a third line to fix their instability, determine their position, and distinguish them definitely from each other." * But man is continually seeking to form an enclosed figure, so to speak, with the two lines, and has thus fallen into many deplorable follies, especially the Materialistic system of sensations, which brings him to the level of the beasts, suggests that all things are indifferent in nature, and that he is hence irresponsible. In virtue of his dual nature he does possess ideas which do not derive from the senses, as, for example, those of law, order, and harmony. These, at the same time, are not of his own creation; thought comes to him, it does not originate within him; he has its germ or principle, but it must be fertilised from without; once fertilised, the germ develops. From this Saint-Martin concludes that "independently of the universal creative faculties of sensible nature, there exist outside man intellectual and thinking faculties analogous to himself and producing thoughts within him." † As a fact, there are two such sources, one of which is the evil principle; the other is "a thinking universal force, having a liberty which differs essentially from those of other beings, because it is itself its own law. From this being all existences emanate continually, and it is what men call God." ‡ From this first fount of

---

* *Des Erreurs et de la Vérité,* Part I. pp. 178-179.

† *Tableau Naturel,* Part I. p. 13.

‡ *Tableau Naturel,* p. 15. This statement should be compared with p. 140, to which it gives the key. "When beings turn criminal, they are really separated

truth our intellectual part receives incessantly both its thoughts[*] and the light which enlightens it, for "in the intellectual order it is the superior which nourishes the inferior, while in the physical order it is the inferior which sustains the superior."[†] While we are passive in so far as we are open to impressions received in the physical order, and to the two kinds of intellectual communication distinguished above, we have the power of examination, adoption, and rejection. In a word, we can judge and discern between good and evil, in which sense the soul is superior to thought because it can pronounce thereon, and is thus in possession of that liberty which is "the faculty within us by which we are enabled to fulfil the law imposed on us or to act in opposition to that law."[‡]

(Continued...)

from the Divine Chief by privation of the exercise of their faculties; and though the virtue of the Creator is communicated to them, if, on account of their corruption, nothing can be returned to Him, they remain in the darkness and death destined for all creatures of falsehood and error."

[*] Subject, however, to a certain sensible modification, which is not clearly described, but is connected by Saint-Martin with the origin of primitive natural signs.—*Tableau Naturel,* i. 224.

[†] Ibid. p. 23.   [‡] Ibid. p. 14.

XII

Immortality and Death

A SYSTEM LIKE THAT of Saint-Martin must not be expected to concern itself with the immortality of the soul in the sense of offering a demonstration, philosophically speaking, of an immortal part in man. The system supposes immortality as it supposes God; it represents man as occupying originally a spiritual state and invested with spiritual splendour. There is no real question as to whether he will live after death; the one question is how he may live now in order after death, and in a measure before it, to ensure his return to the true life and glory of the spirit. Incidentally, however, we shall find the abstract question is touched upon once or twice, when it is worth noting that the appeal is not to psychological experiences, the inferences from theurgic phenomena, the proof palpable of immortality so called. Saint-Martin is content to rest it on considerations borrowed from his philosophy and reflections on the nature and aspirations of man. Man derives from an indestructible source; he has not the same originating principle as matter; he has been generated by unity, "which possesses in itself and also communicates to its productions a total and independent existence. It can extend or contract their faculties, but cannot cause their death, because its works are real, and that which is can never cease to be. Matter, on the other hand, is the product of a secondary principle, subordinate to the first, and its continuation depends upon their mutual action."* Here is the

---

* *Des Erreurs at de la Vérité,* Part I. p. 86.

dogmatic statement which, for Saint-Martin at least, is final, because it is based on his fundamental principles. The argument from human ambition, from human aspiration, from human desire of immortality, from the hunger and thirst after fame, which has been presented so often, but is withal so uncertain in its grasp, did not impress him as it commonly stands and falls in metaphysical discussions, but he takes us through it into the higher field of its application.

If we are made in the image of God, it follows that in God there must be a sacred heart and spirit, but they are so united that they form one only, like all the faculties and powers of this sovereign being. Our rights also extend to the establishment of an indissoluble alliance between spirit and heart, by their union in the principle which has made them. It is, in fact, on this indispensable condition that we can hope only to fashion ourselves anew into the likeness of God, as it is in working to this end that we become confirmed in the mournful conviction of our degradation, and yet in the sublime certitude of our superiority to the external order. Furthermore, in this labour we obtain the inexpressible advantage not only of removing by degrees our privation, but of approaching and enjoying substantially what men who are eager for glory denominate immortality; for the vague desire of the Children of the Flood to live in the remembrance of others is the feeblest and falsest of all those which are employed vulgarly in favour of the dignity of the human soul. Albeit that man is spirit, that in all his acts, regulated or disordered, he has ever a spiritual motive of some kind, and that in his productions he works by the spirit and for the spirit, he is, notwithstanding, filled with this desire of immortality only by a motive of self-love, by the feeling of superiority over others, and by anxiety for admiration, the idea of which always moves and impresses him, and in the absence of which his eagerness and its fruits frequently run a risk of diminishing. We may therefore be assured that such a motive rests rather on an itching after immortality than on a veritable conviction, and the proof is that those who follow it are those commonly who have only temporal works to offer towards its realisation. Possessed of a true conviction of immortality, they would seek rather to labour in and for the true God, and would prove by their own self-oblivion the authenticity of this conviction. At the same time their hopes to abide in immortality would not be deceived, because they would then be sowing in a field where they would be sure of reaping. Working in time only, sowing only in the minds of men, part of whom will make haste to forget their works, while the rest may have never known them, is the most unlikely and clumsy way of securing, as they deem, immortality. Were we willing to reflect a little, we should find proofs of our immortality on every hand. We have only to consider, for example, the habitual famine in which man leaves his spirit, and yet it is not extinguished. It is self-stifled, bewrayed, delivered to errors; it turns to evil, it turns to madness, it does wrong in place of right, and still it does not perish. Did we treat our bodies with the same bad skill and neglect, if we left them to fast so hardly, they would do neither good nor evil; they would do nothing ; they would die.

"Another way of discerning at least the index of our immortality is to realise how, in every respect, man here below walks daily on the edge of his grave, and it can be only by some instinct of his immortality that he seeks to rise superior to this danger, living as if it did not exist. Such carelessness is in itself a sign that he is actually filled with this conviction. Speaking spiritually, his risk is still greater, for he is ever on the verge of being engulfed by the deathless source of falsehood. May it not indeed be affirmed that very many of humanity are walking in their grave itself, too blind to attempt to get out, or to ask if they will ever escape it? When any one of them has the happiness to perceive what they are all doing, he has then a most irresistible spiritual proof of immortality, because he has proof spiritual of his dire mortality, and, figuratively speaking, of his death, the torment and horror of which he could never feel had he not at the same time an energetic conviction of his immortality. This kind of proof is, however, a question of experience, and is one of the first fruits of the labour of regeneration; for if we feel not our spiritual death, how should we dream of invoking life?" *

The issue is exceedingly clear and reasonable within its own lines. Regeneration is a Supernatural experience which is possible only to the immortal spirit; to those who have passed through it the question of immortality is idle; to those who have not passed through it there is no real evidence possible. This is why Saint-Martin did not appeal to proof palpable and "spirits before our eyes," and this is why the

---

* *Le Ministère de l'Homme-Esprit,* pp. 16-20.

strongest "test-cases" of spirit return have so little result in the spiritual order for those who are satisfied as to their character, which will help us also to understand that those of whom it was said that they would not believe though one should rise from the dead were not represented as willingly and perversely obstinate so much as deficient.

The state of the soul after death is another question, the answer to which is rather thinly sketched in the writings of Saint-Martin, though he has much here and there to observe upon the transition of man itself. The key to his reticence is, I think, not far to seek. His books, like his life, were devoted to the way of reintegration. Man could recover his lost estate and glory; he could restore the broken circle of his life; he could go back upon the dreary history of the sin which first taught him the bitter knowledge of good and evil; he could so live that he should lose the consciousness of evil, * and yet be stronger for having passed through it. The one thing needful to know was the right way to set about it; the one thing needful to do was to start about it at once. There was no time for side issues, even if they were not idle. But, so to speak, he relents now and then; he speaks of death; he tells us that, for himself, he adores it; † he asks poetically, perhaps I should say hyperbolically, whether it still exists, whether bodily disease can be accounted anything by the sage; it is only an act of time; "what correspondence can it have with the man of eternity?" ‡ We should have no notion concerning it were it not for the sentiment of immortality with which it contrasts. And then the old ascetic feeling, upon the verge of which the mystic is always standing, comes over him for a moment, and he says that "the wise man should have the moral knowledge of his individual death. He should follow it in all its details; he should see himself dying, since his personal eternity beholds all which passes for him in time." But it is not for the reason of the ascetic, namely, to conquer the fear of death; it is that he may "fulfil worthily the important task of his life, without which he dies in the dark and without knowing it, like the beasts or the Children of the Flood. The sole evil which we can experience on the part of death

---

* *Des Erreurs at de la Vérité,* Part I. p. 21.

† *Portrait Historique, Œuvres Posthumes,* i. 111.

‡ *Pensées sur la Mort,* ibid. p. 144.

is to die before being born; for those who are born before dying, death is henceforth only an advantage." [*]

The gift of Saint-Martin impressed on all subjects which he handled the seal of his peculiar originality. Thus, he tells us in this connection that "death and misfortunes place man under the hand of God's justice, and it is for this reason that manes and the unfortunate are to be respected." [†] Was it some sub-conscious sentiment of this kind which made old ceremonial magic direct that the demons, when they responded to evocation, should be received with the honour due to kings? That the victims of the greater divine vengeance are the more sacred, and it was piety and not devil-worship to recognise it? Sometimes, however, the same gift, because it was so peculiar, and because it was a seeing sense which beheld correspondences so far removed from the usual field of analogy, led Saint-Martin to statements which, even from the mystic standpoint, have a hazardous aspect. Thus he tells us that the moment and mode of our death can and ought to be known to us. "Were man constantly occupied in life by imbuing his spirit with light and truth, he would know the time and manner of his death, because spirit is the universal torch of matter, and the man who is deprived of this knowledge is a corrupted being." [‡] To know how to die we must learn how to live; if we have acquired that knowledge, the mode and disposition of our death will be assured already, and in this sense it is known to us beforehand; its accidents are unimportant, [§] and though the history of premonitions may warrant the possibility, it is not of great service spiritually. Let us rather agree with Saint-Martin in the closing words of the paper which develops this statement. "The wise man who is convinced that this world is only a translation of the unseen world must rejoice and not grieve when the time comes to make acquaintance with the original, because it is a general truth that originals are preferable to translations." [‖]

---

[*] *Pensées sur la Mort, Œuvres Posthumes,* vol. i. p. 144.

[†] *Œuvres Posthumes,* i. 311.   [‡] *De l'Esprit des Choses,* ii. 45.

[§] "Death is merely the quitting of an appearance, that is to say, of the body, or rather it is relinquishing a nothingness. There is an illusion the less between man and truth. Ordinary men believe that they are afraid of death, but it is life of which they are in dread."—*Tableau Naturel,* pt. i. p. 84.

[‖] Ibid. p 50.

XIII

The State After Death

THE DOCTRINE OF Saint-Martin as to the state succeeding death differs so little from that of occult science that Eliphas Lévi may be said almost to have translated it. "Like those globules of air and of fire which escape from corporeal substances in dissolution, and rise with more or less quickness according to the degree of their purity and the extent of their action, we cannot doubt that at their death men who have not permitted their proper essence to amalgamate with their earthly habitation will approach rapidly their natal region, there to shine, like stars, with dazzling splendour; that those who have alloyed themselves partly with the illusions of this tenebrous abode will traverse with less speed the region which separates them from life; and that those who have identified themselves with the impurities which surround us will remain buried in darkness and obscurity until the least of their corrupted substances be dissolved, and bear away with them an impurity which cannot cease till they themselves have finished." * The last clause is perhaps intentionally obscure, but it will be seen that this is a theory of progress and a doctrine of eternal hope. The condition of the evil liver is dwelt upon more particularly in another passage. "Impure men may be separated from their physical bodies without being detached also from their sensible souls"—*i.e.* the astral part of occultists. "If their

---

* *Tableau Naturel,* Part I. p. 111.

146

bodies, though real for other bodies, be apparent only for intellectual beings, they must be after deliverance from this present body what they were whilst imprisoned therein. The death of that body does not change their intellectual situation. The poisons which may have diseased them infect them still; they may still experience impressions relative to those objects opposed to their being with which they have been identified in life; they may nourish themselves with tastes and affections which appeared to them innocent in life, but, unable to offer them a solid and true end, leave their being inactive and in nothingness. All these foreign substances become the torment of the guilty."[*]

To these statements Saint-Martin adds his clearest and most important dictum on the subject of eschatology. "To give additional weight to these truths, I will say that at death the criminal remain under their own justice, that the wise are under the justice of God, and the reconciled are under His mercy. But that which forbids us to pronounce upon the measure in accordance with which these different acts operate, or upon their different numbers of time, is that justice does not work alone, that there are other virtues in combination therewith which cease not to direct its action towards the greatest good of creatures, which is their return to the light."[†]

On one occasion alone does he refer in express terms[‡] to the possibility of probation on the other side of life, and the consolation, if such it may be deemed, is for the lesser measures of humanity. "Men who live only on the surface have only little afflictions and trivial enjoy-

---

[*] *Tableau Naturel,* Part I. pp. 97-98.   [‡] Ibid. p. 112.

[‡] The indirect indications are numerous as to the grounds of hope beyond the grave. It inheres, for example, in the following passage concerning sacrifice partly accepted. "This last sacrifice"—that is, death—"is the true holocaust which man owes to Divine Justice as an atonement for the prevarication of Adam. Therein death finds its nothingness, and the glory of the just is shown in all the pomp of a victor. This holocaust must be prepared by all the acts of man's corporeal life; without this the victim is soiled and disfigured, and the priest, finding it irregular, will either not offer it on the altar, *or will pour on it only a small portion of that holy oil* made use of in the sacrifices of the old law to foreshow the future unction which would be poured one day by the great High Priest on all victims who have remained in the purity of the law."—*Traité des Bénédictions, Œuvres Posthumes,* ii. 191.

ments; they are consoled as soon as afflicted, and afflicted as quickly as consoled. They are only images of men. Hence it is necessary that their life shall recommence when they shall have quitted this visible and apparent region, because they have failed to live during the period when they were passing through it, and it is this prolongation of time which will be their torment, because the combination of their substances will not be in so sweet and harmonious a measure as in this world, where everything is in the proportions of mercy and salvation."[*] Allowing for differences of terminology, there is perhaps, fundamentally speaking, little difference between the conception of this painful probation and the purgatorial state of Christian theology, through which "some Christians shall be saved, yet so as by fire."[†] And this being so, it becomes necessary to record how the vulgar presentation of eschatological doctrine impressed Saint-Martin. Speaking of the punishment of privation to which man and the evil principle have alike become sub-

---

[*]   *Portrait Historique, Œuvres Posthumes,* i. 57.

[†]   There is, however, this distinction, that the state of purgatory, as it is vulgarly understood, is not a state of probation through which the imperfect soul passes to find an opportunity of improvement; it is a state of mechanical punishment, founded on the crass notion that there is good *per se* in suffering. The use of suffering is in its lessons, but purgatory is provided only for souls who are no longer in need of lessons, because by the hypothesis they have acquired already the universal science of salvation. Another distinction is involved in Saint-Martin's idea, that the second chance is harder, for which I confess that I do not see the foundation. It seems more merciful to think that in the great school of the universe those who fail in summation will be sent down to slower form. The mystic, however, develops this distinction in another place. "Having rallied within him the intellectual forces proper to him, man has still to multiply those forces, reuniting them to others which are outside him. Should the opportunity afforded for the accomplishment of this labour elapse in vain, a second, more considerable and painful, is needed, for his task is now doubled. If he still fail to fulfil it, a third, even more rigorous, is dispensed to him, and so of the rest, without the possibility of fixing any term to his evils than that which he may fix himself by sacrificing all the virtues which are in him. If he keep each s part of the holocaust, those who receive it will retain a part of the recompense, until he submits to paying without reserve a tribute which he can render efficacious and complete only by the devotion of his entire being."—*Tableau Naturel,* Part I. pp. 122-123.

ject, and dwelling on the magnitude of that misfortune, he observes: "The pretension to lead us towards wisdom by an affrighting picture of corporeal pains in the life to come is a great error; such pictures are of no effect in the absence of actual experience, and our blind masters, unable to communicate a notion of the torments they imagine, exercise but little influence. They would have enlightened and sustained men by impressing on them that we have only one thing to dread, and that is the loss of the love of our principle, for without this we are in the void, and assuredly that nothingness, if depicted in all its horror, would be a more saving and efficacious conception than those eternal tortures to which, despite the doctrine of these ministers of blood, man always sees an end and never a beginning."* To be perfectly just towards the poor blind masters, who perhaps did their best in the darkness, if they were really apart from the light, it seems right to point out that no Church more eloquently than that of Rome has ever indicated to man that God's love was everything and its loss all loss. These matters are now indifferent; their consideration, I mean, involves now no heat of feeling, and it is easy to be impartial at this day—much easier, no doubt, than in that of Saint-Martin, whom we may exonerate at once from any illiberal intention. For the rest, he leaves, as the keenest and best among us are reduced to do in the end, our eternal issues in the hands of the Eternal; upon the worst of man's notions concerning them man has already done his best, but we are not in reality any nearer to the haven because we have scuttled some bad old crafts on the deep sea. Here, also, I think that we can understand why Saint-Martin would have been silent supposing that he had been empowered to speak. Whether man has a chance of reforming in the future is a dangerous question; we must hope and believe it for others, but must never admit it for ourselves; it is a check on diligence when it is not a source of more overt temptation. We must rather say with Saint-Martin, that "to determine our tribute and labour we have only the moment of our corporeal life, and that this shapes our destinies;"†

---

* *Des Erreur et de la Vérité*, Part I. pp. 45-46.

† *Tableau Naturel,* Part I. p. 124. And yet it is all subject to the larger hope. "If the essential and primitive nature of man have elected him to be the image and expression of the virtues of the Great Principle, and if beings are indestructible by their nature, though their accidents maybe liable to alter

within the space of our waking and sleeping lies concealed the whole scheme of eternity. In his own words, which read like a writing of yesterday, so modern is their accent, this moment "is the matrix of the future man, and in the same way that corporeal beings bear and conserve on this earth the form, sex, and other signs which they have drawn from the womb of their mother, so will man carry into another sphere the plan, structure, and manner of being which he has fixed for himself here below." *

The illustrations of Saint-Martin are sometimes a little inapplicable, but there is one in this connection on "the title of our admission into the future regions" which I cannot resist quoting, because it seems to me quite perfect in its fantasy. "We cannot obtain a seat in our theatres unless we have taken the precaution to secure a ticket which admits us. This ticket is issued only under the seal of the manager; furthermore, unless we book our seats in advance, we risk being crushed in the crowd which is gathered at the doors waiting for tickets to be issued; there is even the chance that we may not get a seat at all. This emblem, altogether temporal and terrestrial, instructs us that we are here below for the purpose of purchasing a title of admission to the divine festivals; that if we neglect the precaution to secure this title, we shall assuredly not enter into that gathering of delight and rejoicing; that we must not put off till the last moment this needful piece of prudence, having regard to the inconvenience to which such delay may expose us; that this precaution is the more easy to take because depots for the sale of tickets are to be found everywhere; that we are, hence, inexcusable if we do not provide ourselves accordingly; that these titles to admission are not transferable, like those of our theatres, because our name is written on them; that there can be no double-dealing, because the names are called out by the manager; and that we must be, therefore, well on our guard against deceivers who offer forged tickets of admission, which carry no title, whatever vogue the vendors may seek to procure for them." †

(Continued...)

and even to perish, man cannot eradicate the law and the convention which constitute him, while the means of operating their fulfilment must always remain to him."—Ibid. i. 138.

* *Tableau Naturel,* i. 124. † *De l'Esprit des Choses,* ii. pp. 61-62.

I should add that Saint-Martin gave an answer after his own manner to the recurring question concerning recognition and reunion in a future state. He concludes that we shall recognise each other not according to our material and actual figures, which indeed are laid aside, but according to the figures of the non-material order, following the analogies formed in our present bodies; that we have, therefore, a great joy and a great hope, "because it is within our actual power to determine our future bonds and recognitions by sowing here below in our souls and in the souls of those around us the germs of all the real blessings and pure pleasures which will then attract us." *

The eschatology of the evil principle remains for consideration in this place. We have seen that the leader of the first emanation fell irretrievably so far as any personal efforts of his own are concerned, and that there is one, therefore, who is indefinitely more unfortunate than ourselves. To reproduce a previous image of Saint-Martin, though it must be confessed that it is a little confused, "not only is he ever walking in his own grave; not only is he ignorant that he is doing so, because a ray of light would be required to perceive it; but in approaching this abyss we become conscious that he is in a continual dissolution and corruption † that he dwells perpetually in the evidence and effective sentiment of his own death; that he can never conceive the slightest hopes of being delivered there from, and that thus his greatest torture is the knowledge of his immortality." ‡ Man, on the other hand, can work out his own salvation; he has not lost the knowledge of good; he is in extra-lignment, but not denaturalised; he is still a "mystic citizen of the eternal kingdom," in exile, but not an outlaw. I must not say that it appears clearly in Saint-Martin how this distinction came about. It is advanced that man was punished by a father, but the fatherhood of God is not confined to humanity; he has sheep which are not of this fold. It is said also that man's crime and that of the evil principle are equally the fruit of their evil will, but that at the same time there is a great difference between the nature

---

*   *Cf.* the "arch-natural body" of occultism.

†   In which the "superior virtues" would appear to assist, so as to put an end to the evil and misery. *Tableau Naturel,* i. 139.

‡   *Le Ministère de l'Homme-Esprit,* pp. 20-21.

of the two trespasses. An affirmation, however, is not an explanation, nor is there any definite assistance from the further statement that the scenes differed. It remains, however, that "man and the evil principle have their sin ever before their eyes, but each has not the same succours or the same consolations." *

Setting this aside, and recurring to the original mission of man prior to his captivity, we have seen that its final end was the restoration of harmony to the universe, and that in this mission the reintegration of the prince of evil was included as essential to the scheme. We have seen that there was a mission of chastisement prior to that of reunion; we have seen how the divine scheme was frustrated for the moment by the junction of primeval man with the leader of the first emanation to his own woe and the aggravated doom of the tempter; we have seen, finally, that the eternal laws cannot fail of their fulfilment; that hence the mission of humanity is not voided, nor has the resipiscence of the evil principle become hopeless. The nature of the chastisement which man is still required to inflict is indicated by the nature of the respite which the evil principle alone tastes in his torment. The sin of man is the ease of the fallen spirit, but it is an ease purchased by further and fiercer suffering; † so also the union of man with his true principle is the loss and pain of evil, but it is a stripping and scourging which hastens the day when the ground of reconciliation may be laid. The material creation is the scene of the punishment of prevaricators, whether human or extra-human, and this punishment has brought into operation a law which acts not only on the spiritual agents charged with the direction of material things but also on the divine emanations; its action is opposed to the simplicity and unity of their nature, and is "a necessary consequence of the horrible scandal which the prevarication of perverse spirits has occasioned throughout the hierarchy of spiritual beings, because the fallen natures are themselves spiritual, and thus could not depart from their law without the entire spiritual circle being set in action to make them feel the effects of the divine justice they had braved, and to reintegrate them in their law by the laborious

---

*   *Des Erreurs et de la Vérité,* Part I. p. 44.

†   *Le Ministère de l'Homme-Esprit,* p. 11.

and painful ways which that justice cannot dispense with employing."[*]
The dissolution of matter which will take place at the end of time will
"restore to all these beings the free exercise of the laws of their first
nature,"[†] and it will give back to the enslaved prevaricators the light
of which they are deprived by the powers of material darkness; it will
"abridge that servitude by restoring their first principles of divine virtue to the just, who now pay tribute to eternal justice in the shadow
of their reconciliation, and preparing for the like reconciliation those
impious beings whose visitation will, however, be still more severe after the destruction of matter."[‡] In a word, it will re-establish universal
harmony by "returning all things to unity."[§]

This dissolution is termed by Saint-Martin the reintegration of
matter. The reintegration of humanity will leave the evil principle,
and we may infer also those among men who have persisted in sin,
still in the state of rebellion, and it will fulfil the mission of chastisement originally assigned to our race. "When this universal envelope
of darkness shall be dissolved. when the Ere of the spirit shall have
consumed all the stains of men, when it shall have purified their essence, then shall all temporal creatures form about the perverse being
a luminous barrier, across which his spiritual eyes may pierce, but
he himself can never break through it until he has disgorged to the
last morsel the iniquity which he has swallowed during all the ages."[||]
Thus the divine event is left in mystery indeed, but not in darkness.
"A period of time is needed for the solar fires to purify those atmo-
spheric regions where clouds form in stormy weather, and a period is
also needed for the purification of the perverse natures, but it is not
given to man to fix the measure thereof."[¶]

---

[*]   *Traité des Bénédictions, Œuvres Posthumes,* ii. p. 168.

[†]   Ibid.   [‡]   Ibid. p. 169.   [§]   Ibid. p. 170.

[||]   *Traité des Bénédictions, Œuvres Posthumes,* vol. i. p. 200.

[¶]   *Rapports Spirituels et Temporels de l'Arc-en-Ciel, Œuvres Posthumes,* ii. p. 250

Book IV

The Doctrine of the Repairer

I

The Active and Intelligent Cause

T HOUGH MAN, as we have seen, did not forfeit by his fall the sublime mission which he was constituted to fulfil, he obscured and retarded it; he became subject in consequence to a double task and double responsibility; he was outside the conditions of accomplishment, and he had to recover the conditions. The history of humanity is that of an imperfect attempt to obtain reinstatement in its true law, pending which the ends of his nativity are in abeyance. Meanwhile, the place which he vacated at his lapse could not remain vacant, and another agent was sent to assume his seat and exercise his power in the direction of the dual law of Nature,* or, otherwise, those two inferior principles which are distinguished in the physics of Saint-Martin from the two intellectual principles of good and evil. Without this direction, which constitutes the third power of the temporal triad,† the operations of Nature cannot be understood. For the providence of this cause man in his blindness has substituted the law of chance. Its operation is, however, so important that without its concurrence corporeal beings could have no visible action. The knowledge thereof leads to that of the sole and the first cause,‡ which is separated absolutely from the sensible as it is also from time.

---

* *Des Erreurs et de la Vérité,* Part I. p. 42.

† Ibid. p. 75.   ‡ Ibid. p. 188.

The provisional definition of this cause as the intelligence behind Nature would, I think, fulfil fairly the intention of Saint-Martin. The existence of such intelligence outside humanity[*] is affirmed by him on the ground that man in his present state has nothing of his own, and must await from without even the smallest of his thoughts. Herein lies all the difference between this spiritual philosophy and the materialism of its period which denied the existence of innate ideas. Saint-Martin conceives man in his actual condition as receptive of thoughts and ideas after the same way that he is receptive of physical sensations. His thoughts come to him from without, and Locke was right in saying that he could give forth only as he received; but the source of intellectual illumination was not in material Nature, but in an Intelligence which ruled Nature; in other words, an Active and Intelligent Cause, having the source of its intelligence and action in itself alone,[†] and communicating action to matter and the light which enlightens the mind of every man coming into this world. It is therefore the true *primum mobile* of matter and of the human understanding. And as it communicated action originally,[‡] so it sustains it now in both classes, and thus it is that in the physical order we have growth, reproduction, and all the effects manifested by the material world, while in that of intelligence we have the growth of the world within, the successive reproduction of thought, the continual correspondence between the receptive faculty of understanding and the fructifying intellect, so that in this Active Intelligent Cause man may be said to live, move, and have his rational being.

Among the thoughts which are communicated to man there are, however, some which are analogous and some repugnant to his nature. These cannot be attributed reasonably to a single principle, and hence the mere experience of daily thought proves, as we have seen, the existence of two principles external to man, and hence also to matter, which is infinitely below man. The evil which we find in Nature, the evil which suggests itself in the silent processes of mind, are the interference of the second principle imprisoned in the temporal production of the good.

---

[*] *Des Erreurs et de la Vérité*, Part I. p. 114.   [†] Ibid. p. 117.

[‡] Ibid. p. 118.

The Active and Intelligent Cause, though it fulfils the purpose of the Good Principle, must not, as might appear almost inevitable, be identified therewith in the sense that it is the Eternal Goodness itself acting on Nature and man. There is no doubt, as we shall see, that it is divine, but Saint-Martin distinguishes it expressly from the First Cause;[*] it forms, with the two inferior agents creating the dual action, an inferior triad operating on the sensible and temporal. Between this and the Sacred Triad the mystic establishes an absolute distinction. "The triad of things sensible has been begotten, exists, and is maintained only by the Superior Triad, but as their faculties and their actions are evidently distinct, it is not possible to conceive how this triad is indivisible and above time when judged by that which is in time, and as the latter is the one alone which we are permitted to know here below, I say scarcely anything concerning the other."[†] Again: "There exists a Cause which is above the three temporal causes whereof I have spoken, since it directs them and communicates to them their action; but it makes itself known only in communicating the temporal causes to our eyes. It is withdrawn into a sanctuary impenetrable by all things under the dominion of the temporal, and its abode, like its actions, being wholly outside the sensible, we cannot reckon it with the three causes employed in the corporisation of matter and all other temporal action."

To this Active and Intelligent Cause, as to the great chief and guide, the order of the universe is committed. From him did all corporeal beings derive their form originally. "It has itself directed the production of the substance which serves for the foundation of bodies, as it directs the corporisation of that substance. Simple in its nature and action, like all simple beings, its faculties are exhibited everywhere under the same character, and though there is a distinction between the production of the forms of matter and the corporisation of the forms derived from them, the laws which direct both do not differ."[‡] While the Active and Intelligent Cause has taken the place of man[§] at the command of the First Principle, and has been invested with the rank which man lost by his Fall, he is neither the rival nor avenger of

---

[*] *Des Erreurs et de la Vérité,* Part I. p. 193.

[†] Ibid. pp. 126-127.

[‡] Ibid. p. 121.

[§] Ibid. Part II. p. 60.

man. He is rather "the ship's light which enlightens all our way," and it is his mission to establish order in the universe, and especially in man.[*]

It may save some confusion to tabulate at this point the metaphysical conceptions of Saint-Martin concerning the noumenal world.

A) The Divine Triad, mentioned once only, never defined or described; the principle of goodness in its eternal, withdrawn condition.

B) The Active and Intelligent Cause, First Principle of all goodness in the world of manifestation, the substitute for humanity in the physical universe since man abdicated his rights at the Fall.

C) Opposed Inferior Evil Principle.

D) Two Inferior Agents:

1. Primary Principle, innate in genus.
2. Secondary Principle, operating reaction, and hence reproduction.

In its junction with the two Inferior Agents, the Active and Intelligent Cause sustains the normal course of Nature, but his most important work is in connection with the destiny of man. He has an absolute discretion over Nature[†] but his operation on humanity can be opposed by the will of humanity, to whose welfare his government is indispensable, and the will of man should therefore be ever in abeyance to give full place to the law of this Active and Intelligent Cause.

"We must, therefore, before all things, recognise the existence of this Cause, and that his assistance is indispensable if we would be re-established in our rights. It is he truly who has been appointed to repair not only the evils which have been permitted, but also those which have been performed by man; it is he whose open eye is ever upon us, as on all creatures of the universe. In approaching him we draw near to the true and only light, the source of all possible knowl-

---

[*] *Des Erreurs et de la Vérité*, Part II. p. 62.   [†] Ibid. p. 142.

edge, and in particular of the science of ourselves. For he is the key of Nature, the love and delight of the simple, the torch of the sages, and even the secret support of the blind."[*]

To forestall the anxiety of his brethren, "who might believe that this Active and Intelligent Cause is a chimerical and imaginary being," Saint-Martin undertakes to inform them "that there are men who have known him physically, and that all might know him in this manner did they place more confidence in him, and take more pains to purify and fortify their will."[†] He adds, however, that he does not use the term physical in the common acceptation, which attributes reality and existence only to those objects which are palpable to the material senses. The actuality of such knowledge rests, as we know, upon the validity of certain theurgic phenomena, but the necessity for a manifestation on the part of the Active Cause is grounded elsewhere on purely abstract considerations, such as man's need of certitude, of defence against deception and self-deception, of a true guide in religion, and so forth. Concerning the general possibility he adds:—"I will not quote my private and personal experience, whatever confidence I may derive there from. There was a time when I should have given no adhesion to truths which I can vouch for at this day. I should, therefore, be unjust and inconsequent if I sought to influence the faith of my readers. I would have no one believe me on my mere affirmation, because I, as man, have no title to the confidence of my brethren; but it would be the summit of my felicity if each one of them would himself nourish a sufficient conception of his truly sublime importance, and of the grandeur of the Cause which watches over him, to hope that by his labour and diligence it may be possible

---

[*] *Des Erreurs et de la Vérité,* Part II. pp. 228-229.

[†] Ibid. Part I. pp. 168-169.

II

The Word and its Manifestation

S Saint-Martin states in his correspondence that the Active and Intelligent Cause is one with the Repairer,* an inference which no reader of the previous section will fail to make independently, nor, indeed, will he require to be told that the Repairer is a title applied to Christ.† Both designations were familiar to the school of Pasqually, and they are therefore not the invention of Saint-Martin, but he made them peculiarly his own, and in all that he tells us concerning the Divine Manifestation to which they are referred we find the suggestions and illuminations of his mystical gift. The Active and Intelligent Cause is a name used almost exclusively in the first period of his philosophy, and it was intended to act as a veil. The reason is given at the close of *Des Erreurs et de la Vérité:* "If I stripped off the veil which I have assumed, if I uttered the name of this beneficent

---

* *Correspondance,* Lettre xix; Penny, "Theosophic Correspondence," p. 77.

† It is Christ also who is described as the Universal Chief of all the spiritual Institutors of the pure and sacred cultus.—*Tableau Naturel,* ii. 160. "The benefits of which this agent is the organ and depositary are neither limited to the places where he appeared nor to the men whom he chose, nor even to all those who then existed on the earth. In communicating his gifts to his elect, he gave them only the germ of the work; it was for him afterwards to develop it, and to effect it at large in all regions which had been involved in the consequences of the crime, that is to say, in all classes of beings, since all had been assailed thereby."—Ibid. 176.

Cause, on which I would direct the gaze of the entire universe, that utterance would move the majority of my readers to deny the virtues which I have attributed thereto, and to disdain my entire doctrine. To indicate it more clearly would therefore destroy my object. I shall leave it to the penetration of my readers, convinced that in spite of the envelopes with which I have covered the truth, the intelligent will understand it, the truthful appreciate it, and even the corrupted will divine it."* The device may seem childish; there was no penetration required, more especially when Saint-Martin adds that all men are Christs."† The aspect under which the Repairer is presented as the Active and Intelligent Cause is, however, of much importance for the proper comprehension of the Martinistic system. That Cause is incontestably the Word as it was understood by St. John, and by all the early Christian fathers—without whom "was not anything made that has been made."

I must confess that as it is presented to us by Saint-Martin this conception of the Active and Intelligent Cause has the aspect of heresy; it suggests the demiurgos of the Gnostics, the *opifex* and æon shaping the plastic matter of the cosmos. Heretical or not, in the last analysis is not perhaps a matter of vital moment, and it is scarcely because of the gravity of such a charge that I desire to exonerate Saint-Martin, but because it is well to know up to what point precisely he connects with accepted doctrine and how and when he diverges. I do not think that the aspect of heresy here in question is more than the offspring of confusion, and that the idea which underlies it is really the manifestation of the Second Person in the Divine Triad under temporal conditions and limitations. If my readers prefer to regard this Cause as a divine emanation or production, as in any case it must belong to the eternal order and must possess a divine priority over the principle which went into corruption, it will create no grievous difference; but I think that the first view adjusts better with the general teaching of the mystic. It is one of those questions belonging to the timeless world concerning which Saint-Martin is never clear, because the gift of his illumination was not concerned with it.

---

* *Des Erreurs et de la Vérité,* Part II. pp. 229-230.

† His actual words are, "Tout les hommes sont des C-H-R."

There is, however, no question as to the identity of the Active and Intelligent Cause with the Word as it was understood by Saint-Martin, and the manner in which it was understood may be established by the definition which he supplies; it is "the eternal unity of the divine essences."[*] And the Word, furthermore, is the Son, who is "the depositary of all the powers of the Father;"[†] the bond which established creation; the consummation which will dissolve it,"[‡] effecting the reintegration of matter in its permanent principle; the energiser of all temporal spirits.[§] The divine faculty which was manifested in this Word has not become separated by this manifestation from those other faculties with which it was joined in the sacred unity constituting their eternal essence before all the ages and independently of them all. "The separation is for us alone who, confined by the limits of our darksome dwelling, can conceive of absolute beings only successively and apart from one another, but all faculties and all actions which thus seem successive and distinct are one, undivided and ever present to the eyes of that one Being who leads and directs them."[||]

In its metaphysical or abstract aspect, the Martinistic doctrine of the Word does not need further elucidation, and the materials are indeed exhausted. I pass on, therefore, to the more important matter of its connection with man. The key to this connection will be found in a single statement which occurs in a posthumous work, and is the more likely to be overlooked because in itself it seems oracular and arbitrary. It is to this effect, that there was no operation of the Divine Word in visible Nature until after the second prevarication. We must infer from this that the Word by which Nature was effectuated resided in man himself, that it was lost at the Fall, by which the intervention of the Divine Word became necessary for the sustentation of the universe, which, in spite of this sustenance, is still in loss and sorrow, deprived through man of the Word which resided in man, and that the recovery of the lost Word is man's first duty towards himself and towards Nature. The way of this recovery is in the union of man with the restoring and repairing Word which has replaced him. The

---

[*]   *Traité des Bénédictions, Œuvres Posthumes,* vol. ii. p. 157.

[†]   Ibid. p. 156.   [‡]   Ibid. p. 165.   [§]   Ibid. p. 172.

[||]   Ibid. p. 204.

correspondences created by this union are treated at great length by Saint-Martin. The indispensable condition is that we should recognise in the first place that there is an Eternal Word, "depositary of the eternal measure, eternal light, and eternal life, which balances continually, and particularly for man here below, the disorder, anguish, and infection wherein he is plunged. Except he cling constantly to the height on which this universal support abides, he must relapse into the abyss of evils and sufferings at the opposite extreme."[*] No middle way is possible.

When it is said that the universe is sustained by the power of the Word, the statement is not mystical in the sense of being indeterminate or vague; it is positively and physically true, and that in all classes. "It is true that if the Word did not sustain the universe in its existence and direct it in all its movements, it would stop instantaneously in its course and go back into the unmanifest. It is true that if the Word did not sustain all animals and plants, they would return at once into their respective germs, and the germ into the temporal spirit of the universe. It is true that if the Word did not sustain the action and display of all phenomena, the phenomenal would come immediately to its end. It is equally true in the spiritual order that except the Word sustain the thought and soul of man, thought would relapse into darkness, and the soul into that abyss which we navigate only by the immeasurable and merciful power of the same Word."[†] We must, therefore, and before all things, aspire without ceasing and support ourselves invariably on the Word. To do otherwise is to deny our very existence, to doom ourselves wilfully to madness, and to be knowingly our own chief enemies.

Referring once more to the distinctive character of the punishment entailed on man by the Fall, namely, his bondage in a universe which is without speech, although ever sustained thereby, Saint-Martin observes that our suffering is of a twofold kind—the consciousness of a shameful disproportion between ourselves and the dumb creatures surrounding us, and the consciousness of the affliction which must be caused to the Word itself by the silence of the universe, since that Word seeks manifestation at all points and untrammelled correspon-

---

[*]   *Le Ministère de l'Homme-Esprit,* p. 319.   [†]   Ibid. pp. 320-321.

dence with all. "The first of these two species of suffering is exhibited not only by the existing state of things, but in a special way by the communication of men with one another. Between human conversation and true speech there is an immeasurable distance, yet if men, when they mix with each other, did not enliven their atmosphere by discourse, or by the ineffective spectres of the Word, the coldness and weariness of death would overwhelm them in the sepulchre which is their abode. The second species of suffering demonstrates that there must be a living source which ever seeks to animate the circle of things with the Universal Word, as men seek to animate their silent abodes by their individual speech, which they have only in virtue of the Universal Word, though put to such puerile uses and so small in its service until it has undergone regeneration." *

If, however, we are punished by the privation of real speech, it is merely because we have sinned against the Word, and we must go back, so to speak, upon our particular phantom of speech to attain once more that grand, fixed, splendid Word, the necessity for abiding with which is ever present in all of us, as that abiding is also the exchange of suffering for gladness. The active possession and enjoyment of this universal instrument is not possible till we have ceased to regard our particular instrument otherwise than as the inverse of the real Word, which can therefore be known only in the silence of all that is of this world. "So long as we converse, either with ourselves or others, only concerning the things of the world, we are acting against the Word, not for it, because we are stooping to the world and naturalising ourselves with that which is void of true speech, and therein is the quality of our punishment." †

But seeing that the true Word is in suffering because the universe is in privation, its internal operation in man must be also by the way of pain, which for the same reason is the only profitable, germinal, fruitful way, and must be sought, not avoided. ‡ The saving and living Word can be born in us only by suffering. "The heart of man is elected to be the depository of the anguish of God, to be His chosen friend, the confidant of all His secrets and all His wonders." § The passion of

---

* *Le Ministère de l'Homme-Esprit*, pp. 323-324.   † Ibid. p. 325.

‡ Ibid. p. 329.   § Ibid. p. 330.

God is in His striving to raise Himself, so to speak, from the death which He suffers in man, and in the hindrances which man opposes thereto. We have, therefore, not only to inaugurate the Sabbath of Nature and the Sabbath of the human soul, but also the Sabbath of the Word.[*] That Word is in labour and anguish because of the false and perverted use to which man has put the divine faculty of speech. We have fallen under the rule of the "dead word,"[†] and to advance towards reality and life we must part somehow with this enormous concourse of rank, empty, earthly, and false verbiage corrupting the atmosphere of the mind. The Divine Word can, however, open continually within us the door to divinity, to holiness, light, and truth.[‡] Both in mind and act it is possible for us to have recourse to this guide, and by union with Him our whole nature will be reborn from death to life.[§] As our criminal thoughts are the result of our contact with the spirit of deception and iniquity, our material thoughts of contact with earth and its darkness, our sidereal or astral thoughts of contact with the astral spirit called the spirit of the great world, so our spiritual thoughts result from contact with the Spirit, and by our alliance with God we can possess divine thoughts. One or other of these alliances we must contract, but we must choose between them, and each, according to our choice, will bear inevitably within us the fruits which correspond to its nature. If we allow ourselves to be penetrated through and through by the Divine Word, it will fructify its seed in all the regions of our nature, and the mere memory of its favours will enable us to rout the enemy, even as the sick were healed by the shadow of the apostles. Nowhere does this Word manifest itself without leaving ineffaceable traces, which we have only to follow with confidence, and it demands only from men that they should maintain themselves in a state of efficacious prayer for universal amelioration, that they should be ready to respond to its impulsion when it calls them to the work of restoration.[‖] "For this Word is the measure pre-eminently, and it tends only to establish men in their original measures in order that the divine measures may be revived in all regions which have lost them. This is the true extension of the kingdom of God."[¶]

---

[*] *Le Ministère de l'Homme-Esprit*, p. 332.   [†] Ibid. p. 344.

[‡] Ibid. p. 421.   [§] Ibid. p. 419.   [‖] Ibid. pp. 342-343.   [¶] Ibid.

It may be added as a conclusion to this section, that the Evil Principle has also its own word; but it is one of lying, and the more he speaks it the more he infects himself; he is ever pouring out his own empoisoned blood, and quenching his thirst therewith. It is a word which would be devoid of all works if men did not daily furnish him the substance of their own works, their acts, and their thoughts, as material for his operations. It is by the operation of this evil word that the enemy himself creates his own extra-lignment, and, exile as he is, the course also of the extra-lignment in the whole universe.[*]

In the few pages which follow we shall see after what manner the Divine Word was really understood by Saint-Martin—that behind it, as behind the Logos of St. John, there was only the charity of God.

---

[*] *Le Ministère de l'Homme-Esprit,* p. 421.

III

The Eternal Love

THE DIVINE HEART, which may be compared to the mother of a family, and is truly the mother of all mankind, even as power is the father, is the organ and the eternal generator of whatsoever is in God or in our principle. The assistance which it condescends to bring to the human soul is solemnised not only by the essential correspondences between the divine source and ourselves, but also by the mythological narratives of a divine made to earth, by the hopes of some other traditions which are known as yet only in promises, and by the fate of certain peoples who believe that they possess it in reality. The Christians, in presenting it under the name of the Word, have divined the second only of its titles, and that consequently which is the more difficult to comprehend. The first of the names which belong to it is Love, in virtue of the ineffable mother of man—Love, which perhaps would be comprehended easily on the part of the human family did it unite in a single focus the love of all individuals composing it, since the perspective of all these united loves has alone engaged the Supreme Love to give itself entirely. By this we feel the necessity of loving one another if we would possess the understanding and key of that Love. The name of the Word is but the expression of the divine movements which this Love has operated eternally in the universality of the divine sphere, of those which it now operates consecutively in time, and of those which it has operated and still effects in man, even as our individual Word is only the expression of the diverse activities which take place in our soul, operating only by explosions or words, for there is no Word which is not an explosion. The Supreme Love is therefore the continuous affection which makes the life of our soul,* wherein innumerable desires originate in unbroken succession, with words analogous to those desires. It is like that azure expanse of heaven, the abode of an incalculable multitude of shining stars, seeming to spring first as a luminous vegetation from a fruitful and translucent earth. We must confess then that this love which has hastened to the help of man is the true mother, of which natural maternity is the emblem; that the name of Word, offering a more imposing and mysterious conception, depicts it less in its essence than in its various modes of operation, and offers only to our soul the act by which it approaches us. The name of Love, which is that also which should be born by our proper essence, since all is Love, unveils to us our correspondence with our source. When considering it under the title of Word, we must tremble with respect and admiration before it, as at once the producer and sustainer of all beings by the power of its speech, whether divine, spiritual or temporal; but in considering it under the name of Love, we quiver only with joy and tenderness, conscious that it shrinks not from penetrating all our substance by its beneficent and inexhaustible desire to modify itself entirely in correspondence with our tainted and broken measures, and that by this unfailing self-devotion we are raised and glorified till we can even regard ourselves as assimilated and identified with life itself. Thus the *verbum caro factum est* of the Christians would seem to them much less incomprehensible did they begin by exalting themselves to the height of this sublime devotion of the love which has gone before man from the moment of his fall, which, by its inflamed desires, has modelled itself into the essences and form of the human soul, which by this act transcending all our thoughts, so occupies the whole capacity of our being that its actual and visible corporisation can scarcely astound us more than ordinary corporisations, if we have experienced the least developments upon

---

* "The Divine Chief in the centre of his pure emanations, radiating into their centre the sweetness of His virtues and of His very being, unites them to Himself by all the rights of love and of beatitude."—*Tableau Naturel,* i. 160.

the generation of beings and the incorporation of man himself in this terrestrial and material envelope. For since the first man came into the world without woman, he has by his fall divided his love, and it was more natural that the second Adam should enter it without man, for he came only to restore unto man that Love which he had allowed to go astray. It is thus that when the mind of man forms in its thought some fantastic objects which mislead and obscure him, a more lively and wholesome light penetrates unexpectedly, and, as it were, without himself, even among his phantoms, to strip off their attractions, and

---

*   Chapter adapted from *Des Trois Epoques du Traitement de l'Ame Humaine, Œuvres Posthumes*, p. 176 *et seq.*

IV

The Great Name

REGARDED IN THE light of the two last sections, the proper
business and study of man is not mankind, in accordance
with the poetical aphorism, but the search for the lost Word.
Now, it is well known that the symbolism of occult philosophy concerns itself a good deal with the recovery of a lost Word, and with
the mysteries concealed in the great and unutterable Name. Outside
occult circles this appears very naturally to be trifling, but at the same
time the quest of the Word and the Name has connections in universal traditions which, quite apart from occult philosophy, are curious,
and within the mystic circle, being confessedly of the things of symbolism, may, also not unnaturally, possess something more of purpose
and meaning than can reasonably occur to the outside world. Here
there is no occasion to enter upon a defence of occult philosophy,
much less upon an explanation of its symbology. It is enough to indicate, firstly, the existence of a very old and far-diffused tradition on
this subject; and, secondly, its particular, and indeed necessary, connection with occultism. As regards the latter point, the connections
are, for the most part, Kabalistic. Now, I have already pointed out
that the body of traditional doctrine conferred upon Saint-Martin by
his initiation has little apparent connection with this school of mystic
thought. His initiation, it must be remembered, was at least in its
forms Masonic, and we know, of course, that the Master-Mason is in
search of the lost Word, and that he receives a shadow or substitution

thereof which may be taken to represent it more imperfectly than the common speech of humanity represents, according to Saint-Martin, the true and life-giving logos of Martinistic philosophy.

The Mystic Masonry of Martines de Pasqually was intended to replace the "spurious Masonry"* which, among other evidences of its emptiness, was not only unable to impart the lost Word, but could not indicate the direction in which it should be sought. Now, spurious or genuine, Masonry, outside the rites of the Elect Cohens, is exceedingly composite in its connections, and that it was open to Kabalistic, among other occult influences, must not be denied by the historians, though the nature and extent of that influence can be and has been exaggerated. In so far, therefore, as the system of Pasqually is Masonic, it has an indirect and fragile thread of affinity with Kabalism, and I may say that so far as Saint-Martin may be accepted as the interpreter of his first master, it is chiefly over the question of the lost Word.† It is not, of course, over the philosophy of the Word itself, and therefore does not transpire in so far as that philosophy has been developed by the preceding sections. As it there stands, it is neither of Plato nor his successors, it is not of St. John or of the Gnostics, whom a certain uncritical mysticism has attempted to connect with the author of the Fourth Gospel; it is not of Jacob Böhme, and though something was indisputably derived from Pasqually, it is, in fine, the Logos philosophy strangely, and withal richly, albeit fantastically, transmuted in the alembic of Saint-Martin's mind. But the lost Word brings us naturally to the Great Name, and to what Martinism has to tell us on the subject of this symbolism, and here one is brought to admit that there

---

* See the *Catéchisme d'Apprentif Élu Coen,* in Papus, *Martines de Pasqually,* where the signs and words of "apocryphal Masonry" are communicated to the candidate, pp. 227-228.

† Other points of contact will be found: (a) In the possible affinity between the primeval man of Saint-Martin and the Kabalistic Adam Kadmon; (b) In the Martinistie doctrine of man's superiority over the angels; (c) In the opinions expressed by Saint-Martin as to the place of Hebrew among the languages of the world. He regards it as their type, itself deriving from a primitive tongue which is no longer spoken generally in this lower world. It has also a spirit which far exceeds its literal sense.—*Tableau Naturel,* i. 268-270; ii. 75-76.

is distinctly a trace of Kabalism, though the alembic has again gone to work, and this time on a mere grain of material, and has not only transmuted but multiplied. I shall not need to tell my readers that the Name or Tetragrammaton of the Kabalists is represented by the four Hebrew letters which we interpret as Jehovah, and they will know also that Christianised Kabalism finds proof of the divinity of the Saviour in the name of Jehoshuah, or Jesus, which is the Tetragrammaton with the mysterious shin in the midst of it. These are the materials which Saint-Martin derived from Kabalism,* and, as he did not "frequent the libraries," I take leave to doubt whether he had heard of the Zohar, except in the distant and unmeaning way that we have heard, all of us, of books which are too far removed from our needs for their acquaintance to be a remote probability. But the Great Name is, notwithstanding, a subject of much importance in the system of Saint-Martin. It is a conception which grew with the growth of his mind; it is the subject of a single allusion in his first book, where it appears parabolically as a lance, composed of four metals, intrusted to man in his first estate.† That is to say, he then possessed the Word which is the Great Name. But it is the subject of frequent mention in his correspondence, and of essays in his later books. "The extract of this name constitutes the essence of man, and thus it is that we are made in the image and likeness of God;‡ this, he says expressly, is "a fundamental quaternion principle," which he derived from his first school.§ He takes care at the same time to distinguish himself carefully and sharply from "common theurgists and mechanical cabalists," ‖ who believe in the arbitrary virtue of names. The Great Name, he says weirdly, should never be made use of by man; we must "wait

---

* "When the Christ came, he made the pronunciation of this word still more central and interior, since the Great Name expressed by those four letters was the quaternary explosion, or the crucial signs of all life; whereas Jesus Christ, by exalting the Hebrew ‫ש‬, or the letter S, united the holy ternary itself to the great quaternary name of which three is the principle."—*Correspondance,* Lettre lxxiv; Penny, "Theosophic Correspondence," p. 242.

† *Des Erreurs et de la Vérité,* Part I. p. 41.

‡ *Correspondance,* Lettre xiii; Penny, "Theosophic Correspondence," p. 55.

§ Ibid. Lettre xxvii; ibid. p. 100.   ‖ Ibid. Lettre xxvii; ibid. p. 101.

always for it to engender, form, and pronounce itself in us," which is the only way to prevent our taking it in vain.[*] But the Name which is above every name, the Great Name of Christendom, he declares to be above the Tetragrammaton, making this pregnant addition: "I am also persuaded that there is one we wait for which is above that." The Name mentioned in the Acts of the Apostles[†] is only the way of deliverance. We still want that of rejoicing; it is the one promised in the Apocalypse; it is that Name which no man knoweth save he who receiveth it."[‡] There is I know not what of strange consolation to the Christian mystic in this announcement; it bears a promise of fulfilment, a promise of completer revelation, and of an answer of assent and encouragement to the poet's question—

> "Wilt thou not make, Eternal Source and Goal,
> In thy long years life's broken circle whole?"

It suggests that period when the five foolish virgins "will at length have obtained oil for their lamps."[§]

It will be seen that we have already transcended the accepted region of Kabalism. Saint-Martin takes care that there shall be no mistake on this head. "There are false doctors who pretend to be acquainted with the true name of God, with the properties which are comprised in it, and with the way in which it should be pronounced.[||] Pay no heed to their instructions. That Name is inseparable from the active properties which it possesses; these properties are in perpetual fructification; it is, therefore, ever now like them, and the Name itself, like every other, can only reveal itself, and that only in such a way that the

---

[*] *Correspondance*, Lettre xiii; Penny, "Theosophic Correspondence," p. 107.

[†] The reference is to Acts iii. 6, "In the name of Jesus of Nazareth, rise up and walk," and Acts iv. 10, 11, 12, concerning the one "name given under heaven among men whereby we must be saved."

[‡] *Correspondance*, Lettre lxxxii; Penny, "Theosophic Correspondence" p. 279

[§] Eliphas Lévi, *La Science des Esprits*.

[||] "I feel myself so drawn towards the inward cultivation of the Word, that if a man were presently to offer me the true pronunciation of the two great names on which both the Testaments are founded, I believe I should refuse the offer, so persuaded I am that it can never be made really my own, except

knowledge in the last analysis remains in the source of knowledge, and cannot fall into the misusing hands of men." * In other words, as to his ultimate source, God is forever incommunicable. At the same time we can be assured that apart from this Name we are in death and sterility, for we are separated from the sole properties that are fruitful and therefore living. So also we can feel that the Name of God is in its fundamental character "the eternal, universal, temporal, spiritual, heavenly, and earthly alliances;" † that all these alliances are developed within us when it descends upon us, and that they discover to us at each epoch the treasures and the wonders of eternal immensity. On our own part we must seek to become the active totality of all these alliances, and thus "the spoken name of that God who comprises them." ‡

Our worship of the Great Name must have three chief characters; it must be, firstly, the offering of incense, the incense of tears and thanks; secondly, attention to its teachings, developed by our own concentration, with such an attenuation of ourselves that the Name of the Lord may be able to communicate with no hindrances its living and penetrating wisdom; thirdly, regulation of our actions in such a way that the Name may itself operate in our works what its light has effected in our intelligence. "In this way we shall, little by little, become the Name of the Lord, and, reintegrated in the eternal alliance, that Name will restore its form in us, will be the universal in works and in lights as it is the universal in essence." § For the liberty of man can oppose the universality of God as regards the circle of humanity by substituting our thoughts and works for those of the divine order. "The character of the Name of God is that of a physician, so gentle,

---

(Continued...)

so far as it may take root within me naturally, and shoot, as it were, out of its own stalk or its own root, which is also my soul's root."—*Correspondance,* Lettre lxxiv; Penny, "Theosophic Correspondence," p. 244. At the same time he did consider that "great virtue is attached to this true pronunciation of the Great Name, and that of Jesus Christ, which is as its flower."

* *De l'Esprit des Choses,* 65-66.   † Ibid.   ‡ Ibid. p. 67.
§   Ibid. ii. p. 68 .

so beneficent, that he comes within us and comforts us without ever being hidden, and what, therefore, will he not do if we invoke him? That Name seeks ever to diffuse itself in the world, but is repelled by so many obstacles that it is forced to return upon itself and withdraw into silence. The man of truth experiences the same opposition when he seeks to diffuse the individual lights which he has received, and is forced upon numberless occasions to interdict speech to himself." *

There is, therefore, nothing conventional or arbitrary about Saint-Martin's symbolism of the Great Name. For him all names are indexes of the properties of things; and as all things must manifest their own properties, so he says that they pronounce their own names, or otherwise reveal themselves. "Thus God utters his own name unceasingly, so that his properties may be shown forth before all faculties and organs of his productions." † The pure and divine beings who minister to his glory and his light, all beings of Nature, from the fundamental pillars of the universe to the creatures of a day, do likewise; and this also is the object and the duty of man, who, being in the likeness of his principle, was born to make a constant use of his Word. ‡

---

* *De l'Esprit des Choses,* p. 69.

† Ibid. p. 63.

‡ It is also said that man in his fallen state has lost the knowledge of his own true name.—*Tableau Naturel,* i. 124.

V

The Mission of the Repairer

T HE HUMAN PERSONALITY of Christ is not often referred to by Saint-Martin, who was absorbed, as we have had full opportunity for remarking, in the contemplation of His divine nature. But when he distinguishes between the mission of the Repairer and that of the first man, he seems for a moment to approach the human nature, and we see that the divine history was not for him only "a symbol and a sign," and that had he ever treated the subject of the union between the two natures in Christ, he would not have offered us a doctrine which differs seriously from that of the Catholic Church.

The object of the Repairer's mission* was to reunite us to the living act of the Divine Principle, because that union would have been also the object of the first man if he had remained in the lineal way. The emanation of the first man was drawn from the eternal model unceasingly present to the divine thought. The generation of his race could not be otherwise than defiled when man himself became defiled by his crime; and had Christ been born according to the generation of man, he could not have escaped pollution. In other words, had the Great Name, or Jesus, not become Jesus Christ, had it remained in the degree of sublimity and glory where it was when the divinity became Christ, in that same eternal image whence the first man was

---

* Adapted from *De l'Esprit des Choses*, 301-304.

178

derived, the restoration could not have been effected, because the remedy would have been too remote from the disease. Christ, at the moment when he was engendered from the eternal image of man by the Great Name, found himself filled with omnipotence and with the eternal living essence; in other words, with that great and divine Name which is at once the principle and sustentation of all things. This sublime term could not have been reached by the first man except by immense labours, and would have indeed been his reward, towards which he would have tended unceasingly, acquiring at each stage of his progress a degree of that glory whereof the Great Name is at once the organ and the source. Christ, in possession of these treasures, held them in abeyance when he clothed himself with matter, content to develop them gradually, and he continues now to manifest them, and will yet do so, in the same progressive manner till he brings us to perfect union with the principle at the end of time.

The reason of the divine homification, both spiritual and corporeal, heavenly and earthly, depends on that mandate issued by God to man, that he should subdue the earth. In spite of our fall, this decree was so respected that God became man in order to fulfil it in our name, as if to leave us the glory while he experienced all the weariness and bitterness. Moreover, man was dead spiritually without accomplishing his mission, and hence it was necessary that the Repairer should die corporeally without fulfilling the common course of human life, and this at an epoch which corresponded symbolically at all its points with the divers progressive degrees of the disease and the healing of man.

Book V

The Way of Reintegration

I

Regeneration

A S THERE IS no system of mystical philosophy which does not insist upon a reversion of the natural man, and as mystical experience is the history of this change and its consequences, as, finally, it is referred to and known universally under the name of Regeneration, Conversion, or the New Birth, so it is inevitable that we should find in Martinism that the way of reintegration is through the gate of a second birth. On the other hand, we should scarcely look for any new note in the account of this process, on which the great masters of spiritual science, long before the days of Saint-Martin, had set the seal of the completeness of their sanctity. We know approximately what errors of enthusiasm would be avoided by the French mystic, who, though also a man of enthusiasm, regulated zeal by light. The sensationalism, somewhat sordid in analysis, which makes the conversion of exploded English Protestantism mere froth of spiritual experience, would be, of course, absent; the startling illustration and the sudden change had no place in his system; he was not a disciple either of report or suddenness. "I have desired," he says, "to do good, but I have not sought to make a noise; for I was convinced that noise did not work good, as that good did not make noise."* And as to the slowness with which the supernatural life in man passes from conception to birth, and through what stages from

---

* *Portrait Historique, Œuvres Posthumes,* i. 96.

birth to growth, we might learn from many places of his writings, but one instance must suffice. "Come down, as we have, into this dark realm of affliction and misery, we can only recover progressively the different faculties of which we are deprived; and the law laid down by the principle of all laws being that things which are most spiritual are also most elevated, we must perforce begin at the lowest, because we are at the inferior extremity of progress." [*]

The theory of regeneration is expressed by Saint-Martin in an aphorism when he speaks of "the profound feeling that we must un-earth ourselves completely if we would attain to say of God, *Habitavit in nobis. Amen.*" [†] The birth of the spiritual man supposes in some sense the death of the natural man; but Saint-Martin, who, when he is most purely mystic, is always most sane and reasonable, exhibits here his freedom from another error of enthusiasm, though it is this time a mystic and not a Protestant error. The price of the new birth is not the wanton torture of our nature proposed by unbridled asceticism. There is indeed a self which must be dispossessed, not because it is our own, but because it is a spurious *propriété* which has been fastened on us by the spirit of the world. "There is the true death we have to undergo, the true self-hood which we have to part with; but when the Divine Self-hood condescends to replace it, and be its substitute within us, we are permitted to cherish it with the greatest care." [‡]

There is another point which it will be well to mention here, because it applies in a particular manner to that class of persons who are likely to be the chief readers of this study, in whose interest it has been, indeed, undertaken. It concerns the real value of initiation as a help to the new life. Now, all initiations are theurgic, or at least I know of none which belong to another order, and Saint-Martin did not deny that there were stages and states in which the "physical communications" might be proitable. [§] There are aids from all quarters, and things inferior help to things superior. It may even be said that the inferior are sometimes necessary steps. But with every allowance

---

[*] *Loix Temporelles de la Justice Divine, Œuvres Posthumes,* ii. 94-95.

[†] *Correspondance,* Lettre xxxviii; Penny, "Theosophic Correspondence," p. 130.

[‡] Ibid. Lettre viii; ibid. pp. 36-37.

[§] *Correspondance,* Lettre xxxii; Penny, "Theosophic Correspondence," p. 111.

for the concealed possibilities which may reside in the *Magia Divina,* and for some initiations as the gate thereof, in the last analysis the help from initiation fails, or at least it ceases at a certain point. Now, the point at which it ceases is short of the communication of spiritual life. This position is made very clear by Saint-Martin in connection with the present subject. "The knowledge which might formerly be transmitted in writing depended on instructions which sometimes rested on certain mysterious practices and ceremonies, the value of which was more a matter of opinion or habit than of reality, and sometimes rested on occult practices and spiritual operations, the details of which it would have been dangerous to transmit to the vulgar, or to ignorant and ill-intentioned men. The subject which engages us, not resting on such bases, is not exposed to similar dangers. The only initiation which I preach and seek with all the ardour of my soul is that by which we may enter into the heart of God and make God's heart enter into us, there to form an indissoluble marriage, which will make us the friend, brother, and spouse of our Divine Redeemer. There is no other mystery to arrive at this holy initiation than to go more and more down into the depths of our being, and not let go till we can bring forth the living vivifying root, because then all the fruit which we ought to bear, according to our kind, will be produced within us and without us naturally."* This, he says elsewhere, is "the work we ought all to work at, and if it be laborious, it is also full of the consolations of help extended when we undertake it courageously and resolutely."† But these conclusions have an application outside the field of initiation, and if we accept them, we must agree with Saint-Martin when he observes that "our understanding forbids us to regard as a means of regeneration anything which belongs to the realm of external facts, wherein our inmost essence counts for nothing, since such facts are no more linked with ourselves than the works of a painter with an uninstructed person who glances at them. Furthermore, it forbids us to consider as a means of regeneration all secondary agents and all the private ways so often trodden by erring men; as regards our inward birth, all such things are like the out-

---

* *Correspondance,* Lettre cx; Penny, "Theosophic Correspondence," pp. 374-375.
† Ibid. Lettre ii; ibid. p. 5.

ward application of medicaments for a disease which has poisoned the blood." [*]

The agent of our regeneration is the Divine Word or the Great Name, concerning which we have learned enough from the doctrine of the Repairer to know that these terms are not used in any conventional or mechanical manner. They signify that our regenerator is Christ. By immersing ourselves continually in his living waters, by approaching the furnace of his fire, by directing our own word ever towards that central and interior Word, will our tongue be unbound, for only that interior Word can engender true speech within us. [†] "It is precisely on this account that the world fails to advance; its word is frittered on the external, never carried to the interior, where it can be joined with the living Word. Forcibly and painfully we must be ploughed, so to speak, by the Word of the Lord, to uproot all the thorns and briars which cover our field. That Word must leave deep traces in our humility, which is its cherished earth; therein must its seed be sown, that it may produce in due season an abundant harvest. We must feel in this earth of humility how much we deserve the severity of God, since we were destined to be the channel by which he would make himself Kinsman to the nations, and we have set obstacles and bounds to his divine manifestation. Having bewailed this impiety, we must open our soul to hope that he will still take us to himself, and that we yet may walk with him in the regions of peace." [‡] As regeneration begins by this agency of the Word, so it is made perfect by our full alliance therewith. It must possess us sensibly and actively; it must speak its language within us; it must vivify us with its benedictions, its power, its light; it must enable us, unworthy as we are, to speak its holy works, and to exercise the saintly ministries and all the divine properties which are inseparable from the Name of God.

"The first stage of our regeneration is our recall from the land of oblivion or kingdom of death and darkness, for this is indispensable for our entrance into the path of life." [§] The last stage is not of this world; our renewal here is but the preparation for our perfect regen-

---

[*]   *Le Nouvel Homme,* p. 23.

[†]   *De l'Esprit des Choses,* ii. 70.   [‡] Ibid. pp. 70-71

[§]   *Le Ministère de l'Homme-Esprit,* p. 223.

eration, which can only take place after the separation of our corporeal principles. "After our death we are suspended, so to speak, from the Great Triad, or universal triangle, which extends from the First Being to Nature, and each of whose three actions draws to itself one of our constituent principles—divine, spiritual, and elementary—to reintegrate them if we are pure, and so set free our soul and enable it to reascend to its source. But if we are not pure, the enemy, who does not oppose the separation of the corporeal parts which belong only to form, will combat the reintegration of the principles over which the soul has permitted his usurpation, and will retain the whole under his dominion, to the great detriment of the unfortunate soul who has become his victim." * The protection against this future tyranny is the conception now within that soul of "an eternal in whom the Son of Man may be incorporated, with his virtues and his powers;" but this conception is impossible until we have "reanimated within us our primitive body or pure element." † The here mentioned is the Sophia occasionally referred to in Saint-Martin's correspondence, where he remarks: "I have no doubt that she may be born in our centre. I have no doubt that the Divine Word can also be born there by her means, as he was thus born in Mary," ‡ who "had her share of Sophia, like all saints and all the elect." § I must confess that I can understand from Saint-Martin neither the nature nor the operation of this virgin; it is clear, however, that she is not that Holy Spirit of whom Mary was the spouse, for a masculine aspect is involved by this symbolism, and, moreover, Saint-Martin says, using the uncouth metaphors of Böhme: "There is a vegetable land which is material, that of our Helds; there is a spirituous one, which is the pure element; there is a spiritual one, which is Sophia; there is a vegetable land divine, which is the Holy Spirit and the *Ternarium Sanctum*." ‖ The subject is not elucidated by these seeming distinctions, but perhaps Sophia is that portion or gift of the Spirit which is individualised in each man by grace.

Lastly, while the process of regeneration is a process of growth, and therefore slow, like growth, while it is not completed till the new

---

*   *Le Ministère de l'Homme-Esprit,*p. 287.   †   Ibid. p. 288.

‡   *Correspondance,* Lettre xxx.; Penny, "Theosophic Correspondence," p. 107.

§   Ibid. Lettre xxxiii; ibid. p. 103.   ‖   Ibid. Lettre xxxiv; ibid. p. 117.

man receives his crown, there yet are quickening influences, and even during the early stages one phase may follow upon another with a certain swiftness. Hence Saint-Martin says that "when a man comes to be regenerated in his thought, he will soon be so in his speech, which is the flesh and blood of his thought, but when he is regenerated in his speech he will be so soon in the operation which is the flesh and blood of speech." *

---

* *Le Nouvel Homme*, p. 21.

II

The New Man

"THE ENTIRE BIBLE," says Saint-Martin, "has man alone for its object, and man also is its best and fullest translation."[*] Like man, it begins in Paradise and it ends in eternity, and since in eternity there is no end, the canon of Scripture will never close while man remains to amplify it; his soul is its text, his life is its commentary, its history is his history.[†] We shall not, therefore, be surprised to find that the great story of Israel is that of universal election, and that every individual who responds to the call of grace applies in his own person the whole providence exercised by God towards the chosen people. Man's own nature is thus the Promised Land, which should be filled with the altars of the Lord, with the monuments of his glory, his love, and his power, but since the Fall it has been possessed by wicked and idolatrous nations who should have had no part therein—that is to say, with the dark, false, illusory substances which act in our corporeal form. We must proceed to the conquest of these nations and put them to the sword "without distinction of

---

[*] *Le Nouvel Homme,* p. 98.

[†] "If the Holy Scriptures be the spiritual history of man, their living law must pass through us and work within us, accomplishing all the processes peculiar to the spirit of their agents, or of those who are proclaimed by them as having been the ministers of truth and the materials of its universal edifice."— *De l'Esprit des Choses,* ii. 160.

age or sex."* These few words give the key to Saint-Martin's biblical exegesis as regards the Old Testament. After what manner the Ark of the Covenant must be borne into the Land of Promise,† the Mount of Sinai exalted therein and its marvels manifested,‡ the law proclaimed by the higher part of our nature for the rule of the chosen people within us, all these are illustrations and developments which the discernment of the reader may be left to work out for itself. The application of New Testament history to the regeneration of man is more important; it is more intimately characteristic of Saint-Martin, and demands further treatment§ For him the life of Christ is the life of the new nature conceived and born within us for the operation of our redemption. But this conception, this birth, this operation are the stages of pain and passion by which the New Man passes into glory, and he must be crucified before he can be crowned. ‖ From the large volume which is devoted to this mystical commentary on the gospel narrative, it is possible only to offer a few selections; but I do not know that its entire presentation would make it more complete, for it is at once discursive and fragmentary. Nor can such interpretations be regarded as of solid value; they belong to the fantastic order. At the least, they are an arbitrary framework which is not essential to the scheme, though they help to set out the scheme and give it a certain consistence; at the most, they are indications and suggestions which show us that on the other side of every spiritual history there is the infinite with all its riches. The temporal history of the Repairer may well correspond with the inward legend of the soul, though it may be merely a confusion of thought to say that the Christian gospel is actually the soul's history. All great books are allegories, or material upon which the genius of allegory may be exercised, though apart in most cases from any such intention in their writers. On the other

---

*   *Le Nouvel Homme,* p. 99.   † Ibid. p. 84 *et seq.*

‡   Ibid. p. 136 *et seq.*

§   "The Old Testament had for its object the restoration of the human soul, that is to say, the work of man. The object of the New Testament is the work of God." All its earlier part belongs, however, to the spirit and purpose of the old covenant; the new covenant was only inaugurated at Pentecost, and it is still in course of development.—*De l'Esprit des Choses,* ii. 300-301.

‖   *Le Nouvel Homme,* p. 29 *et seq.*

hand, the intended significance of some formal allegories is beneath the dignity of the outward sense, as in the alleged significance of the Round Table present to the mind of Tennyson when he conceived the "Idylls of the King."

The general standpoint of Saint-Martin is that there is an unknown world within man, and that it is vaster and fuller and greater than the visible universe. To the man of sense who can conceive of nothing in humanity outside the capacity of his skin, this, of course, is the conception of delirium; but the spiritual philosopher will know that on his inner side man is in communication with the infinite, and that the inner world extends in proportion as we recover consciousness therein. The mystical legend of the fall of man and his descent into matter is the history of the constriction of consciousness at the external. Saint-Martin, however, regards the unknown world of humanity, as it appears to his philosophy, wrecked and desolated by the Fall, and he compares it as such to the Promised Land, overrun by idolatrous nations. Those nations must be exterminated by the Israel of God, that the Sun of Righteousness may rise over it with healing in its wings, and the Orient from on high visit it. Had the mystic adhered to this allegorical method, treating the Covenant of the Law as the ethical reparation of the soul, giving place in due season to the Covenant of Grace and manifesting the Christ in the spiritual Israel, he would have produced a consistent and perhaps truly significant allegory; but, unfortunately, with the confusion so frequent in mystical writers, and Saint-Martin's besetting defect, the New Testament is spiritualised after another manner, and yet without abandoning the previous method, with results that are at times almost ludicrous. In the sketch which here follows, I have done my best to harmonise the conflicting elements and to produce something like order in the symbolism.

The aspirant towards the new life must be content to regard himself for the moment as typified by Mary, in whom the Divinity becomes flesh. Mary, that is to say, is the soul when it aspires towards the life of the eternal world. That aspiration is either the first consequence of election, of the call of grace, or it is the free act which opens the door to the election which, at one or other period, enlightens every human being born into this world, though it is not accepted by all.

The election itself is represented by the annunciation of the angel,* foretelling that the Holy Spirit shall brood over us and the glory of the Most High shall cover us, and that for this reason the New Man, anointed and sanctified, who shall be born of us, may in some mystical sense be termed the Son of God. In order that this annunciation may be made, we must be restored in veritable innocence,—that is to say, we must put off the concupiscence of the flesh and give place to the desire of the spirit, after which we shall discern within us that sacred conception which will qualify us to utter the canticle of Mary, while our kindred, the cloud of regenerated witnesses, salute us with rejoicing, as Mary was saluted by Elizabeth.† When once this conception has taken place, we must spare no pains to bring it to a happy termination,—that is to say, we must avoid the dangers of relapse towards the life of sense, which are very great at the beginning of the life of the spirit. We must watch with vigilance over all movements that occur within us; we must neglect none, lest we do harm to our spiritual child; but we must also defend ourselves against false motions, which belong only to fantasy, that other danger of the spiritual life; for these will give weapons to our enemy, who will not fail to use them, that he may set his seal and character upon some part of the body of our offspring." ‡

When the higher powers have operated within us by the Spirit the conception of our spiritual Son, and have deemed in their wisdom that the moment of his nativity has arrived,§ that birth takes place within us, as in the stable at Bethlehem; the shepherds hear the midnight song of the angels; the behold the star in the east, and come to adore him, offering their gold and frankincense, while Herod, the prince of this world, dwelling in the heart of the unregenerated man, trembles because his throne is menaced by the birth of him who shall be called the King of the Jews. ‖ In vain he massacres the children of Rachel to pacify his terrors; this Son can never be destroyed, because he is born not of blood, nor the will of the flesh, nor the will of man, but of God; and God, who has formed him, will watch over all his days, will lead him to an asylum in Egypt,¶—that is to say, into the

---

* *Le Nouvel Homme*, p. 31.   † Ibid. p. 32.   ‡ Ibid. p. 33.

§ Ibid. p. 51.   ‖ Ibid. p. 52.   ¶ Ibid. p. 53.

hidden life, till the time of wrath shall have passed and that of glory be at hand.

The New Man is born in the midst of humiliation, and his whole history is that of God suffering within us. We may also regard his advent as the manifestation of the archetypal, primeval man reappearing on the scene of the desolation caused by his departure, to restore that scene and to recover his lost titles. He is warmed by the breath of the cattle who are housed in the stable, referring to our animal nature, but it is his spirit which should have enkindled them.[*] He is the son of sorrow, the secondborn of Rachel, costing the life of his mother, and we must nourish him daily with the divine elements which gave him birth; we must pour over him the blood of the covenant, that he may be preserved from the destroying angel; it must be infused into all his veins, that he may be the death of all the Egyptians,[†] and may one day despoil them of their gold and silver vessels, wherewith they make unto themselves feasts of iniquity. It is the blood of suffering, which is the sign of life, for life increases with suffering, and thereby the true sacerdotal element shall penetrate the fibres of his being.[‡]

As the Divine Child grows in years the wisdom of his Father manifests; he confounds the doctors in the temple of the human heart; those doctors are the doubts which matter and the darkness of false teachers have created;[§] they are the incessant suggestions which have come from the spirit of falsehood all the days of our life till this son beheld the day. His first progress in knowledge dispels incertitudes and anxieties; before our eyes, our heart, our mind, the most differentiated of our faculties, he sets the unity, and we see that all our extra-lignment occurred because this unity was not yet born within us. Now the doctors who seduced us discern the empire of his word, the analogy between the light which he offers and our own natural illumination. The innumerable nations within us—for at this point the allegory of Mary disappears and we return to the original line of symbolism—are converted by his instruction and become themselves the advocates of truth; we are each of us as a great assembly of the

---

[*] *Le Nouvel Homme,* p. 53. [†] Ibid. p. 54. [‡] Ibid. p. 55.
[§] Ibid. p. 90.

faithful, ceasing not day or night to raise up altars to the Supreme Author and Ruler of all things.

"Be not astonished," says Saint-Martin, addressing the man of desire, "to behold this cherished Son exhibit most high faculties, since he has partaken of the Word from his birth, and, seeing that he is truly thyself, his sole mission is to change into that self all that has ceased to be thee. He is consecrated to the Lord by his birthright, as the Eternal Word is consecrated to the Ancient of Days before the foundation of the ages, since it is the Word that has founded the ages." [*]

Developing his allegory, Saint-Martin represents the New Man entering upon his mission, when the period of the hidden life of growth is over, even as Christ entered upon his public ministry, and submitting, like Christ, on its threshold, to the law of corporeal baptism, which, he says, must be received from the hand of the Guide, in order that the New Man may receive subsequently a divine baptism from the hand of his Creator. [†] At this point the allegory becomes not only obscure, but almost unintelligible. The Guide is the guardian angel of Catholic doctrine, who stands in the same relation to the New Man as the Baptist stood to the Repairer. The baptism received from his hands is, however, a humiliation, [‡] because man in his true estate is not only superior to the angels, but is also their judge, as will be seen in a later section. "Such is the outcome of the immense transposition which took place at the moment of sin, and it is a grace of infinite magnitude, extended by the divine compassion to permit that the hand of the spiritual creature should burst our chains and enable us to receive the higher and creative life from which we are so remote."

When this corporeal baptism, which, however, appears unconnected with the corporeal rite of the Christian Church, or the Church might be regarded as the Guide, has been fulfilled upon us, [§] the New Man emerges from the waters in which he was immersed, and as he sets foot upon the earth—that is perhaps to say, as the mission of the regenerated man becomes manifest to the outward world, or correspondingly is realised in the inward, a voice cries from heaven: "This is my beloved son, in whom I am well pleased." Heretofore the New

---

[*] *Le Nouvel Homme,* Ibid. pp. 91-92.   [†] Ibid. p. 171.

[‡] Ibid. p. 172.   [§] Ibid. p. 173.

Man was indeed the Son of God, because he was conceived and born of the Spirit, but his name and his divine parentage had not been announced, and until that barrier fell before the waters of the Spirit, he could not receive from his Father the authentic avowal proclaiming his sonship and his inalienable title to his inheritance. Hence it is then only that the Divinity begins truly to enter within us, that the three Divine Principles descend and accomplish a close union with the three principles which constitute ourselves personally, converting them into a single principle and manifesting them invariably in the same powerful and harmonious unity. This entrance of God within us is the chief desire and essential object of the Divinity* and we can have, only a feeble idea of the efforts which He makes to accomplish it. "If there be anything deplorable in our existence, it is to know that we ourselves bar the approach of Divinity; it is to be physically aware that the Divinity is ever moving round us, striving to enter our hearts and thus raise us from the dead, to enliven us by the fire of the Spirit. The least ray of the Divine Word suffices to operate this prodigy within us, substituting virtues and characterised faculties in place of the tenebrous state which is peculiar to the region we inhabit. Yet it is the ray of this Word which we drive zealously away as though it were death." †

The New Man does not follow these errors; he was conceived in Nazareth; he has dwelt among the Nazarenes; at his coming of age he has approached the Jordan, which is the frontier of the Promised Land; there he has submitted humbly to the hand of his Guide, and this baptism, the understanding of which is imparted by the visible baptism of the Restorer, ‡ produces a twofold effect upon the New Man—he hears the Divine Words proclaiming his sonship, and he discovers concealed treasures in the depths of his being. "The Divine Voice enters within him as into its proper form, permeating all his faculties, exhibiting not only the wealth wherewith he is endowed by his divine nature, but also the use which he should make of it for His glory from Whom he has received it." § To consider this wealth,

---

* *Le Nouvel Homme,* p. 174.   † Ibid. p. 175.

‡ The term "corporeal" is, therefore, used by Saint-Martin in some obscure transcendental sense.

§ *Le Nouvel Homme,* p. 176.

and to resolve within him the ends to which it must be applied, the New Man passes into the desert of the Spirit, into the desert of God. He returns, as it were, apart from the Spirit and the Divinity into his own individual being, conscious of that trespass in his far past which makes him, in his own eyes, unworthy of both, and bent upon gathering all his forces, collecting all his lights, so that when he has restored them to unity "he may offer himself in juster measure to Him who is measure itself."[*] During this period he traverses the most remote tracts of his being, resting not day or night till he has expelled all impurities, all malefactors, all venomous animals. Therein also he is tempted after the same manner that the first man was tempted in the spiritual domain entrusted to him, and he defends himself, like the Repairer, by opposing to his enemy the Word which cometh out of the mouth of God. His exile continues for forty days and forty nights "to accomplish the rectification of the tetrad which characterises the human soul, and has been disfigured by sin."[†] This rectification consists in its total separation from all that is devoid of correspondence with man's primitive elements, after which the time of exile ends, the desert is abandoned, and the true period of ministry begins."[‡]

It is the moment now of the Sermon on the Mount, when the New Man sheds upon the world unknown within himself and us the light of a living instruction, which is also inward, and not an external, superficial, and dead doctrine, like that of the doctors and the Pharisees.[§] This mountain, according to Saint-Martin, is an interior temple more ancient than the temporal structures of the two covenants; "it is that temple wherein the preacher of the Word is not only seated on the seat of Moses, and on the seat of the second law, but on that also of the truly first law, of that law which is old enough to be itself placed upon the Seat of Unity."[||]

We may pass lightly, with Saint-Martin, over the analogies of the earlier public life, which, in the miracle of Cana, first exhibit that the New Man has revivified within him "our six elementary actions which compose the visible circumference of material things, and has thereby attained to their central septenary principle, which imparts to

---

[*] *Le Nouvel Homme,* p. 178. [†] Ibid. p. 179.

[‡] Ibid. p. 196.   [§] Ibid. p. 221.   [||] Ibid. p. 203.

them motion and life," and note after what manner he understands the Ministry of the New Man.* "The moment has arrived when the New Man, after the example of the disciples of the Restorer, sets out to preach in the towns and villages of the Israel which is Man; it is the moment when, in the Name of the Spirit, he may repeat the election of twelve apostles by developing within him the gifts which glorified the ambassadors of the Restorer. He will offer in his own person a likeness of that election, by reason of the secret power and continuous, though unseen, operation of an ancient law, which established primevally twelve channels for the communication of light, order, and measure among the nations; to which law all the dispensers of Divine things have remained faithful, which has been observed in all times, even by the simple professors of the elementary sciences, who have set apart twelve signs invariably in the region of the material firmament. He will not carry the fruits of this election to the Gentiles, nor into the cities of the Samaritans, because these nations are the figurative representatives of the peoples reserved for judgment; he will go rather to the lost sheep of the House of Israel, towards those regions round about him which have been disturbed and led astray by the consequences of crime, but have not yet shut their hearts to repentance. He will testify for their encouragement that the Kingdom of Heaven is at hand. By his tears, his prayers, his labours, he will restore health to the sick who are among them, life to the dead, liberty to those who have been bound by the demon; he will spare no pains to fill his whole earth with the abundance of his works. When he enters into a certain town or village of the earth of man, he will seek out one who is worthy to give him lodging, and will abide with him till the time comes for him to depart. Upon entering a house he will salute it, saying, May peace abide herein; and if the house be worthy thereof, peace will come upon it, but otherwise it will return to the owner. For peace is not to be confused with the nations who are unmeet to receive it. But when the New Man finds within himself some house or city which will not bid him welcome or give ear to his words, going out there from, he shall shake the dust off his shoes, and that house or city shall become more guilty than Sodom and Gomorrah, which heard only an exter-

---

* *Le Nouvel Homme,* p. 196.

nal doctrine addressed to their corruptible senses, contempt for which brought down the wrath of the Lord upon their material bodies and abodes, whereas the disciples of the New Man will be the bearer of the doctrine of the New Man, which will knock at the inmost foundation of their being, and will invoke on them, if disdained, the most appalling scourges and punishments. The Spirit who thus commissions the New Man into his own land will forewarn him that he goeth as a stranger amidst wolves, and will commend him to be wise as the serpent yet simple as the dove; he will foretell all the opposition which he will experience from the impious and unbelieving nations who dwell in the country of the New Man. But the Spirit of the Lord shall be with him, and he shall conceive within him those answers which shall secure the victory of him who hath sent him. For the New Man cometh not in the Name of the Spirit save to give battle to his enemies." *

After this manner the New Man within us accomplishes gradually the conquest of his primeval dominion, puts an end to the usurpation of the false self, and assumes into his own nature all that has remained innocent in our fallen humanity. In the fulfilment of his mission he becomes more and more conscious of the Divine Life acting upon himself, establishing itself with him, sustaining him by its sacred influences, and communicating to him the well-spring of its joy. † In a word, he becomes so penetrated by the Divine Light that there is, as it were, a bright sun shining within our world, which no man of desire will fail to discern when he turns his eyes inward. And herein is the transfiguration of the New Man typified by the mystery of Tabor, in the light of which we discern our correspondence with the source from which we derive, ‡ and thereby the New Man within us is able to proclaim to his disciples, the virtues and faculties of our being by which he is surrounded, that "He who hath seen me hath seen the Father." §

And thus Saint-Martin brings his fantastic allegory to the period of the triumphal entry into Jerusalem. As the ass used by the Repairer in his progress signified the old covenant and the colt signified the new, ‖ so for us the first covenant is the image of the old Adam, while the second is the New Man, "that divine soul in its purity on which

---

*   *Le Nouvel Homme,* pp. 228-230.   †   Ibid. p. 297.

‡   Ibid. p. 299.   §   Ibid. p. 302.   ‖   Ibid. p. 336

alone the Repairer rests when he makes his entrance into the Jerusalem of Man." * It is from the temple within this city that the New Man casts out the money-changers and merchants who have converted the house of prayer into a den of thieves;" † and it is therein also that the priests and the doctors of the law begin to conspire against him,‡ because it is necessary that, after the example of the Repairer, the New Man should pass into Gethsemane § to accept the chalice of expiation, that he should appear before the high priest of the law of time‖ to confess that he is the anointed of the Lord for our personal regeneration, as Christ is the anointed of the Lord for universal regeneration, and that, in a word, he should reproduce in his own person the divine majesty of the passion.

At this point the allegory becomes once more exceedingly forced, and it is not a little difficult to understand amidst its confused cloud of imagery what is really signified by the immolation of the New Man within us. There is a touch of pathos and suggestion when it is said that Barabbas was preferred before Christ because Christ came not to save himself but to save the guilty, not to deliver himself but to set free the slave; ¶ and we also must immolate the sinless man within us that we may unbind our individual Barabbas. ° We must enter into the work and sacrifice of the Repairer, and apply them to our particular work and sacrifice, for we must die in our spirit before we die in our body, but after the death of the body we live in the spirit by death only, and not by life. ** In a general sense the symbolism is no doubt concerned with the spiritual man's crucifixion to the world and the world's crucifixion to him.

However this may be, when the New Man has accomplished his sacrifice within us, it is followed by the same signs which were manifested at the death of the Repairer. "The material sun is darkened, because that sun operates within us only the death of life, whereas the spirit born within us must operate the destruction of death." †† We may take this sun to signify the gross intellectual light before it has been clarified by the Divine Light. So also the veil of the temple is

---

* *Le Nouvel Homme*, p. 337.   † Ibid. p. 338.   ‡ Ibid. p. 354.

§ Ibid. p. 388.   ‖ Ibid. p. 390.   ¶ Ibid. p. 393.

° Ibid. p. 394.   ** Ibid. p. 402.   †† Ibid. p. 405

rent in twain; that is to say, the iniquity which separates our soul from the true Shekinah is riven and dispelled. The earth trembles because the blood of our sacrifice penetrates the foundations of our spiritual being. The tombs open, and the bodies of the saints appear in the holy city; that is to say, our spiritual substances are re-born, or awake from the sleep of death. In a word, everything within us confesses that this New Man was truly the Son of God.[*] And he meanwhile passes into the depths of our nature, as Christ descended into Hades, to pass judgment on the prevaricators and unbelievers, to accomplish a complete separation between himself and those substances within us which have not been cleansed from their sins, to preach to all spirits that are imprisoned within us,[†] that they may concur in his sacrifice, and thus obtain regeneration. Then he returns alive; he shows himself to his own that are within us; he commissions them to bear his word through all the regions of our nature,[‡] while he himself ascends to his Father, that he may obtain us the gift of the Spirit.[§] He departs, but he is destined to return, communicating heaven to our soul, accomplishing our complete restoration, transferring our particular Jerusalem into the truly celestial city, and it is within vision of his second advent, or glorious manifestation within us, that the mystic vision terminates.

"It is insufficient for the New Man to have passed through all the temporal epochs of regeneration and all the individual progressions attached to the restoration of human posterity; he must attain, also, the individual complement of that restoration, if not permanently, by reason of the imperfection of our sphere, then at least partially, and as by a foretaste of that abiding reintegration which he will one day enjoy, when, after having represented his principle here below in a confined manner, he shall represent it in the heavens above in one as vast as durable. Hence, beyond the particular judgment which we have seen him pronounce in Hades, he must utter prophetically that Last Judgment, separating those who, having escaped within him by penitence the sentence of the first death, will be spared also the second, from those who are the victims of both. When this terrible judg-

---

[*] *Le Nouvel Homme,* p. 407.   [†] Ibid. p. 409.

[‡] Ibid. p. 419   [§] Ibid. p. 420.

ment shall have been executed within thee, O human soul! there shall be then, and for thee, a new heaven and a new earth, for the former things have passed away. Then shalt thou behold the New Jerusalem descending from heaven within thee, like a bride made ready for the bridegroom, and a great voice shall cry from the throne, 'Behold the tabernacle of God with men I' And he shall abide with thee, and God himself dwelling in the midst of thee, the same shall be thy God. He shall wipe away all tears from thine eyes, and death henceforth shall be no more.

"If thou wouldst learn the proportions of this heavenly city, transport thyself to that great and high mountain which is within thee, and thou shalt behold it illumined by the splendour of God, as if by a precious stone, a stone of jasper, transparent as crystal. Thou shalt behold it built four-square, and the measure of the wall is one hundred and forty-four cubits of the measure of man, to signify that it is on the individual dimensions, at once threefold, sevenfold, and fourfold, of thy sacred essence, that this eternal town of peace and consolations must be raised, because thou alone art in correspondence so close with the Eternal Source of all measures and numbers, that He has elected to make thee His representative amidst all the regions of the visible and invisible universe. Thou shalt discern that thou art thyself the tabernacle of God, with all those who dwell in thee, and this is why He would abide within thee, that thou mayest be His people, and, so abiding, that He may be thy God. So shalt thou behold no other temple in this holy city, even this heavenly Jerusalem, because the Lord God Almighty and the Lamb are the temple thereof; nor hath this city any need of lighting by sun or moon, because it is the glory of God which enlighteneth it, and the Lamb is the lamp thereof The nations shall walk in the grace of His light, and there the kings of the earth shall bestow their glory and their honour.

"Remark, O human soul, how men who are still in the earthly material kingdom shut up the gates of their fortified cities after expelling enemies and malefactors. In the spiritual kingdom men do likewise, for without this they will be in danger of falling victims to their neglect. But in that divine kingdom which the New Man establishes within thee they will close no longer the gates of the holy city, because there shall be no more any night therein, nor aught which is unclean, nor one of those who commit abomination or lying, but those only who are written in the book of life.

"Thou shalt behold in the holy city a river of living water, clear as crystal, which floweth from the throne of God and of the Lamb, for thou knowest at length that man himself is a stream derived from this river, and issuing therefore eternally, even as that which gave birth to it. Thou shalt find also in the middle of this city, on either bank of the river, the tree of life, bearing twelve fruits and producing its fruit each month, and the leaves of this tree are for the healing of the nations. For this tree of life is that light of the spirit which cometh to be enkindled in the thought of the New Man, and shall not be quenched for evermore. The fruit which it bears is the spirit of this New Man, who must fill henceforth the universal ages with all his wisdom. Those leaves which are for the healing of the nations are the works of the New Man, diffusing round thee unceasing harmony and happiness, as thou shouldst have diffused them formerly in virtue of those three sacred which constitute thee at once the image and the son of the God of beings.

"Work without ceasing that this holy city may be built within thee, as it should have ever subsisted there, had it not been destroyed by crime; and remember all the days of thy life that the invisible sanctuary wherein our God deigns to be honoured, that the worship, the lights, the incense, of which external nature and material temples give us salutary and instructive images, that, in a word all the marvels of the heavenly Jerusalem may be found still to this day in the heart of the New Man, since therein they have existed from the beginning."*

It was impossible to pass over this allegory, to which a position of importance has been assigned always by the admirers of Saint-Martin, but I must confess that I have presented it with reluctance, firstly, for its obvious defects, and, secondly, because of the slender spiritual ministry exercised by devices of this sort. There are better things than this in Saint-Martin, as there is evidence that he also thought, and in the little Steps of the next section, which will be permitted to speak for themselves, we shall find some of them ingarnered, though here also there is a trace now and then of his fantasy as distinct from his illumination.

---

* *Le Nouvel Homme,* pp. 425-432.

III

Steps in the Way

1 – The Door of the Way[*]

I N THE EARTHLY journey to which we are all condemned, and in the various spiritual paths which man may traverse during the passage, we have all of us an individual door by which truth seeks to enter us, and by which alone it can enter. This door is separate and distinct from that general door of our origin by which radical life comes down to us and constitutes us spirits in our nature, because the latter is common to us all as well as to the perverse principle. The purpose of our individual door is to revivify us by the fountain of life and the eternal light of love, but there is no such door as this for the perverse nature. It is designed specially that we may recover communication with the sources of love and of light; without it we may pass our days in the vain pursuit of vain sciences, as vainly perhaps in the following of true sciences. So long as the fountain of life does not find this door open within us, so long it tarries without till we open it. By this door alone can we obtain our sustenance; if we fail to open it, we remain altogether destitute; if we open it, it brings us nourishment in abundance. Hence, if we were wise, we should never go about any work till we had fulfilled our daily duty in this respect, and also the kind of task which it sets us. But seeing that this door has been ordained by God as

---

[*] *Le Ministère de l'Homme-Esprit*, 169-171.

that of our entrance into the ministry, when we are numbered among those who are called to the work, the tempests and tumults will in vain torment us to retard our work, while the fountain of life will not fail sooner or later to End this door in those who are fit to be employed, and in them will God's glory triumph, to their great satisfaction.

Though God opens this door in those who are called to the work, others who are not so called must not fall back on a pretended impossibility of themselves undoing it, because there is in all men a door for desire and justice which we must and can open. As to the other door which belongs only to the work, it is right that God alone should open it, but this is not the door of our advancement should the one remain closed through our indolence, for in His name we may cast out demons, and yet He may have never known us.

The reason why things that are acquired by external ways become truly useful to us only after much difficulty is that they are in strife with those which enter and issue by our true door. It is like the sap of a plant which has been grafted struggling with the sap of the tree on which the graft has been set, a strife which continues till the sap of the tree has taken its natural direction and has drawn the new sap after it.

2 – The First Work of Man[*]

The first work of man is to labour for his reconciliation, without which it is impossible for him to obtain anything, or to say that he has done anything.[†] He has only to reflect on our nature in its actual situation; there is nothing so clear as that we are denuded of all our powers and plunged in such a state of privation that nothing can be worse than our condition. If repelled by this state, it is probable that man is not condemned to it of his own choice, and that he cannot of himself break bonds that he has not forged. Hence it is useless to

---

[*] *Œuvres Posthumes,* i. 372-375.

[†] "The object of man on earth is to employ all rights and powers of his being in rarefying as far as possible the intervening media between himself and the true sun, so that, the opposition being practically none, there may be a free passage, and the rays of light may reach him without refraction."—*Tableau Naturel,* ii. 164.

reckon on his own powers to soften the misery of his environment, and if his greatest misery be the want of an initiative of his own, it will follow that he can recover his activity only by the restoration of his liberty; in other words, his bonds must be broken for him. But to know that the rights of man can be recovered by reconciliation is not in itself sufficient; he must also seek the means of attaining reconciliation. The first and most wholesome is the conviction of our privation, to be grounded so firmly in humility that our position shall earn the goodwill of those who keep us in bondage.* Such sincere humility produces persistent desire; desire produces the serviceable and indispensable solicitude and effort which we are conscious cannot be dispensed with, at the same time that they cannot be learned from any one. This disposition conciliates unerringly the chief with the inferiors, and sets us in the way of favour. If we are easy of access to favours, the same will increase speedily, they will indeed become identified with us, and so naturally that we shall be even their instrument. It is then that man enters into the enjoyment of his rights, and may hope to obtain the crowning favour, which is to preside over favours. These truths are indicated palpably by the cultus, in which the beginning of everything is fast and prayer; sacrifice is preceded by confession, and so forth.

Yet to know that humility and the abhorrence of self lead to reconciliation is again insufficient, or it is at least no less necessary to become familiar with the ways which lead to these sentiments. In a sense, all men have known them; in a sense, all have taught them; but there are few only who practise them. It is, therefore, permanently true that these ways are open to all, and to be aware of this we need only to remember that if the prison of man be the enemy of man, it is by holding this enemy in subjection that man can re-conquer his privileges; by the punishment of the corporeal part is the spirit made humble, and the spirit when humble recognises all that it lacks. Then

---

* "The dispositions which are essential to our advancement consist in a profound self-annihilation before the Being of beings, retaining no will but his, and surrendering ourselves to Him with boundless resignation and confidence; I will add, in suppressing every human motive within us, and reducing ourselves (if the comparison may be permitted) to the condition of a cannon waiting for the match to be applied."—*Correspondance*, Lettre iv.

does that Being who watches over it take pity thereon, and attaches Himself thereto, for then He becomes mindful that man, all weak and wretched as he is, notwithstanding is of His own nature; He accommodates Himself to that weakness, and lends a helping hand to raise it towards Himself. So spake Moses to the Jews, that God would remember His covenant when they had sought pardon for their impieties.

3 – Man the Thought of God [*]

Man is a species of sacred text, and his entire life should be its development and commentary, which is equivalent to saying that the soul of man is actually a thought of God.[†] From this sublime truth one no less sublime follows, that we are not in harmony with our law if we think by ourselves; we should think only by God, for otherwise we can no longer say that we are His thought, but act rather as if our thought and principle were in ourselves, and by disfiguring our own nature destroy that from which alone we derive—an impiety and blindness which account for the development of all prevarications.

It follows also from this truth that the final cause of our existence cannot be concentrated in ourselves, but must be referred to the source which engenders us in the form of thought, detaching us from itself to effect externally that which its undivided unity does not permit it to operate, but of which it should be notwithstanding the term and the end, as we are all here below the end and term of those thoughts to which we give birth, which are so many organs and instruments employed by us to co-operate in accomplishing the plans which have our ego for their invariable object. This ego, or thought of God, is therefore the channel through which the entire Divinity must pass, even as we introduce ourselves daily and entirely into our own thoughts to direct them to that end of which they are the expression, so that whatsoever is void of us may be filled therewith.[‡] Such is the

---

[*]   *Le Nouvel Homme,* pp. 11, 14, 15, 16, 17, 18, 19, 21, 22, 24-26.

[†]   Human nature is also the universal figurative picture of divinity.—*Tableau Naturel,* i. 166.

[‡]   "All the physical means employed by man, and all the material works which he produces, have for their object to assimilate beings outside himself and

secret and universal intent of man, and such also is that of the Divinity of which man is the image.

This operation fulfils itself by laws of spiritual multiplication on the part of the Divinity in man when He opens to him His integral life, and then does the Divinity develop within us all the spiritual and divine products relative to His plans, as, in that which relates to our own, we transfer constantly our powers in our thoughts, previously developed, so that they may attain their perfect fulfilment. There is, however, this difference, that the Divine plans, joining us with unity itself, open up inexhaustible resources, and as they are essentially alive, they effect within us a succession of living acts, which are like unto multiplications of lights, multiplications of virtues, multiplications of joys growing continually. It is more than a golden rain descending upon us; it is more than a rain of fire; it is a rain of spirits of every rank and faculty, for God never thinks without producing his image, while only spirit can be the image of God. It is thus, I say, that we receive within us multiplications of sanctification, multiplications of ordination, multiplications of consecration, and can dispense them in turn, after an active manner, to objects and persons around us. One of the signs of our advancement in this order is the sensible experience that the things of this world are illusory, and the ability to compare them physically with things which are. A single sensation of life will then instruct us more than all documents, and subvert, as if by magic power, all the scaffolding of false philosophy; for this comparison instructs us in the whole difference which subsists between a thought of God and that confused and tenebrous assemblage of mixed, wandering, and voiceless substances which compose the material region wherein the laws of our body confine us. This operation is an indispensable condition of entrance into the rank of catechumens and for setting foot upon the first round of the sacerdotal ladder.

The man who has submitted his own faculties to the direction of the source of all thoughts has no longer uncertainties in his spiritual conduct, though he is not ensured from them in temporal matters. He

---

(Continued...)

to make them one with him. This universal law of reunion is that also of physical nature."—*Tableau Naturel,* Part I. pp. 37-39

who has attained the regeneration of his thought will soon find it in his speech, which is like the flesh and blood of his thought. But when there is regeneration in speech it will soon be present in the operation which is the flesh and blood of speech. Not only does the spirit penetrate him, circulating in all his veins, and clothing itself with him to impart movement to all his members, but whatsoever is within him transforms into spiritual and angelic substances, to bear him upon their wings whither of truth in all regions which are susceptible thereof.

It is then that man finds himself in spirit and in truth the priest of the Lord; then has he received the life-giving ordination, and can transmit it to all those who consecrate themselves to the service of God. That is to say, he can bind and loose, purify, absolve, expel the enemy into the darkness, rekindle light in souls; for the word "ordination" signifies an ordering; it is the restoration of everything to its rank and place. Such is the faculty of the Eternal Word, which by number, by weight, and by measure produces all things unceasingly. Such, finally, is the zeal of the Word for this sublime work, that it would be transformed into man himself, so that it may order and consecrate us, if men be wanting to impose their hands on us; for it seems that truth, in order to be of use to us here below, must have corporeal humanity for its organ. It is not thus a simple mystical result or a simple metaphysical operation which takes places within us when the Divine Word regenerates us; it is a living work, for this Word is life and activity, and our whole spiritual and corporeal being experiences the sensation physically.

But if man be a thought of God, and if the regeneration of his thought is followed by that of his speech, which is equivalent to saying that he becomes the speech of God, it will follow that man was originally both speech and thought of God, and must be such once more when he is happily re-established in his original nature. To this end should all our efforts be directed; without this we persuade ourselves vainly that we are advancing on the path of return towards our principle. Let us never cease to contemplate this divine and indispensable end; let us never rest, never spare an effort, till we feel ourselves reborn in that living faculty which is our essence, or until, by its potent virtue, we have expelled from us all the buyers and sellers who have established their traffic in the temple.

If we feel that we can only be regenerated in so far as we become a speech of God, this is proof that God is himself a living and effective speech; our similitude with him will then be manifested to us in the most natural, most instructive, most winning manner, since at any moment we may convince ourselves of this similitude by showing that we can instantaneously connect with God as God connects with us. Now, that which manifests entirely the glory of this Supreme Being and our own spiritual nature is the fact that whatever the dignity and power of the speech which is in us, we cannot hope for its re-birth and development, except in so far as the Divine Word comes to quicken our own, and restore the activity which has been arrested by the bonds of our prevarication. It is, finally, to feel irresistibly that speech is an absolute necessity for the establishment of speech, by which we learn that all our work must take place in the man within, as in the invisible storehouse of our divine life, and that such work can only be accomplished truly by the Divine Word or the Divinity itself.

The re-birth of our internal speech is not confined merely to a partial effect concentrated in the one point of our interior being; it is propagated in all the regions which constitute us, and revives life at every step; it imparts, so to speak, the names which are proper and active for all substances—spiritual, celestial, elementary—collected within us, to reestablish them in the vivacity of their motions, in the effective exercise of their original functions, as Adam formerly imposed names on all animals and introduced his living power into all creation. Now, these two testimonies, that of our experience and that of tradition, instruct us that such also is the progress of eternal Divinity in its holy operations, restorations, and rectifications, whence the life of His Divine Word spreads successively in all beings that it would regenerate and that do not oppose its action. But if by our own experience and the tradition of the operations of Adam we know the restoring path of the Divine Word, it is proof that such also was the creative course of that same Word; since things are not regenerated by another path than that of their creation. Thus St. Peter rightly told us that there is no other name under heaven given unto man whereby we may be saved, for St. John also has affirmed that in the beginning was the Word and the Word was God, and without Him was made nothing that was made. Hence we cannot find the saving God, the sanctifying God, the fortifying and quickening God, except in the creative God, as we cannot find the creative God save in Him who is of Himself, whose life is eternity, of whom eternity is the life, albeit these diverse powers may act in divers times and may exhibit different properties.

If speech be necessary for the establishment of speech, and if hence we cannot be re-born in our speech otherwise than by the Word, we cannot be re-born in our other faculties save by faculties analogous, in our thought except by thought, in our movement except by movement, in our life save only by life, in our spirit otherwise than by spirit, in our virtues by anything but virtue, as in our lights by light. We should be thus in a continual mobility and activity, since the least rays of that which is within us should be reacted on perpetually by similar sparks, given forth unceasingly by the eternal furnace of life.

Such is the state of those who, after having vanquished the dragon, have ascended through death into the region of repose and bliss; such also here below is their state who have broken the chains of their bondage, have opened all their faculties to Him who asks nothing but to penetrate and fill them; such, in fine, is the state of those on whom the Spirit has laid hands, for by this imposition He collects into unity within them all the spiritual subdivisions which they have allowed to take place; it is even by this means, and in virtue of the indivisible unity of which this Spirit is the depositary, that He places them in a position to lay hands in their turn on their like, and to effect the same concentration within them. Such is the object of the priesthood, these are its powers, this is its fruit for the worthy who are included in the Divine election. It is a fruit which appears to be without limit, when the principle, having been set in motion, is transmitted in the same measure and without alteration, because it acts invariably by the same law and on the same species of disorder, which is nothing but a subdivision. So also it is the same spirit which, in things physical as in things moral, by the imposition of hands, causes the blind to see, the deaf to hear, the lame to walk, makes whole the sick man, raises the dead to life, and sets the bondman free.

4 – The Communication of Spiritual Life*

We find in the physical order that the remedy comes after the disease, which is itself preceded by health; it is thus the disease which causes the cure to be discovered, and this rule obtains in the spiritual order, where also a state of health preceded that of infirmity, and the medicine, as in things physical, must be analogous to the complaint. The first stage in the cure which man has to operate on himself is to remove all the vicious and foreign tumours which have accumulated within him since the Fall, whether those which have become engrained in the human species by the many errors of the posterity of the first man, tendencies derived through our parents from departed generations, or those which our own neglect and daily prevarications have permitted to accumulate. Till all these have been purged off we cannot enter the way of our restoration, wherein we must traverse that grim and darksome region into which the Fall has precipitated us in search of the natural elixir with which we can alone restore the senses of a sorrowing universe. There is here no further question as to the spiritual nature of our being, of our essential correspondence with our principle, of our degradation through wilful wandering, of the burning love which has caused our generative source, and still prompts it daily, to call us in the midst of our impurities, nor of the cloud of witnesses to these fundamental and self-evident truths. The question is whether we are purged of all the secondary impurities, or have at least a great desire to be delivered from them, whatever the cost, that we may restore that life which has become extinct by the primitive crime, and without which we can be neither the servant of God nor the consoler of the universe. We must indeed realise that the sole science for our study is to become without sin. If man were in this state, it might well be that he would manifest naturally all sciences and all lights. The work of man calls for manmade new; others will attempt vainly to share in the construction of the building; the stones

---

* Adapted from *Le Ministère da l'Homme-Esprit*, pp. 59-69.

which they bring will be wanting in polish as well as in the required dimensions, and they will be sent back to the workshop until they are fit for use.

The test of our purgation is whether we are above every fear save that of not being in perfect anastomosis with the divine action and impulsion; whether, far from regarding our personal trials as misfortunes, we confess that we deserve all, and that if we are spared it is by grace and by indulgence of our weakness, so that in place of lamenting because we are denuded of joys and consolations, we give thanks that there are any left us. Assuming these conditions, and passing on to the beginning of the regeneration which replaces man in his primitive rights, titles, and virtues, let us recall how in our material bodies we are conscious frequently of pains in limbs which have been amputated. Now we have lost all the members of our true body, and the first proof that we are beginning to exist as spiritual beings is to be aware of lively suffering in those lost members. Life must be reborn in all those organs which we have allowed to perish, and this can take place only by the generative power of life substituting those renewed organs for the weak and foreign members which constitute us at this day. All the foreign bodies which oppose our vegetation and fruitfulness must be torn up; whatsoever has entered within us by the way of seduction must pass out by the way of suffering. Now that which has entered into us is the spirit of this world, with all its essences and all its properties, which have been transformed into corrosive salts, into poisonous tumours, and have become so coagulated that they cannot be separated from us save by the most searching remedies. This is why regeneration must take place amidst the acute suffering of our whole nature, till all the false bases of our errors having vanished, they may be replaced by the spirit and the essences of another universe.

As it is in our inmost parts that these foreign substances are implanted, it is also in our most secret being that the same sufferings must be felt; there must be developed the real sense of humility and contrition, because we are found united to essences so unrelated to ourselves. There we must learn to walk in the universe as along a road bordered by groves and having at every step the dead asking us for life. There by our sighs and our sufferings we must attract the substance of sacrifice on which the fire of the Lord cannot fail to descend, consuming the victim but giving life to the operator, and filling him with potent supports or permanent virtualities to pursue the universality of his work. By this union of the secret and living substance of the sacrifice with ourselves does our regeneration begin, for the purifying pains are its prelude, designed to remove what is hurtful, but not supplying what is wanting. In this union the balm of life is applied to the soothing of our pains and the healing of our wounds, and it renews us in all our faculties, in all our powers, in all the active principles of our being, oppressed heretofore by the weight of the universe, and so dessicated by the fire which burns them within that they turn with longing to the one refreshment which can restore their free activity.

This refreshment so adjusts itself that it is small with the small, weak at the beginning, because man is so weak and so little, even as a child with us who are less than children, and, speaking generally, growing with our growth. Or it acts like a tender mother towards her wounded child, fixing all her thoughts on his cure, and expending herself in all his suffering members. But it does even more than this, for it puts on the very form of the child, and substitutes itself for all that is bruised and broken therein; there is nothing too painful, there is nothing too minute; whatsoever may do good is for it a necessity. The means which it adopts, thus graduated and measured, are restoring tongues directed by the true Word, or such at least, with all the denominations and expressions contained within them, are the means which it prefers to employ.

There is no reason for astonishment that it is necessary for this living and active force to enter within us so that it may dispose us towards its own work. Whosoever is acquainted with the true condition of things is conscious that he must become both alive and powerful before that work can be accomplished, since evil itself is a power and not a mere fiction. It is not by discoursing that we can destroy its reign in nature or in the soul of man; the learned discourse to no purpose; that does not put evil to flight; on the contrary, it spreads wider under the shadow of their apparent palliatives.

It is this substance of life which sustains Nature against the foes that harry it, which sustains the political life of peoples, which sustains man individually even amidst his ignorance, extravagance, and abomination. It is that substance which, entombed everywhere, everywhere cries for liberation. Its first and its chief seat is the soul of man, wherein it seeks especially to develop and manifest. And did man concur therewith by his persistent action, did he feel that, in virtue of his original nature, he is a divine oratory wherein the truth desires to offer pure incense to the Eternal Source of all things, he would soon behold the substance of life diffuse its roots within him, and spread innumerable branches laden with flowers and fruits over himself and all around him. Soon also the spirits, overjoyed by the delights we should have thus procured them, would go so far in their charity as to forget the injuries which we have heaped upon man heretofore by our errors;* for each act of this substance is a flowering season, which begins at the root of our being, at our animic germ; thence it passes to the life of our mind or intelligence; lastly, to the bodily life; and each of these things being joined to its corresponding region, so every blossoming which takes place within us must be communicated to its particular atmosphere. But as this threefold operation of the substance imparts to us a new life everywhere, the great work is effected by a threefold transformation, which gives us a new soul, a new mind, and a new body. But this also is a transmutation accompanied by suffering, because it is a strife of the healthy with the diseased, of the physical act of the true will against our own diseased will. Hence our wills effect nothing until the divine will is infused into them. By these different operations does life substitute a pure essence for the corrupted essence of our triple nature; our desire becomes one with the divine, with the divine hunger for the manifestation and reign of truth in the universe; our intelligence is united with the Divine Eye, which sees both before and behind; the false and corrupt in our body is replaced by diaphanous substances, and becomes a medium for the divine marvels.

---

* This reference is elucidated by the observations on the "Angelic Ministry of Man" in No. 7 of the present section.

5 – The Divine Contemplation *

Among the various privileges of the human soul, that which we should first seek to develop, because it is not merely the most eminent of all, but the one which gives value to the rest, is to draw God from the magical contemplation of His wonders, which are eternally before Him, which spring forth eternally from Him, which are in truth Himself, whence therefore He cannot separate, since He cannot be divided from Himself. This is, in a sense, to divert Him from the imperious and alluring attraction which entrains Him ever towards Himself, being, in fact, that law whereby the things which are turn ever from those which are not, and cleave to their like as by the necessary effect of a natural analogy. It is to awake Him, and, if it be permissible to express it in such terms, to reclaim Him from that ecstasy in which He experiences perpetually the quick and reciprocal impression of the sweetness of His own essences, and the delicious consciousness of the active and generative source of His own existence. It is, finally, to invite His divine regards towards this darksome and deviated nature that their life-giving power may restore its ancient splendour. But where is the thought which can reach Him unless it have kinship with Himself? which can operate this species of awakening unless it be alive as He is? which can draw from His sweet and restoring fountains unless it has been restored to sweetness and purity like His own? which can unite with what is unless it has become like to what is by separation from all that is not? In a word, who can be admitted to the house of the Father and to the Father's intimacy till he has proved himself the true child of the Father? If ever thou shouldst succeed in awaking this supreme God and withdrawing Him from His own contemplation, can the state in which He shall find thee be to thee a matter of indifference? Be thy nature re-born, therefore, as a new nature! Be each of the faculties which constitute thee revivified in its deepest roots! Let the simple, living oil flow forth in an infinity of pu-

---

*   *Le Ministère da l'Homme-Esprit,* pp. 44-46.

rifying elements, and be there nothing within thee unstimulated and unwarmed by one of these regenerating and self-existing elements!

6 – The Universal Ameliorator [*]

Of all the titles which serve to characterise man when he is restored to his primitive elements, that which most satisfies the laudable desires of the soul and most fully corresponds to its conception, is the title of Universal Ameliorator. For the human soul experiences a pressing and importunate need for the reign of order in all classes and all regions, so that all may concur and participate in the sovereign harmony which alone manifests the majestic glory of the Eternal Unity. Brotherly love can in truth exercise no more sublime office than the forgiveness of our enemies and the service of those who hate us. But those who do not hate us, those also who are unknown and will always remain unknown to us, must our love be condemned to inaction in their regard? Should it even be limited to those vague prayers which are meant commonly when we are directed to pray for all? In a word, the entire human species, past, present, and to come, may not this be the object of our real benevolence? May not the heart of that God who is dear so eminently to all the faculties of our being, that God who, for infinite reasons, is entitled to be called our friend *par excellence,* may not His heart be afflicted because the marvels which He has distributed to man and the universe are shrouded by darksome clouds, and should we relax for one moment our efforts to procure it repose? Assuredly there can be nothing so important for us as to return into our mother country without having contracted the manners and customs of this land of iniquity; but though it is much to escape from its defilements, is it not still more to neutralise its corroding poison, or even to transmute it into life-giving balm? We are told to do good to our enemies, and it cannot be denied that, in several respects, Nature is to be included in their number. As to those who are called the enemies of God, it is for God and not for us to measure the justice which is due to them. God himself is too mild and too lovable to have enemies;

---

[*] *Le Ministère da l'Homme-Esprit,* pp. 38-41.

those who would so appear are only foes to themselves, and remain under their own justice.

There are several tasks to be fulfilled in the spiritual career. Most men who enter it seek virtue and knowledge therein only for their own amelioration and their own perfection, and happy are those who are filled with such a desire. But if they rejoice the Father of the family by striving to be numbered among His children, they would rejoice Him still more by endeavouring to be included among His workers; the others serve themselves, but these give Him true services.

Since God has designed man to be the Ameliorator of Nature, He has also given the order to accomplish the amelioration. But He has not issued that order without providing the means; He has not provided the means without conferring an ordination; He has not conferred the ordination without imparting a consecration; He has not imparted consecration without a pledge of glorification; and He has not promised glorification to man save that man is the organ and distributor of the divine admiration, taking the place of that enemy whose throne is cast down, and developing the mysteries of the eternal wisdom.

7 – Angelic Ministry of Man *

Since that period when the first man was drawn from the abyss into which he had fallen, it is our task to discover by every possible means the eternal marvels of the Father manifested in visible Nature, and it is the more possible because the Son, Who contains them all and opens all, has restored them to us by incorporating our first parents in the natural form which we bear, and that He brought with Him the key of all when He was made like unto us. Be assured that there is a deep knowledge which we might impart even to the angels did we return into our rights; and this should by no means astonish us, because, according to St. Paul, we shall judge the angels. Now, the power of judgment supposes that of instruction. Administrators, physicians, redressers of wrong, warriors, judges, also governors and guardians, all

---

*   Adapted from *Le Ministère de l'Homme-Esprit,* pp. 51-54.

these may the angels be, but without us they can have no profound knowledge of the divine marvels of Nature. They are hindered not only because they know the Father only in the splendour of the Son, and that, unlike the first man, they do not comprise in their envelope any essences derived from the root of Nature, but also because we close to them that central eye which is within us, that divine organ through the medium of which they would have contemplated the treasures of the Father in the profundities of Nature, and it is in this manner that the men of God might and ought to instruct the angels, unfolding before them the depths concealed in the corporisation of Nature, and in all the wonders which she includes.

The high privilege of penetrating the profundities of Nature, and becoming, so to speak, its possessors, has been partly restored to us since our degradation; it may even be regarded as an inherent heritage of man, constituting his true wealth and his original possession. Man since his fall has been grafted anew upon the vital root which should produce within him all the living vegetation of his principle; did he therefore raise himself to the living source of wonder, he could himself communicate the real evidences thereof. This, indeed, is the one way by which the divine plans can be accomplished, since man is born to be the chief minister of Divinity. At this day even our material body is far superior to the earth; our animal soul is far superior to the soul of the world, through its junction with our animic spirit, which is our true soul; and our animic spirit is far superior to the angels.

But man would deceive himself if he dreamed of advancing in his work as the minister of Divinity until he has revived that sacred sap within him which has become thickened and congealed by the universal alteration of things. That which has been coagulated must be dissolved and revealed to the eyes of our spirit, so that the depths of our nature may be visible, wherein we shall find the foundation on which the work reposes. Except that basis be re-shaped and levelled, our edifice can never be erected. Only in the interior light of our being can the Divinity and its marvellous powers be experienced by us in its living efficacy.

8 – The Secret of the New Man [*]

The faithful friend who accompanies us in our misery here below[†] is, so to speak, imprisoned with us in the elementary region, and though he enjoys his spiritual life, he can only participate in the divine light and the divine joys of the divine life through the heart of man himself, since man was chosen to be the universal intermediary between good and evil.[‡] We look to this faithful friend for all the assistance, all the protection, all the counsels which are needful in our darkness, in a word, for strength to undergo the sentence of our ordeal, which he is in no way empowered to change; but he in return expects to experience through us, that is to say, by the divine fire with which we should be kindled, the warmth and influx of that Eternal Son from which he keeps himself separated out of pure and living charity for unfortunate humanity. It is for this reason that Jesus Christ has said: "Despise not one of these my little ones, for I say unto you that their angels in heaven behold continually the face of my Father which is in heaven." They behold the face of God only because the children whom they accompany have a pure heart, which is the organ of these angels, who are not in heaven with the Father; but, reciprocally, the heart of man is pure only when faithful to the voice of his angel, in other words, when man has become as a child and so acts that his angel may behold the face of God. So, also, there is a deep meaning in those other words of Christ: "Unless ye become as little children ye shall in no wise enter into the kingdom of heaven." The angel is wisdom, the heart of man is love; the angel is the recipient of the divine light, the heart of man is its organ and modifier. Neither can dispense with the other, one

---

[*] *Le Nouvel Homme,* pp. 6-10.

[†] This is the guide mentioned in the previous section by whom the New Man is baptized on the threshold of his mission.

[‡] The free agents who are the ministers of Divine Wisdom, though they did not participate in the crime of man, share in the painful consequences which this crime has entailed.—*Tableau Naturel,* i. 133.

cannot be united to the other except in the name of the Lord, who is at once love and wisdom, and binds them thereby in his unity. There is no marriage which can be compared with this marriage, and there is no adultery like that which makes it void, whence it is said: "What God hath joined together let no man put asunder."

In this great truth we may discern also the sense of the injunction, "Love thy neighbour as thyself," as also of that other passage which tells us that "he who humbleth himself shall be exalted." In this triple alliance all is living, all spirit, all God and the Word. O man! if thou canst perceive the least ray of this exalted light, lose not a moment in fulfilling every law which it may impose on thee; make thyself living, active, pure, even as the two correspondences between which thou art placed! So shall thy regeneration be hastened, so shalt thou prepare thyself a place of refuge in the time which is to come. Thou art the lamp, the spirit is the air, the heat and fire of the divine light are contained in the oil; the air breathes upon thee that it may awaken thine activity, whereby thou wilt transmit to it in return the gentle and living warmth, the holy brightness, of that oil which must pass of necessity through thee before attaining to it.

In this operation man becomes a veritable light amidst the darkness, because he exhibits the living principle which willeth indeed to procure it for him, and cause it to How through his heart; thus, man may rejoice indeed, but he may not glorify himself; the angel, too, is overwhelmed with consolations and gladness; by means of the divine delights which we procure him, he cleaves and unites more and more unto us, not only by his living and native charity, but by the need of increasing his own felicity. The Divinity, on its part, does but seek continually to penetrate further into the heart of man, for the extension of his glory, life, and power, and to fill with these the angel who so ardently desires them.

Is there anything more exalted in its sublimity than the vocation which designs us to be the instruments of communication between the Divinity and the spirit? Can we delay a moment over so sacred a work, and thus retard the accomplishment of that active triad which, in spiritual and distinct characters, represents the Eternal Triad? By each moment thus lost we render ourselves guilty towards God, whose designs we hinder; towards the spirit, whom we deprive of nourishment; and towards ourselves, whom we wrong not only by the non-fulfilment of our law, but actually destroy by depriving of the double subsistence, divine and spiritual, afforded in this sacred function. When the Divine Life enters within us, it attracts the spirit; when the spirit enters, it attracts the Divine Life. Then is God made spirit, and the spirit is made divine. Our spirit then receives the nourishment prepared by the wisdom which ordains all its operations for the supreme good of existences. Without it, the advent of Divinity alone would consume us, while the spirit by itself would not suffice for our nourishment, because, albeit we are less than God, we are more than the spirit.[*]

9 – The Two Species of Mystery[†]

Mystery is of two kinds. The one comprises the natural mysteries of the formation of physical things, the laws, mode, and purpose of their existence; the other encloses the mysteries of our fundamental being and its correspondences with its principle. The final end of a mystery in general cannot be to remain inaccessible either to intelligence or to that sweet sentiment of wonder for which our soul is made, which is therefore an indispensable nourishment for our immaterial being. The end of the mystery of Nature is to elevate us, by the discovery of

---

[*] There are some Kabalistic teachings which present a certain analogy with this unreasonable doctrine concerning man and the angels, which, it should be observed, is quite distinct from recent attempts to identify man with the fallen portion of the angelic hierarchy. There is, moreover, no trace of it in the Masonic catechisms of Pasqually, or in the curious treatise of Fournié, which is supposed to represent the original instruction of Martinism. In another section of *Le Nouvel Homme* there are said to be two doors in the heart of man, the one below, through which the enemy of mankind may receive the elementary light, from which he is also shut out, and the other above, by which the spirit who is imprisoned with us can alone have access to the Divine Light. By the opening of the lower door we torture the imprisoned angel, for according to *L'Homme de Desir* (No. 146, p. 217), the serpent thereby intrudes his poisoned head. The attempt to open both doors is so fatal that Saint-Martin refuses to dwell upon it. It is our duty at all costs to keep the enemy in darkness and to open the door of the spirit.

[†] *Le Ministère de l'Homme-Esprit,* pp. 47-50.

the laws of physical things, to the knowledge of the higher laws by which they are governed. The knowledge of the mysteries of Nature and of all that constitutes it cannot be interdicted at this day, in spite of our fall, for if it were, the final end of its mystery would be wanting. The final end of the mystery of divine and spiritual things, linked as it is with the mystery of our own being, is to move and excite within us the sentiments of wonder, tenderness, love, and gratitude. It should therefore penetrate our fundamental being, in the absence of which the dual mystery that binds us to things divine and binds things divine to us, would fail absolutely of its effect.

There is at the same time a great difference between the two kinds of mystery. That of Nature can enter into our cognisance, but Nature of herself only affects us feebly, or even fails to touch us in our essential and fundamental being. If we all of us find pleasure in her contemplation, and in penetrating her mysteries, it is that we then ascend higher than herself and attain by her means to regions which are truly analogous with us, whilst, viewed from thence, she appears as but a beacon which points us to the height but cannot of itself communicate its sweetness. On the other hand, divine and spiritual things do infinitely more affect our fascinated and wondering faculties, even when they do not minister to all the needs of our intelligence; they seem to impart a larger measure of wonder on account of their reluctance; could we subject them completely to our knowledge, our admiration would be diminished and our enjoyment would be proportionately lessened; for if it be true that our felicity is in wonder, it is also true that wonder is more sentiment than knowledge, whence it is that God and spirit are so sweet and yet are known so little.

For the opposite reason it may be affirmed that Nature is more cold for us, being rather adapted to our knowledge than our sentiment. Thus the plans of wisdom are so disposed that those things on which our true pleasure is founded do not yield themselves enough to our comprehension for our wonder to be exhausted, while those not primarily intended for the nourishment of this faculty, having less analogy with us, do accord us a species of compensation in the pleasures of the intelligence.

From the way in which men have administered the two domains, they have dried up both the springs which should have yielded us sweet waters, each after its own kind. Human philosophy, treating the natural sciences, has confined itself merely to the surface, and has not put us in a position to taste those very pleasures of the understanding which Nature is ever ready to procure us; while the institutors of divine things, by making them dark and unapproachable, have prevented us from feeling them, and have consequently deprived us of the wonder which these would have excited unfailingly, had they been only permitted to approach us. The complement of the perfection of mystery is to unite in a just and harmonious combination that which can at once satisfy our intelligence and nourish our admiration; it is that which we should have always enjoyed had we kept at our primitive post. For the door by which God issues from Himself is that door through which He enters the human soul. The door by which the human soul issues from itself is that by which it enters the understanding. The door by which the understanding issues from itself is that by which it enters the spirit of the universe. The door by which the spirit issues from itself is that by which it enters the elements and matter. Hence men of science who pass not through all these ways never enter into Nature. Matter has no door by which to issue from itself and enter into an inferior region. This is why the enemy has access to no regulated region, either spiritual or material. In place of watching vigilantly at his post, man has opened all these doors to his enemies, and, not contented with this, he has also shut them on himself, so that he is without and the robbers are within. Can any situation be more deplorable?

10 – The Concealed Being[*]

There is assuredly a profound reason for that law by which the origin of all things is concealed and unknown, even by those who derive from that origin. Beneath this impenetrable veil the roots of all procreations inosculate with the universal force. It is not until this secret inosculation has taken place, and the root has received its living preparation in mystery, that substantialisation begins, with the assumption of external form, colour, and property. Even in time this inosculation is insen-

---

[*] *Le Ministère de l'Homme-Esprit,* pp. 150-151.

sible, and disappears into immensity, into the eternal and permanent, as if to instruct us that time is only the region of the visible action of existences, while that of their unseen activity is the infinite. The eternal wisdom and eternal love are solicitous both for their glory and our intelligence; they shrink, as it would seem, from suggesting that anything has commenced, that there is anything save the Eternal, since truly no being, and especially no man, has any notion of a beginning on his own account, unless indeed for his body, and even in this case the notion is excited as much by the tyranny of the body over the spirit as by the daily lessons of reproduction. As a fact, only disorder and evil can have a beginning; and since man connects with unity, as with the centre, however much he may grow old corporally, he does not less regard himself as in his prime. Thus, the concealed origin of things is a speaking witness of their eternal and unseen source; we feel, as already said, that death and evil have indeed begun, but that life, perfection, bliss can be only because they have ever been.

11 – The Three Epochs in the Treatment of the Human Soul [*]

When a man by abandoning himself to injustice has permitted the appetite for virtue to grow weak in his soul, but afterwards by saving remorse endeavours to revive that precious desire within him, it is imperative that he should set to work without delay. The first result which he experiences is a painful situation, which is in effect one of combat between the laudable intention that impels him and the disorder with which he is filled. This is, so to speak, the first dressing of his wound, and, as in one of the physical kind, it is necessary that the remedy should assist the blood by prolonged suppurations to purge itself from all vicious humours. When this purification has been accomplished, when this powerful and well ordered desire has swollen, as it were, all the faculties of the man, the second stage of his cure begins, and its symptoms may be compared with those slight quiverings or irritations which surgery regards as of happy augury in

---

[*] *Œuvres Posthumes*, i. 173-174

corporeal treatment. The difference between the two stages is, that in the first death still prevailed over life, while in the second life asserts itself over death, and, being in a condition to subdue it, has already a foretaste of victory. The third degree, as in the physical so in the moral, is that of the overflow of life itself, which places the patient once more in the enjoyment of all his faculties, and sets no bound to his development but that which he may himself create by further prevarications, or Nature may raise on her part by the law of death imposed on all bodies.

12 – The Medicine of Man *

The truth has no greater end than to form an alliance with man, but it desires the man alone, free from combination with anything which is not fixed and eternal as itself. It wills that the whole man should cleanse and regenerate himself continually in the pool of fire and in the thirst for unity; it wills that he should daily pour forth his sins on the earth, that is, his material part; it wills that his body should be prepared at all times for death and for sufferings, his soul prepared for the operation of all the virtues, his mind prepared to avail itself of all lights, and to make all show forth the glory of that source whence they come to him; it wills that he should look upon himself, in his entire being, as an army ever in the field, and ready to march at the first order issued; it wills that he should possess a resolution and constancy which nothing can enfeeble, and, forewarned that in the progress of his career he has suffering alone to anticipate, since evil will present itself at every step; it wills that this prospect should in no way impede his advance, nor divert his eyes from the term which awaits him at the end of his course. If it find him in these dispositions, here are the promises which it makes and the favours it designs to bestow on him. No sooner does the interior man open to the truth than it is seized with a transport of joy, which is not only like that of a tender mother for a son unseen for years, but like that of the most sublime genius in presence of a most sublime production, which, though at first it

---

*   *Le Nouvel Homme*, pp. 1-5.

seems strange to the mind, and, as it were, effaced from the memory, soon adds the most lively affection to the first admiration when genius recognises that the production is its individual work. No sooner does truth then perceive desire and will in the heart of man than it precipitates itself therein with all the ardour of its divine life and love. Very often it demands merely that the man should renounce that which is empty, and for this negative sacrifice it overwhelms him with realities; in the first place, setting signs of warning and preservation upon him, that he may no longer exclaim with Cain, "Whosoever findeth me will slay me." Next, it impresses on him the marks of terror, so that his presence becomes redoubtable and he puts his enemy to flight. Thirdly, it invests him with the tokens of glory, so that he may blazon forth the majesty of his master, and receive everywhere the honourable rewards which are due to a faithful servant.

Thus does truth treat those who put trust in the nature of their being, who suffer not its smallest spark to become extinguished, who regard themselves as a fundamental idea or text, of which our entire life should be only the development and commentary, all our moments concurring to elucidate and explain it, not to obscure, efface, and cause it to be forgotten, as happens almost universally with our unfortunate posterity.

To co-operate in our cure, the truth possesses a real medicine which we experience physically within us whensoever it thinks fit to administer it. This medicine is composed of two ingredients conformed to our disease, which is a complication of good and evil, inherited from him who could not forego the desire of familiarity with this fatal science. The medicine is bitter, but it is the bitterness which cures, because this quality, which is justice, joins with what is vitiated in our nature to induce rectification, while, on the other hand, what is regular and quick within us joins with what is sweet in the medicine, and health is restored to us. So long as this medicinal operation does not take place within us, in vain do we believe ourselves whole, in vain prosperous; we are not even in a condition to make use of pure and saving elements, for our faculties are not open to receive them. It is not, therefore, sufficient for our re-establishment to refrain from unwholesome and corrupt sustenance; we must also make use of this spiritual medicine which the doctors of the soul administer to excite that painful sensation which may be termed the fever of penitence, inducing, however, the sweet sensation of life and of regeneration. Those who are in the way of regeneration receive and experience this medicament whensoever the enemy infects them, vitiating something in their nature. Others neither receive nor experience it, for they are in an inveterate condition of derangement and infirmity, which forbids any medicine to operate within them.

This medicine is, at the same time, so necessary to our restoration, that those who have not received it cannot partake with profit of the bread of life, nor can they become refined gold. It must search and work our soul unceasingly, even as time tries all the bodies of nature to renew them in the purity, simplicity, and lively action of their constituent principles. Thereby a living spring, nourished and sustained by very life, opens within us; thereby, also, we possess ourselves of joys which do not pass away, which establish beforehand within us the eternal kingdom of the true.

It will be easy to discern that this medicine must not be confounded with earthly tribulations, with the wrongs we may suffer from our fellow-creatures; such trials are either for the punishment of the soul or for its proving, but they impart only temporal wisdom; now we cannot receive the divine life except by preparations of its own order, and the medicine referred to is exclusively such a preparation. Blessed is he who shall persevere to the end in desiring it and in profiting thereby whensoever he shall have the happiness to experience it!

13 – Prayer *

The beginning of all truths is in Nature, but their consummation is in Prayer, because Prayer comprises all. † It includes also all religions, because it immerses our soul in that sacred charm, that divine magism, which is the secret life of all beings. It is this magism, indeed, which explains the diversity of the religions of men and justifies even their exaggerations, since wherever we find God we meet with this mag-

---

* Adapted from *Œuvres Posthumes,* p. 403-443.

† "Prayer is for our intellectual being what breathing is for our body."—*Tableau Naturel,* i. 178.

ism, which is in fact the operation of the faculty of wonder. By its aid we can pass through all dangers without perceiving them, and endure fatigues without feeling them; it diffuses peace, almost pleasure, over evils, and over death itself, by imparting to our imperishable being, in such cruel moments, the wizard powers which support it to its end, as by some indefinable fascination; by veiling, so to speak, the perilous paths which we are compelled to traverse; by showing, finally, in a palpable manner, that all our actions, all our progress in the career of life, even our death itself, should be vested with this character, should be the flower-season of admiration, or the summit of that edifice of generation which we should build during the whole course of our existence.

But when does Prayer attain in reality this sublime term? When we succeed in making prayers which themselves pray in us and for us, not those which we are forced to stay up on all sides, seeking them in formulae, or in childish and scrupulous observances; when we feel only God present in his works, and that his works are spirit and life; when we realise, therefore, that we can look for Him to dwell in us only in proportion as we ourselves become life and spirit,—that is to say, in the measure that each of our faculties becomes one with the works of God.

Men are far, alas! from attaining the height of this ineffable region of Prayer. They do not raise themselves even to the height of the religion of intelligence; they are so surrendered to the sensible, not to say the material, that without the religion of facts or prodigies it is almost impossible to win access to their souls, and to awaken the principle of life within them. It is even necessary, for their own good, to begin by regarding them as enemies before seeking to treat them as brothers. Where are those who have not merely ceased seeking for signs, which was the reproach of the Jews, but do not content themselves, like the Gentiles, with the wisdom of the mind, and plunge rather in this immense abyss of Prayer to prove effectually that whatsoever does not connect with this active and living religion is but a phantom at best? Where are those who realise how far the appetite for the marvellous absorbs and hides for us the marvels which we might meet with in Prayer? Where are those who have made a firm resolve to abide in the temple of the Lord till they feel that the temple of the Lord comes to abide in them?

The eternal and divine wisdom maintains all the productions of the everlasting immensity in their forms, their laws, and their living activity; in the physical order the air operates the same effect upon all beings in Nature, for in its absence all forms would dissolve; in connection with man, Prayer has a like distinction and a like office; it must weigh on all the faculties which make up our existence, and maintain them in their activity, as the universal power weighs unceasingly on all beings and causes them to manifest their innate life. This eternal wisdom is the air which God breathes; it is one in its measures, and hence the form of God is eternal; it has nothing to strive with, or any labours to endure, like that temporal wisdom which we need in our passage through the region of composites. Here is the model for our Prayer, which obtains nothing till it has acquired that character of active unity, which carries it beyond time and makes it the natural channel of the marvels of eternity. For this it is which, pressing thus on all our spiritual channels, purifies them of all their corruption and places them in a condition to receive the treasures which they should transmit to us. When we say in the *Pater,* "Hallowed be thy name," we do but invoke the fulfilment of this law. The soul is the name of God, and if we obtain the sanctification of that name within us, from that very moment the channels of the marvels of eternity open for us, and they may be diffused not on us alone, but over all the immensity which surrounds us. For it is by uniting ourselves with all the elect of God, all patriarchs and apostles of God, that we can say "Our Father" in the most sublime sense of the words, because thereby we become their brethren, participating in all their works. Once they obtain free approach to us, these marvels are no longer held back, for we are then initiates of the divine movement, of that movement which is never interrupted because it is the son of desire, and desire is the root of eternity. Now, this divine movement within us takes place only in the absolute repose of our being, and by the stilling of all storms amidst which we abide in the temporal region. Oh, how grand, terrible, and superb would be the man who had not reproduced sin! There are no powers, no lights, no virtues which would not be found in him. But what sorrow for man to feel that he cannot look for Prayer at his ease and in full liberty except in proportion as the whole universe shall dissolve; to feel that all which surrounds him, approaches him, constitutes him at this day is an obstacle to Prayer!

Let a man, therefore, search himself before offering the Prayer of the Centurion. For woe unto such an one if this word be said before he is ripe for its understanding. It will be uttered only to his dismay and his loss. Who is he that shall endure the Word of the Lord when it reverberates in his ear? But the man who is possessed by Prayer encounters this Word everywhere and at all times, for as there is no time, so is there no space for the spirit. Are not these two measures proportional? Earth, stay thy course; heaven, suspend thy voice; and thou, prince of darkness, away, plunge into thine abyss! A man is about to pray, to pray till he enters that region where man is tormented forever by the pursuit and importunity of prayer and speech.

Nothing but prayers of thanksgiving should, however, be addressed to God; nothing should be asked of Him, for He gives all things, yet that only which is ever perfect and ever excellent. He showers delights and favours when even we feel by our defilements that we merit only punishments and should expect only tortures. Miserable men know this, yet they unceasingly destroy God, that is to say, they prevent Him from penetrating within them that He may thereby manifest Himself outside them. For if it be our felicity to know God, the felicity of God is to be known, and whatsoever is opposed thereto is for a death. Weep, and yet again weep, over the sins of men and over our own; seek to understand how much God loves us; promise Him to work that we may proclaim it, never resting till we have had speech with Him. Let us even go so far in our penitence, and in the consciousness of our ingratitude, as to devote ourselves without regret, and even with pleasure, to sufferings, to dangers, to terrors of every kind; that is to say, let us submit ourselves with delight to the chastisements which we have all so justly merited. The chief prayer that we should offer, the chief work that we should perform, is to ask of God the single passion for His search, His finding, for union with Him, permitting ourselves no movement which does not derive from this passion. By this path are we brought to become the true image and likeness of God, because we do nothing any more, have no thought any more, produce no blossom within us, which is not preceded by, which issues not directly from, the holy, interior, and divine speech, even as there is nothing in all the universe of spirits and of worlds which does not continually proceed from the eternal and universal generative and creative speech of all things.

But it is insufficient to demand of God that He should descend in us; we have accomplished nothing unless He remains there; and herein is the greatest misfortune of which men are the victims, for daily does God descend within them, but daily do they allow Him to depart, or rather they themselves expel Him, and seem unaware of it, so to speak. Prayer is a vegetation, for it is but the laborious, progressive, and continual development of all the powers and properties of man, which have been withheld and entombed by sin. Thou canst never, therefore, know the prayer of penitence until thou hast compassed the vast field of the necessity of the first man—that of immortal, spiritual, thinking and speaking Nature—and that of the horrible privation which so evidently demonstrates a punishment, thence a fault, and thence also a justice anterior to thyself. Thou canst never partake of regeneration until thou hast experienced this living purification or penitence, which produces the Baptism of Water by thy tears; thou canst never exercise the works and gifts of the Spirit till regeneration has restored thy powers. This indicates the vastness of the domain of Prayer, and the grandeur of the work which it imposes upon thee. Every degree of this enumeration awaits thine activity, in order to offer thee its fruit, and thus remind thee unceasingly that thou art a living extract of a living source, and that all should be born of thee in its image, so that it may be accounted unto thee and abide with thee. God is a King who enters ever into His kingdom and never departs therefrom. For the human soul He is even as a tender and devoted spouse, watchful, with untiring solicitude, to spare His cherished bride not only evils and dangers, but even the smallest fatigue.

Prayer is the principal religion of man, because this it is which rebinds our heart to our spirit, and it is only because these are disunited that we are guilty of so many errors and abide in the midst of so much darkness and so many illusions. In the unification of mind and heart God is naturally joined with us, since He has said that where two or three are gathered together in His name there is He in the midst of them. Then can we say with the Restorer, "My God, I know that thou dost hear me always." Whatsoever does not issue constantly from this source belongs to the order of dead and separated works; and even the works of the Spirit, which operate by this source within us, who are the organ thereof, are not to be compared with such union. The safeguard against pride in this kind of works is to keep our eyes fixed continually on the source, for we shall then feel that we are labouring for its glory alone, while, on the other hand, when we draw from the works of the Spirit in external ways and intentions, we feel that we are toiling for our own glorification.

When Prayer has thus rebound our mind and our heart to God, and has opened the divine treasury within us, we feel ourselves warmed and vivified by all the divine forces; the foundations of the covenant are laid within us; all patriarchs, prophets, and apostles of the Lord do there perform their several functions, because the Holy Spirit itself operates within them; and all such functions operate within us in a delicious bond and harmony, depicting the holy fraternity of all those elect of God, with their ardent and mutual zeal to advance God's work within us, because they are themselves directed and influenced by the harmony of unity.

I have said that our Prayer should be a continual act of thanksgiving, reciting the preserving graces of which we are the recipients. As to evils, we should mention those only from which we do not ourselves suffer; as to tribulations, those which we are spared; as to privations, those which we do not experience. We might extend Ps. 43. to infinity, for it is no longer the mercies accorded to our fathers and celebrated by the Jewish hymn, but those which are shown daily to ourselves. Did we follow this course, we should soon experience joy, peace, and consolation, while the Supreme Hand would shield us even from those more serious ills which seem inevitable to our nature, but are at the same time almost invariably the consequences of our faults and our follies. But to attain this height of sublimity to which we may be raised by Prayer, we must buy it at the price of the pangs of childbirth; the memory of the suffering which it has cost us will thus remain with us, and thus also will our treasure be the price of love.

I have said that we should ask only for God and Prayer to pray themselves within us. But since it has been promised us that whatsoever we ask the Father in the name of One shall be given us, we must, with industrious faith, demand Himself in His name, that our prayer may not be refused. The Scripture tells us that the Holy Spirit prays within us unceasingly with ineffable groanings. Our sole task is, therefore, not to hinder God from thus praying within us. For if He pray everywhere within us, and with all the faculties of His being, we shall then be that veritable emptiness which we ought to be in respect of Him, doing nothing but hearkening continually to the various and divine prayers which He makes in us and for us, and shall be only their object, their living sign and testimony for the instruction of the external regions. Herein is the true abandonment, that state in which our being is led continually and secretly from death to life, from darkness to light, if we may dare say so, from nothingness to being—an exodus which fills us with wonder, not only by its sweetness, but still more because the work rests in the Divine Hand which effects it, and is fortunately incomprehensible for us, as are all generations in all classes to the creatures who are their agents and organs. Such is the bliss of this ignorance, that were the Knowledge and the Key of this divine generation offered us, we should err if we accepted it. As to the eternal and divine generation itself, let us never dream of attaining its real and effective knowledge, whatever sublime glimpses may be caught concerning it in the abysses of wisdom. A universal magism surrounds all generations, all feel it, none understand it. I will not shrink from maintaining that even God is everlastingly ravished in His own generation, but did He comprehend it a beginning must be assigned to it, since His thought would precede it. Lastly, could any being have knowledge of its own generation, there would be no more magic, and, without magic we might indeed have knowledge and truth, but we should no longer possess pleasure.

When we have the happiness to attain this sublime abandonment, the God whom we have obtained in the one Name, according to the promise, who Himself doth pray within us, can no longer leave us, since He has infused into us His own immortality, and we are henceforth simply the centre of His operations. Possessed of Him, we have no longer any defilement to fear, because He is that purity which nothing can soil. We have no longer to dread the assaults of the enemy—demoniacal, astral, or terrestrial—because He is force and strength, before which all powers are broken. We have no longer any cares to distress us concerning our progress, our conversation, our needs, for in all these things He is present, having the fulness of all means which suffice for them, and thus may be realised the truth of those words spoken to the Apostles, warning them to be in no wise solicitous about the needs of life, like the Gentiles.

When God, in answer to our Prayer, has established Himself within us, another prodigy will come speedily to pass for the increase of our happiness. In Isaiah, Jeremiah, Amos, and other prophets, God swears by His name, by His right hand, by His soul, to break the staff of bread, to destroy the guilty cities, to remember no longer the wicked nations; but how much the more will He be ready to swear after the same manner that He will never more desert us, since He cannot do so without separating from Himself! How much the more will He be desirous of swearing all these things in His name and by His love than the contrary in His name and by His wrath?

What then should be our hope and security, since God, who forbids us to take His name in vain, would never take His own word in vain, and hence none of His promises can fail in their effect, nor all His blessings and mercies to follow and accompany us everywhere. Happy therefore is the man whom Divinity deigns to choose for His temple. Labour and suffering he must look for, and must be subject in all things to the master's orders, but the compensations which await him are far above the services to be rendered, and it will even come to pass that he shall no longer need to ask of God to enter within him and invoke Himself in His own name, for this Deity of love and desire will come without supplication, when the only prayers possible will be acts of thanksgiving and jubilation. There will be no need of the injunction to pray without ceasing, for the unceasing dwells within him and cannot do so without praying, without His eternal desire leaping out universally, that is, without pouring over us the waves of spiritual worlds and the incalculable numbers of divine universes.

But the Prayer which He offers within us is a Prayer of pain, because it is an operation of rebirth. When He seeks to enter within as the Reconstructor, He must encounter suffering, and He performs penance within us. Shall we not ask Him, when our cure has been effected, the grace of sharing His affliction in respect of the defilement and darkness of other men? But we must do more than share the pangs which bewrayed and blinded humanity occasion Him. The judgment of the human race must also enter within us; we must experience it in all its extent, in all its horror. At the same time, this operation is so important that we must beware of desiring it before our substance is sufficiently strong and pure to support it, a precaution which is equally indispensable before we ask the Great Being to pray Himself within us; for sympathy is possible only between analogous natures. When, however, we watch diligently over ourselves, we may be sure that He will delay not in electing Himself to Prayer within us, and this is the first sign of regeneration, which takes place in proportion as the progressive course of all elections and the purposes of all alliances is accomplished within us, since it is thus alone that the Eternal Word of the Father descends in us with free operation and makes itself comprehended by our spirit with all the sweetness which it engenders. Then shall we experience true faith, the faculty of regarding God as the owner of the house we assign to Him by the compact mutually agreed upon—of permitting Him full liberty to use all therein as He pleases—of reserving nothing for ourselves, since it is God Himself who must permeate all that composes us. We must realise, above all, that we can do nothing unless we are continually engendered of God. But to reach this exalted state we must pass through one which precedes it, the determined employment of all the powers of our will. So also we should pray ever to reestablish our analogies with that which is beyond time; we should link ourselves inseparably with that profound Name which seeks to be linked inseparably with all; we should make constant efforts that this fundamental Name may not be apart from us even for a moment; without it no works of ours can be lawful or free from our own reproach.

But there is one marvel which must not be spoken aloud; it is that man prays always, even when he knows it not; the prayers which he utters consciously are but the extension of those which he offers unaware, the flowing out of the eternal stream engendered within him. Their sole object is to vivify all his members, all his ways, and in him all places, that life may be everywhere. Nevertheless, if this secret and unknown prayer be not united to active and voluntary prayers it will in no wise serve him, and its proper peace, or that, namely, which it engenders, returns upon itself.

Book VI

Minor Doctrines of Saint-Martin

I

The Doctrine of External Religion

1 – The Exoteric Church

THE MINISTRATIONS OF a priest were declined, it is reported, by Saint-Martin on his dying bed, though the authority, it should be added, is only a newspaper of the period, which does not seem to have satisfied his biographer, M. Caro.[*] There were grave doctrinal differences between the mystic and the Church of his childhood, but equally in religion and in politics he always exhibited respect for the established order; and on one occasion observes expressly that his object being the general welfare of mankind, he would refrain above all from creating discord by the direct attack of received dogmas or existing institutions.[†] The man of desire was essentially a man of peace. Respect, however, is not concurrence, and there can be no doubt that there were personal convictions of Saint-Martin which, far more strongly than any arbitrary dogma, made his reconciliation with the Latin Church impossible. When the Spanish Inquisition, after a delay of many years, condemned his first book, he is said to have been exceedingly cast down;[‡] but it was not because he accepted that

---

[*] *Du Mysticisme au XVII Siècle,* p. 71.

[†] *Des Erreurs et de la Vérité,* Part i. p. 9.

[‡] The statement is on the authority of Mrs. Cooper-Oakley, writing on the subject of the Unknown Philosopher in *Lucifer,* January 1897. I am not

condemnation as proof of his error; he was grieved that the Church, like the world, was unable to receive his truth and made common cause against it with philosophers and infidels. For his own part he had nothing to recant, while the policy which he had dictated to himself left him also nothing to reply. If Martines de Pasqually, his master, pursued a different course, it must, I think, have been either because he was less discerning, less consistent, or less sincere; in any case, initiation is incompatible with the ecclesiastical discipline of the Church.

When Saint-Martin fell under the influence of the Lutheran mystic Böhme, there are, I think, indications that his sympathies were still further alienated, but he remained mild and reasonable to the end. His most extreme statement does not occur in any work which he had designed for publication, but in a letter to Baron Kirchberger, where, speaking of the power of the Word passing through impure organs, and admitting that the fact was undeniable, "even if we had no other example than the prophet Balsam," he adds: "I do not reckon the pretended transmission of the Church of Rome, which, in my opinion, transmits nothing as a Church, although some of its members may sometimes transmit, whether by their own virtue, by the faith of the hearers, or by a particular will of goodness." *

To deny that the Church transmits in the sense intended by Saint-Martin is to assail its title to existence, and it is worthwhile to investigate at some length the considerations which actuated this statement, because the feelings of a Christian mystic towards the most mystical of all the Churches, more especially when nurtured therein, are always a point of interest to other mystics who are disposed to seek their guidance from the Light of the West.

I find no reason to suppose that the outward respect of Saint-Martin was simply a matter of policy and prudence. It was not like that

---

(Continued...)

acquainted with the source of her information. Matter says that "although it was the heaviest blow which could be indicted on a religious soul, he bore it with all the moderation of a strong reason, and all the calmness of a conscience assured of itself." But even this is an interlinear reading, for in his Portrait Historique, Saint-Martin simply records the fact of the condemnation without one word of commentary.

* *Correspondance,* Lettre lxxiv; Penny, "Theosophic Correspondence," p. 240.

which was paraded long afterwards by Eliphas Lévi, part verbiage, part mockery, and appealing to *la haute convenance* for its justification. It was honourable and sincere, nor was it founded upon one consideration only, though Saint-Martin seems to have been most impressed by the doctrinal reserve of the great religious institutions. He speaks of the wise motives, outside all vulgar appreciation, which have caused the ministers of religion to announce doctrines with prudence and with a reserve which is beyond all praise. Penetrated undoubtedly with a sense of the sublimity of their functions as depositaries of the keys of knowledge, they have preferred that the people should venerate that key without themselves possessing it, rather than expose its secrets to profanation.[*] There is no need to say that this title to respect is one that the Church would reject, because it involves the symbolism of dogmas, as it would reject also the connected statement that "darkness and silence are the asylums chosen by truth,"[†] because again the Church does not interpret its mission as embroidering a veil for the truth, but as the teacher of truth literally. Still we are enabled to see how Saint-Martin regarded the ecclesiastical office at the beginning of his own ministry,[‡] namely, as an initiate speaking of initiation. As he abandoned all formal initiation at a later period, so he ceased to regard the Church in the light of a depository of secret knowledge, but his respect remained.

To understand his position, we must seek first of all for his definitions. The Church, according to Saint-Martin, is the spirit of Jesus Christ; where that spirit is found, there is the Church of Christ; where it is wanting, there are only skulls and stones.[§] In harmony with this he defines religion as the science of the heart;[||] that is to say, the higher sense of the Logos is Love, and religion is the method by which our human love is united to the divine. It is not, therefore, reducible by analysis like other sciences. It is the fruit of humility and good faith; faith is confidence; confidence is love, hope, "all sentiments that are

---

[*] *Des Erreurs et de la Vérité,* Part ii. p. 199.   [†] Ibid.

[‡] Observe also the following statement: "I maintain not only the necessity of a cultus, but I shall manifest even more clearly the necessity of a single cultus, since one chief or one Cause should alone direct it."—*Des Erreurs et de la Vérité,* Part p. 195. The reference here is to the Active and Intelligent Cause.

[§] *Œuvres Posthumes,* ii. p. 212.   [||] Ibid. p. 292.

more living, more satisfying than those which can be occasioned by evidence."[*] The cultus is the means by which the religious necessity of man, or the desire of truth and love, receives its satisfaction,[†] and it is also the law in accordance with which the Supreme Being receives the honour due from humanity.[‡] It has passed into the hands of the ignorant, and its utility has suffered in consequence, but the lower senses are fixed by its pomp, and their extra-lignment is thus checked by its influence, which is also profitable to pure and strong souls.[§] "Woe therefore to those," says Saint-Martin, "who are the causes or instruments of its abolition!"[||] The majority of religious institutions he regards as extra advantages offered by the Divine Mercy to man, and auricular confession is named expressly in this connection. "Prior to this practice man confessed his sins in his heart; now he confesses them also with his lips; the more he multiplies the organs of his humility and the avowal of his errors, the more he advances towards reconciliation."[¶] It is difficult to agree that a system which includes institutions of such efficacy, and apparently of divine origin, can at the same time transmit nothing. It becomes more apparent, in fact, as we proceed, that the failure in transmission is not in the Church but in the ministers. The Church assists us towards regeneration by operating divers effects at divers seasons. The celebration of the corporeal advent of our Saviour at Christmas has His rebirth in us for its object, in order that we may be reborn in Him; "and those who join with the Church at this holy period by the prayers and practices of religion will not fail to experience this birth."[°] The administration of

---

[*]   *Œuvres Posthumes,* ii. p. 293.   [†]   Ibid. p. 306.

[‡]   Ibid. p. 271.   [§]   Ibid.pp. 93-94.

[||]   According to mother definition, "a cultus is simply the law by which a being, seeking to possess what it needs, draws near to other beings attracted by its analogy with these, while it flees those which are opposed to it. Thus, the law of a cultus is based on a first and evident truth, namely, on the law resulting exclusively from the state of beings, and from their respective correspondence."—*Tableau Naturel,* i. 176. I should add that Saint-Martin finds no difficulty in admitting some wholesome office and ministration in all varieties of the culms, because they are all one as to their end, which is to provide for the necessities of man in the different stages of his development.—Ibid. i. 182.

[¶]   *Œuvres Posthumes,* 270-271.   [°]   Ibid. p. 287.

its favours is full of divine charity and sweetness. "The mortal organs which it uses, sinners like ourselves, are exalted notwithstanding by their character to the rank of privileged agents, whose sole occupation is to intercede with the Divine Mercy, to soften it by prayers, to offer their tears to obtain not only the pardon of our iniquities, but the abolition and destruction of that root of sin sown in us by the Fall and vegetating so cruelly all the days of our life. I confess that I have been filled with respect and penetrated with great tenderness on beholding confessors who have fulfilled their ministry among the penitents, prostrate themselves at the foot of the altar, and supplicate the God of souls in favour of the infirm beings whom they have just healed and absolved, taking also the place of the sinner, and by their aspirations assisting the restoration of life to their wounds. Such a religion may have seen abuses arise within it, even on the part of its ministers, but it is incontestably the true religion, and no such faults in the ministry will cause a reasonable mind to waver. For if it be given them here below to be the representatives and co-operators of the superior agents, and thus at times to be more than men for the good of other unfortunate prevaricators, why should we insist that it is impossible for them to be also men like the vulgar, and sometimes even less than men by abandonment to the depravities of the most iniquitous? There is nothing fixed on earth, and we can pass so easily from one to the other extreme, that we should not be astonished at any variation of which our nature offers us an example."[*]

I do not know, and there is indeed no means of knowing, at what period of his life Saint-Martin wrote this panegyric, but I conceive that it was prior to the "Ministry of Man the Spirit," possibly to his correspondence with Kirchberger, and even to his acquaintance with Böhme. I do not pretend to judge between the earlier and later standpoints, though I think that the mysticism of the Church Catholic is preferable to the most exotic plant of Lutheranism; moreover, the panegyric is a piece of special pleading which is not altogether convincing, though it has high and strong claims. But it is quite clear that the early views of Saint-Martin, if this was his early, and not, as it may also be after all, his later judgment, should be balanced against

---

[*] *Œuvres Posthumes,* ii. 326-327.

extreme statements in the opposite sense, more especially as there is no sign in his writings from first to last of any leaning towards a substituted Church; he believed that it wanted life, that it had lost transmissible virtue; but he disbelieved utterly, as I read him, that it was a human institution or that it could be abrogated by any act of humanity. The duty of those who had attained life, who possessed virtue, was not to replace, but to restore. This feeling comes out quite unexpectedly in a passage on the Catholic Catechism. "Some poorly enlightened parents fear to harm their children by beginning their education with the Catechism, but they look at the matter from the point which they have reached themselves, and not from that of the children. The Catechism explains nothing, yet it contains all. The obscurities and even the incoherencies which it may be possible to find therein do not puzzle the child, for he is not of an age to notice them, while the good things which are met with sow the seeds of goodness within him, the seeds of love, sensibility, order—all faculties to which the soul is destined primitively. The work of the understanding is subsequent, and when it is of an age to remark obscurities, above all, when it is in a state to rectify them, all these things become apparent."[*]

There was no period, however, when Saint-Martin looked at the Church from a standpoint which she would have tolerated herself. For example, he says that she is universal, but it is because all places are proper for the celebration of her mysteries, because all men may become priests by the Spirit, because everything may serve for sacrifices, and because natural law and conventional signs are the same for all men.[†] Of these reasons, the first is fantastic, the second begs one of the questions at issue, namely, the transmission of ordination by the Spirit outside the ecclesiastical vehicle, and the last two are unintelligible.

If we pass now to Saint-Martin's impeachment of the ministry, we shall see more clearly that it is not the institution but its corruption which he condemns, and that here again he desires rectification and not removal. I think, had we lived at his period, we should have agreed with his caustic aphorism, that " the priests have begotten the

---

[*] *Œuvres Posthumes*, 281.　　　　　　　　　[†] Ibid. p. 294.

philosophers, as the philosophers have begotten death and nothingness."[*] The unintelligence of the hierarchy has revolted reason, and reason, in the excess of rebellion, has forfeited herself. The sarcasm is now ineffective because the order of things has changed; we know now the limits and inefficiencies of reason, and we have ceased to expect either from the hierarchy or humanity an undeviating right conduct of the understanding; we shall agree therefore with Saint-Martin when he invites us to respect the functions of priests, and seek to appropriate the virtues which they represent, but not to look to them for vast instruction or to rest on their knowledge. "Let us remember rather that all religion is written in man, and that otherwise it would not be indestructible."[†] We shall agree with him also when he says, that "the ignorance of the priests has infinitely weakened faith in their holy ceremonies, and in all the helps which we may expect from the Messiah. Yet let us abase our pride a little; let us bring to these ceremonies all the dispositions of which we are capable and not intermeddle by judging the power of the ministers. The Word is immutable, and, however scanty the light of the priest, the holy thing will ever be profitable to those who unite with it in fear and yet with confidence, respect, and humility."[‡]

In the "Ministry of Man the Spirit "there is an inclination to make much of the sacerdotal failings, which previously we have 'been solicited to deplore and yet to regard with charity. Priests have been placed in the position of teachers, and they have impoverished the pupil without enriching themselves; they have reduced the office of the Word to figurative institutions, discourses, and external pomp; they have seized the key of knowledge, but the domain to which it gives entrance they have not themselves entered, while they have forbidden it to others; they have paralysed the divine work, neutralised the cure of the soul, forbidden the exercise of reason without recognising that there is a reason which opposes truth and one which espouses its cause.[§] Yet it is not a bitter denunciation; it is rather a questioning complaint, an invitation to confession on the part of one who has forgiven already, with an indication of the path of priestly

---

[*] *Œuvres Posthumes,* p. 306.   [†] Ibid. ii. 270.   [‡] Ibid. p. 310.

[§] *Le Ministère de l'Homme-Esprit,* p. 406 *et seq.*

duty. There are profound and saving truths, and the ministers of holy things are above all persons those who should instruct us in their wonders, because they are the envoys of the Lord sent to proclaim His ordinances.*

I think, therefore, on the whole, we are warranted in concluding that Saint-Martin looked for the regeneration of the Church as for that of man. But he looked also for a new dispensation; the ministry of nature preceded the ministry of the law; the law preceded the ministry of grace, which has been made of no effect by the fall of the priesthood from grace; there is now a ministry of living action to follow, about which Saint-Martin made the same error of proximity as other prophets have made before and since.

But the Church visible is the Church external, and that which is external, though it may serve as an organ, belongs to the order of accidents, and in the last analysis it did not concern Saint-Martin. He looked to the interior, invisible, spiritual Church in the heart of regenerated man, that Church which is unfortunately for the majority of humanity latent rather than unseen. "When man prays with constancy, with faith, and seeking to purify himself in the great thirst of penitence, it may befall him to hear inwardly what was said by the Repairer to Cephas, 'Thou art Peter, and upon this rock I will build my church, and the gates of hell shall not prevail against it.' This operation of the Spirit in man instructs us in the dignity of the human soul, since God does not fear to make it the corner-stone of His temple; and it shows us, in like manner, the nature of the true Church, as also that there can be no Church where this invisible operation of the Spirit is not to be found." † This operation constitutes the true Church, because it is the Eternal Word which sets its seal ,on the chosen corner-stone, even as the Repairer set that of His own Word on the soul of St. Peter. From this Word come those seven virtues or gifts, which are the seven pillars of the edifice, based on the living rock, "the Eternal Church of our God." ‡

---

* *Le Ministère de l'Homme-Esprit,* p. 411 *et seq.*

† *Le Novuel Homme,* pp. 41-42.   ‡ Ibid. p. 101.

2 – Christianity and Catholicism[*]

True Christianity is not only anterior to Catholicism, but to the word Christianity itself, which does not once occur in the Gospel, though the spirit which it contains is clearly exposed therein, consisting, according to St. John, in "the power to become the sons of God;" while the spirit of the children of God or of the apostles of Christ is, according to St. Mark, "the Lord working with them, and confirming the word with signs following." From this point of view, before we can be truly in Christianity we must be united to the spirit of the Saviour and must have consummated our perfect alliance with Him. Hence the true genius of Christianity is less a religion than the term and resting place of all religions, and of all those toilsome ways whereby the faith of men, and the need to be cleansed from their defilements have ever obliged men to travel. So also it is a memorable fact that in the whole of the four Gospels, based as they are on the true spirit of Christianity, the word "religion" does not once occur, while in the apostolic writings which complete the New Testament it is found only four times: once in the Acts, where the reference is to the religion of the Jews; once in the Epistle to the Colossians, where the cultus of angels is condemned; and twice in St. James, who remarks that religion is vain in the man who cannot curb his tongue, while "religion pure and undefiled before God and the Father is this, to visit the fatherless and widows in their distresses, and to keep one's self unspotted from the world." In the last examples, Christianity more closely approaches its place of repose in divine sublimity than it assumes the vestures which we are accustomed to call religion.[†]

Here then is a tabulation of the differences between Christianity and Catholicism.

---

[*] *Le Ministère de l'Homme-Esprit,* pp. 369-374.

[†] The criticism is inept, for the definition of St. James concerns only natural religion, which is not even the first step towards spiritual religion, but the condition which is necessary to make that step possible.

Christianity is the very spirit of Jesus Christ in its fullness, after this Divine Repairer had ascended every step of that mission which He began with the fall of man, when He promised that the seed of the woman should crush the serpent's head. Christianity is the complement of the priesthood of Melchisedec; it is the soul of the Gospel; it is that which permeates this Gospel with those living waters required by the nations for the quenching of their thirst. Catholicism, to which belongs properly the title of religion, is the path of ordeal and labour to attain Christianity.* Christianity is the region of emancipation and liberty; Catholicism is but the seminary of Christianity; it is the region of the rules and discipline of the neophyte.

Like the spirit of God, Christianity fills the Whole earth. Catholicity occupies but a part, though its name represents it as universal.†

By Christianity our faith is taken into the luminous region of eternal divine speech. Catholicism confines this faith within the limits of the written word or of traditions.‡

Christianity enlarges and extends the use of our intellectual faculties; Catholicism binds and circumscribes their exercise.§

Christianity engages us to find God in the depths of our own being, without the help of forms and formulae. Catholicism leaves us at variance with ourselves to find God concealed under the apparatus of ceremonies.‖

---

* The distinction in itself is sound, but the tone is grudging and the form that of disparagement. The Church, by her own hypothesis, is not Divine Grace, but its channel.

† I infer that the term universal, as applied to herself by the Church, does not concern a geographical fact, but a mission and a capacity.

‡ When the soul is in communication with the Divine Word, it is clear that faith has passed and knowledge has begun. The Church claims to be the channel of the Divine Voice; the written word is an accident; she claims to be in conformity with her traditions, which, from her standpoint, simply indicates the consistency which is a characteristic of Divine Mission; her traditions are not her words, but her testimonies.

§ There was never a more fantastic distinction. The proper exercise of the intellectual faculties is in the assimilation of truth; Catholicism would circumscribe its believers to the work of assimilating what it regards as truth, and Christianity can have no better intention The Church may be mistaken, but even Christianity has been challenged.

‖ Perhaps no Church has more consistently taught that God is within us.

Christianity has no mysteries,* and the name is repugnant to it, since it is evidence essentially and universal clearness. Catholicism abounds in mysteries and rests on a hidden foundation. The sphinx might be placed at the threshold of temples made with hands; it cannot dwell on the threshold of the heart of man, which is the true portal of Christianity.

Christianity is the fruit of the tree; Catholicity is only its fertiliser.†

Christianity makes neither monasteries nor anchorites, for, like the sun, isolation is impossible to it, and it seeks, also like the sun, to diffuse its splendour everywhere. It is Catholicism which has peopled the wilderness with solitaries and the town with religious communities, those to devote themselves more profitably to their individual salvation, these to present a corrupted world with some images of virtue and piety to stir it in its sleep.‡

Christianity knows no sect, for it embraces unity, and unity, being one, cannot be divided from itself Catholicism has witnessed within its heart the birth of innumerable schisms and sects which have established the reign of division rather than that of unity; and even Catholicism itself, while believing itself in the highest degree of purity, finds scarcely two members of uniform views.§

Christianity preached no crusades; the unseen cross which it bears in its heart is for the consolation and the felicity of all creatures. It is a false imitation of Christianity, to say no more, which invented crusades; it was Catholicism which adopted them subsequently; afterwards fanaticism commanded them, Jacobinism composed them, anarchy directed them, and they were executed by brigandage.

---

* There is, for example, no "mystery of the kingdom of God" (Mark 4:60); no "wisdom of God in a mystery" (1 Cor. 7); no "mystery of God" to which stewards were appointed (ibid. 4:1); no mystery of the resurrection which is to come (ibid. 15:51); no "mystery of Christ" (Ephes. 4); no "great mystery," in the union between Christ and His Church (ibid. 5:32); no "great mystery of godliness"(1 Tim. 3:16).

† The Church is not greater than her Head.

‡ It is therefore not the object of Christianity to raise up examples of virtue and piety.

§ Even in the Catholic Church there are things doubtful as well as things essential. Moreover, Christianity has seen apostasies as well as the Church schisms.

Christianity has waged war with sin alone; Catholicism has declared it against men.

Christianity proceeds only by certain and continuous experiences; Catholicism by authority and institutions. Christianity is the law of faith; Catholicism is the faith of law.

Christianity is the complete installation of the soul of man in the rank of minister and labourer of the Lord; Catholicism limits man to the care of his personal spiritual health.[*]

Christianity unites man inseparably to God as two beings inseparable by their nature; Catholicism, while employing occasionally the same language, at the same time nourishes man so largely with forms that it makes him lose sight of his real end, and leaves him or leads him to contract many habits which are not profitable to his true advancement.[†]

Christianity rests immediately on the unwritten word; Catholicism in general on the written word, or on the gospel, and on the mass especially.[‡]

Christianity is an active and perpetual immolation, both spiritual and divine, either of the soul of Jesus Christ or of our own. Catholicism reposing, as already said, mainly on the mass, offers therein only an ostensible immolation of the body and blood of the Repairer.

Christianity can only be composed of that holy race which is primitive man, or the true sacerdotal race. Catholicism, once more, reposing particularly on the mass, since the pasch of Christ, has been only the initiatory degrees of this priesthood;[§] for when Christ celebrated the Eucharist with His disciples, and said unto them, "Do this in remembrance of me," they had already received the power to cast out demons, to heal the sick and to raise the dead; but they had not yet

---

[*] A curious commentary on the annals of the propagation of the faith, on the lives of Xavier and Damien.

[‡] It may be seriously doubted whether forms and ceremonies have ever restrained any soul in its progress when that soul was fit for advancement., but Saint-Martin knew well enough, and has expressed well enough, the real ministry of forms to the unadvanced in spiritual culture.

[§] The system of the Church is sacramental; the Eucharist is the crown of the sacramental system.

[||] In other words, the Church is the school of saints.

received the most important complement of the priesthood, since the consecration of the priest consists in the transmission of the Holy Spirit, and the Holy Spirit had not yet been imparted because the Repairer had not yet been glorified.

From the moment that the soul of man is admitted to it, Christianity becomes for it a continual multiplication of lights; Catholicism, which has made the Holy Supper the most sublime and the final degree of its cultus, has allowed veils to fall over this ceremony, and has finished by inserting these words in the Canon of the Mass, *Mysterium Fidei,* which are not in the Gospel and contradict the universal lucidity of Christianity.*

Christianity belongs to eternity; Catholicism to time.

Christianity is the final end; Catholicism, despite the imposing majesty of its solemnities, and despite the saintly magnificence of its admirable prayers, is only the means.†

Finally, there may possibly be many Catholics who as yet cannot judge what Christianity is, but it is impossible that a true Christian should not be in a position to judge not only what Catholicism is but also that which it should be.‡

---

* The contradiction is, in any case, canonical, for St. Paul commands the deacons to hold "the mystery of faith in a pure conscience" (1 Tim. 3:9).

† The definition of such a mission cannot be the statement of an objection, and it is unfortunate that it should assume its form.

‡ The distinctions of Saint-Martin are of no effect, because, as regards Christianity, they move in a world which has not been realised, and, as regards Catholicism, they ignore its higher sense. The discussion is of no importance at the present day, because we are all aware that no institution has ever realised its own ideals. But even in idly criticising it is graceful to be fair.

3 – The Mysterium Fidei

The position of a mystic who denies mystery to Christianity and the sacramental system to the Church, who is yet a fervent Christian and convinced that even the visible household of the faith will be transfigured by some wonderful regeneration when the time of glory comes, is one which would appear inaccessible. The rejection of the *Mysterium Fidei* by Saint-Martin involves both points, for the sacrament involves mystery. One is led irresistibly to suspect that we are dealing here simply with some confusion of thought, and such assuredly is somewhere at the root of the difficulty. We have seen that the *Mysterium Fidei* is confessed by St. Paul, and having regard to the unity of Scripture from the standpoint of the Church, the introduction of these words into the Canon of the Mass is not an interpolation but a transfer, and that Saint-Martin is specifically wrong when he denies mystery to Christianity, for it is affirmed with every warrant of Scripture in the most express manner.[*] I think, however, that he was carried beyond his intention in the attempt to form a. chain of antithesis, and that what he meant to indicate was an over-devotion to symbolism and outward sign on the part of the Catholic Church, thus obscuring the real mission of Christianity as a revelation and not a veil of mysteries. It does not follow that this rectification would constitute a right view, but it is not open to the sharp reproof of a score of accessible facts, and it just possible that in the soul of the average Catholic there is occasionally:

---

[*] It is equally affirmed by Saint-Martin: "Among all the most illustrious learned and religious institutions which have ever flourished, there is not one which has not covered science with the veil of mysteries. Judaism and Christianity are alike examples. The traditions of Israel inform us of the judgment on King Ezechias for exhibiting its *treasures* to the Babylonian ambassadors; and we see by ancient Christian rites, by the letter of Innocent I. to Bishop Decentius, and by the writings of Basil of Cæsarea, that Christianity possesses *things of great force and great weight which neither are, nor can ever be, written.*"— *Tableau Naturel,* ii. 192

"Too much presuming
  To turn the frankincense's fuming
  And vapours of the candle starlike
  Into the cloud her wings she buoys on."

But the recognition of a natural exaggeration should not be converted into an impeachment of the mystery of faith, and that least of all by Saint-Martin, for whom the world, as we have seen, was a parable or allegory,* and therefore even the system of Nature was a universal sacramentalism.† To reject sacramentalism in the order of spiritual things is a divorce of Nature and Grace which no mystic could countenance. It is not necessary to pursue the subject further as it is not seriously challenged; but admitting that Saint-Martin has either failed to explain himself or is in error concerning it, it will be well to observe briefly his position concerning the central sacrament of the Christian Church—I refer, of course, to the Eucharist. He has already told us that she errs in regarding the importance attributed to the sacrifice of the Mass, which he describes as an ostensible immolation, replacing to some extent, and that unwarrantably, the active and perpetual spiritual and divine immolation of the soul of Jesus Christ and of our own. The charge of replacement seems entirely fantastic; we know that the Christian who sins is thereby supposed to crucify the Son of God afresh, and that in the eyes of the Church the unbloody sacrifice operates somehow as an atonement, in which case the Mass enters so far into the spirit of Scripture. But as none of these things are acceptable in a literal sense, and as every Church has mistaken *signum* for *signatum,* we may accept the statement of Saint-Martin as an obscure registration of this fact, and endeavour to

---

*   *Tableau Naturel,* ii. 207

†   This is clearly implied by another teaching of the *Tableau Naturel,* namely, that the manifestations of the image of the First Principle is in accordance with a law which is bound up in the temporal and successive order, i. 162. It follows also from the statement that man, in his fallen condition, can only receive the communication of the Divine potencies under an innumerable multitude of facts, signs, and emblems, i. 164. It follows, finally, from the Martinistic doctrine of the necessity of visible signs, i. 174.

regard the Eucharist as apart from the Mass, that we may elucidate his position.

Though the sacrifice of the Repairer has enabled men to fulfil as far as possible here below the sublime task of their regeneration by entering into union with Him, and serving Him in spirit and truth, He desired, when He departed from them, to bequeath a sign of alliance which might recall daily His manifestation and devotion. He desired also that it should be a development of that divine seed which He came to sow in our infected and barren region; and as we are composite beings He selected diverse substances of operation, so that our constituents might find their nourishment, support, and preservation, each according to its class and its needs. He desired further that this institution might derive all its value from the Spirit which produces all and sanctifies all." [*]

But we must be spirit to approach spirit, and hence the sign of the second covenant can be only profaned by communication to the man of earth. [†] The institution is intended to assist us in working efficaciously at a living labour, namely, the recovery of the pure element or primitive body which can only be restored to us as we return towards the image of God. [‡] It retraces for us our spiritual death and our spiritual resurrection, and also it enforces the lesson that we must die and rise again with the Repairer. It can effect within us a universal and perpetual production, emanation, creation and regeneration; it can transform us into the kingdom of God and make us one with Him. [§] If this be not the communication of the living Christ there is no meaning in words, and hence Saint-Martin does teach the Real Presence in the Eucharist. But as the effect of that communication is the restoration, or should be, of our arch-natural body, I do not know that it is either gross or anthropomorphic to suppose that the elements of that body may be communicated from the arch-natural body of Christ, in which case that body is also effectively and virtually present in the Eucharist. As a fact, Saint-Martin does confess that a true flesh and a true blood corroborate all our faculties of intelligence

---

[*]   *Le Ministère de l'Homme-Esprit*, p. 279.   [†] Ibid. p. 280.

[‡]   Ibid. p. 284.   [§] Ibid. p. 283.

and activity towards the accomplishment of the great work in the communication of the Eucharist.[*]

There is, therefore, a sacramental system as there is also a mystery, and the difference between Saint-Martin and the Church is that the one spiritualised what the other had materialised in his opinion. The opinion itself is, of course, not altogether true, but it has its side of truth, though from the standpoint of mystic Christianity the system which has perpetuated the sign must be forgiven much.

---

[*] *Le Ministère de l'Homme-Esprit,* p. 282. In a sense he had always held this view. Cf. *Tableau Naturel,* ii. 186-188, where he maintains that it is not inadmissible to suppose that the Universal Repairer chose a material substance as a base of spiritual and divine virtues, which substance, therefore, received from him "a virtuality foreign to its nature." He even argues the special suitability of the materials selected, namely, bread and wine, while he condemns the figurative interpretation of their "sacrifice."

II

Political Philosophy of Saint-Martin

THE POLITICAL PHILOSOPHY of Saint-Martin has three characteristics: 1) Originality, that is to say, it is without precedent, and this to such an extent that it has established none. 2) Impossibility of application, because it presupposes the return of at least a portion of humanity to the primeval state. 3) A certain quality of insincerity, though assuredly of the unconscious order, because it appears to support existing institutions, especially monarchical, but makes void all their claims.

At the period of Saint-Martin two theories, both equally artificial, were current concerning the origin of human association and political institutions, the one maintaining that authority was seized by the strong and skilful;[*] the other that society was established upon the common consent and by the unanimous will of the individuals composing it.[†] Saint-Martin rejects both views, the one on account of its barbarism, the other because it is impossible, while also fundamentally unjust and unreasonable; objections which, it will be needless to observe, possess no jurisdiction if the social order emerged from a savage condition. He lays down that all just association is a commerce of moral actions, and that, speaking broadly, the errors of political philosophy as to the basis of political bodies have the same source as those of the ordinary observers of nature.[‡] They have considered only

---

[*] *Des Erreurs et de la Vérité,* Part ii. p. 4.   [†] Ibid. p. 5.   [‡] Ibid. p. 14

the envelope of man. They have sought in man isolated the principles of government, and have not found them, even as the other observers have failed to find in matter the true source of the effects which it produces.[*] The man who has best preserved himself from admixture with the elements, who has therefore least disfigured the idea of his principle, and has thus strayed the least from his first estate, possesses an advantage over those who have not made similar efforts, have not found the same success, or are deficient in the required gifts; he is therefore their superior and they should be ruled by him.[†]

"If there be anywhere a man in whom the obscuration of the real faculties reaches the point of depravation, that other who has preserved himself from both is thereby his master, and not in fact only, nor even from necessity alone, but also by duty. He must take possession of him and deprive him of the liberty of action, to satisfy the laws of his principle and for the safety and warning of society; he must, in fine, exercise upon him all the rights of slavery and servitude, which in such a case are no less just and real than they are unwarrantable and void in any other."[‡]

The case is entirely Utopian, but if the perfect man did indeed appear among us, he might well be the saviour of society, and in his rule we might expect the administration of the Prince of Peace.

"Such," continues Saint-Martin, "is the veritable origin of the temporal empire of man over his kind, as the consanguinity of corporeal nature was the beginning of primeval society. But such an empire, far from compelling and repressing, would be the firmest support of natural society, its defence against crimes in its members and against the assaults of all other enemies. As the man who was clothed with this power would find his happiness only in preserving the virtues which obtained it, he would seek likewise for his own interest the welfare of his subjects. Let no one believe that such an occupation would be useless, for he could not be that which we represent without in himself possessing an unfailing guide of conduct and the ability to attain his ends. The light which enlightened man in his first estate being also an inexhaustible source of faculties and virtues, the closer he now approaches thereto the wider will be his empire over those who

---

[*] *Des Erreurs et de la Vérité,* Part ii. p. 16.   [†] Ibid. p. 18.   [‡] Ibid. p. 19.

withdraw there from, and the better will he know what is needed to maintain order among them."

The authority of such a ruler would extend even to religion and the cure of diseases,* while he would be also the supreme judge in matters of art and taste. Sacred institutions in particular should have "the same end, the same guide, and the same law" as those of the political order. "They should be, therefore, in the same hand; so long as they are divided they lose sight of their true spirit, which consists in a perfect understanding and in union."†

Saint-Martin could be no otherwise than conscious that his picture seemed entirely chimerical, but he believed that it was in conformity with the universal conception of kinghood in its last analysis.

"Reflecting on the respect that we bear them, must we not conclude that they are regarded as the image and representatives of a superior hand, and as such the custodians of more virtue, more force, more light, more wisdom than belong to other men? Is it not with a species of regret that we find them subject to human weakness? And would it not be entirely desirable that they should be known only by great and sublime acts, even as that hand which we acknowledge has placed them on their thrones?"‡ From these considerations he infers that the origin of kingship is superior alike to the powers and to the will of man. The interesting point is not that such a view has a claim on serious contradiction, but that it was held sincerely by a philosophical Frenchman on the eve of the French Revolution and through all its searching fire, while in his capacity as a citizen he accepted the changed order, its trials and its duties, with submission and even with zeal, and did not only recognise therein the chastening visitation of God, but was in frank and liberal sympathy with the blind needs and blinder aspirations of that volcanic epoch.

It is in connection with this subject, thus unusually regarded, that we meet with one of those statements, seemingly unconcerted in Saint-Martin, which have the air that he was guarding a greater secret than the metaphysical doctrine of a theurgic school. He affirms that lawful sovereigns and governments of the kind which he has delineated are not imaginary, that they have always existed, still are, and

---

* *Des Erreurs et de la Vérité,* Part ii. p. 20.   † Ibid. p. 24.   ‡ Ibid. p. 20-21

will continue through all, because they are part of the universal order and connect with the Great Work.[*] If we bring into contact with this a passage in a letter of his fellow-adept Willermoz, which shows that after a patient labour of something like fifteen years he had proved that there was an exalted and even Divine Agent charged with the work of initiation;[†] and if we will then compare both with certain wonderful testimonies which are given by Eckartshausen,[‡] we shall not exactly grasp, but may, I think, have a clue to what is conveyed by this pregnant utterance, and that the conception which it shapes points towards an unseen but physical government of the Church and the world. The issues may be dark and the way strange, but there is a providence, and though the hand is unseen it is a hand that may be grasped; it is that which once prepared the way for a Liberator, and did not there end, but is now awaiting, or rather actively ensuring, a certain fullness of time to place another freedom within reach of humanity.

"It is with confidence," says Saint-Martin, concluding his thesis on government, "that I establish on the rehabilitation of man in his principle the origin of his authority over his kind, that of his power, and of all the titles of political sovereignty."[§] Now, it would seem that in the absence of such a rehabilitation things must go as they are while they can and may change when they must, but that in no case is there any true title to existing government, for that is vested in conditions which, if not impossible, are at least unfulfilled. The sympathies of Saint-Martin are monarchical because the pageant of earthly kinghood is for him a type of the true royalty, but it is only pomp and pageant, and there is a flavour, as I have said, of insincerity in his message of peace to existing governments and in his condemnation of rebellion.

"Let me seek, however, to disarm the suspicion of governments, who might possibly mistrust my sentiments, and fear that in unveiling their defects I shall destroy the homage which is due to them. I have

---

[*] *Des Erreurs et de la Vérité,* Part ii. p. 25.

[†] Papus, *Martines de Pasqually,* p. 113.

[‡] "The Cloud on the Sanctuary," *passim.*

[§] *Des Erreurs et de la Vérité,* Part ii. p. 28.

expressed already my veneration for sovereigns, as to their persons as well as their office, but I desire to convince all my readers that I proclaim only peace and order, that I lay submission towards their chiefs as an indispensable duty on all subjects, and that I condemn without reserve all insubordination and all revolt as diametrically opposed to the principles which I have attempted to establish."* So far this is reasonable enough; some usurpations and some rebellions may well be worse than a monarchy with forged titles, but the assurance of a philosopher attempting to tranquillise princes after explaining the abysmal difference which separates their conventional authority from substantial and true royalty, might be anything but palatable if it were worthwhile to take it in earnest, and I think that the principles of Saint- Martin, had anyone been ready to adopt them, were scarcely less subversive than a frank revolutionary propaganda. More than this, he carries the duty of submission to the established order into superlative absurdity when he adds: "I condemn rebellion absolutely, even in the case where the injustice of chief and government are at a pinnacle, where neither one nor the other preserve the smallest traces of the powers which constitute them, because, iniquitous and revolting as such an administration would be, I have proved that political laws and leaders have not been set up by their subjects, and cannot therefore be overthrown by them." † Could the honesty of Saint-Martin be questioned, it might be thought that he was assailing here the institutions he appears to defend, but in reality he is only establishing the supreme paradox of his standpoint. It is scarcely possible to accept the testimony of Robison upon any doubtful matter independently of less impeachable witnesses, but is it not possible that Saint-Martin produced in some minds the opposite of the impressions that he intended? And admitting that, as Robison says, the treatise "On Errors and on Truth" was a text-book for Masonic illuminati of the Avignon and Philalethes type, may there not be a grain of foundation for his other statement that the lodges of these rites became active embers of political disaffection? ‡

The theocratic principle of Saint-Martin inspired more than one of his tracts and pamphlets; it is the motive of his essay on "Human

---

* *Des Erreurs et de la Vérité,* Part ii. p. 30. † Ibid. p. 31.

‡ "Proofs of a Conspiracy."

Association," which was so much admired by his biographer Matter.[*] It is the subject of some interesting observations in the posthumous works;[†] it underlies many theories which do not connect with it on the surface; and it follows logically enough from his central doctrines. That he looked for its ultimate triumph is evident in every line that he penned on the French Revolution, and above all in his expectation of a "Sabbatic reign on earth as a termination to time, like that which terminated the formation of the universe."[‡] It is difficult for a mystic to abstain from prophecy, especially on the subject of the millennium and the septenary repose of the earth. Saint-Martin anticipated a "complete solution" of the "grand problem" in about two centuries from the date of the French Revolution.[§] Meanwhile, it was possible and peremptory that all should approximate to the individual new reign which is open and promised to all who are men of goodwill. The condition of its realisation is that all our "thoughts, lights, desires, movements, words, prayers, our very breath, our spiritual works, our life even as our death, should become divine within us, and this without restriction and without exception, without distraction and without admixture."[||] "Happy," exclaimed Saint-Martin, is he who "beholds the approach of the universal new reign behind the formless cloud of the human passions which darken the revolution!" That revolution was, in his most firm conviction, a preparation of the Sabbatic way, and not the last reason was that it threw so many men, as it were, into the arms of God's will because all other protections, all other resources, had been taken from them.[¶] "Do not believe," he says in a letter to Kirchberger, "that our French Revolution is an indifferent thing upon the earth. I look upon it as the revolution of human nature; it is a miniature of the Last Judgment, with all its features. France has been visited the first, and that with great severity,

---

[*] "After the 'Letter on the French Revolution,' which its author, who valued everything that he wrote, himself placed so high, I know of nothing which represents him so fully, or is more entirely his own."—Preface to L. Schaver's edition of the treatise on "Numbers," pp. xi-xii.

[†] *Sur le Gouvernement Divin ou le Théocratisme,* vol. i. pp. 396-398.

[‡] *Du Nouveau Règne, Œuvres Posthumes,* i. 399.

[§] Ibid. p. 402.   [||] Ibid. pp. 402-403.   [¶] Ibid. p. 405.

because she has been very guilty. Those countries which are no better than she will not be spared when their time comes."* Conscious of the predilection of God, he had no anxiety for himself during the terrible scorching of his country; he was dealt with, he says, as though he were without reproach, while innumerable persons who would have profited far better by the favour were not only deprived thereof, but treated as if they had abused it.† There were so many indeed who seemed to be abandoned by Providence that for a moment even his faith quailed, but he remembered that there was an edifice in construction, and that the blood of expiatory victims was required to cement it.‡ The scourge was cleansing those who were capable of being made clean.§

When a saviour of society appeared for a moment in the person of the great Consul, Saint-Martin recognised a temporal instrument in the hands of Providence for the fulfilment of its plans towards France,‖ and he was confirmed more than ever in his convictions. "It cannot be denied," he wrote early in 1801, "that great destinies attach to this remarkable man."¶

In connection with his theocratic sentiments there are many views of Saint-Martin on the subject of human power, on the civil and criminal codes, on the right of torture, and especially on the malfoundation of the rights and privileges of sovereigns, which offer curious material for reflection as to the influence which they may have had at his period in the centres of illuminism and political plotting; but as there is an insufficient warrant only to follow a doubtful line of inquiry suggested by a prejudiced writer° who understood nothing so little as mysticism, the student who desires to follow this line of inquiry may be referred to the originals.**

---

* *Correspondance,* Lettre lxxii; Penny, "Theosophic Correspondence," p. 226.

† *Portrait Historique, Œuvres Posthumes,* i. 61.

‡ Ibid. p. 88.   § Ibid. p. 112.   ‖ Ibid. p. 117.

¶ Ibid. p. 120.   ° Robison, "Proofs of a Conspiracy."

** *Des Erreurs et de la Vérité,* Part ii. sec. 5, *passim.*

III

Some Aphorisms and
Maxims of Saint-Martin

1

God is all; the tongue of God is the spirit; the tongue of the spirit is science; the tongue of science should be the learned man. But the ordinary man of learning is like a signboard, and full too often of errors in orthography, like the signboards of small shops.[*]

2

Nature and the Scriptures should be compared. The priests misread the Scriptures: the philosophers misconstrue Nature. Hence they are always at war, and never compare their differences.[†]

3

When we speak of the Divine Sensibility, men tell us that God's feelings are not as ours. But, this granted, it is for us to strive that we may feel like Him, without which we can in no wise become familiar with His operations, and still less be numbered among His servants. In truth, this Divine Sensibility is so absolutely the one thing needful,

---

[*] *Œuvres Posthumes,* i. 199-200.   [†] Ibid. p. 197.

that, apart there from, we are corpses, less even than stones, because stones abide in their law, and are that which they should be, whereas the soul of man was never designed to be a dead thing.*

4

There is nothing more easy than to come to the gate of truth; there is nothing more difficult than to enter it. This applies to most of the wise of this world.†

5

Great progress in truth is difficult in the midst of the world and under the favour of fortune; duplicity and double-seeming are needed in dealing with the one and anxiety for preserving the other. Our rest is not therefore in God.‡

6

It is in vain that we pretend to arrive at the fullness of truth by reasoning. By this way we reach only rational truth; still it is infinitely precious, and full of resources against the assaults of false philosophy. The natural lights of every man of aspiration have indeed no other font, and it is therefore of almost universal use; but it cannot impart that sentiment and tact of active and radical truth from which our nature should derive its life and being. This kind of truth is given of itself alone. Let us make ourselves simple and childlike, and our faithful guide will cause us to feel its sweetness. If we profit by these first graces, we shall taste very soon those of the pure spirit, afterwards those of the Holy Spirit, then those of the Supreme Sanctity, and, lastly, in the interior man we shall behold the all.§

---

* *Œuvres Posthumes,* vol. i. p. 202. † Ibid. p. 200.

‡ Ibid. p. 216. § Ibid. pp. 261-262.

7

The sole advantage which can be found in the merits and joys of this world is that they cannot prevent us from dying.[*]

8

It is easy to understand why wisdom is a folly in the eyes of the world; it is because it shows by our own experience that the world is a folly by its side; for where is there a seeker after truth, however ardent, who has not delayed by the way, and has afterwards regarded himself as a fool when he has resumed the path of wisdom?[†]

9

If this world will seem to us, after our death, as nothing but magical illusion, why do we regard it otherwise at present? The nature of things does not change.[‡]

10

Were I far from one loved and cherished, and did she send me her picture to sweeten the bitterness of absence, I should have certainly a kind of consolation, but I should not have a true joy. So has truth acted in regard to us. After our separation from her, she has bequeathed us her portrait, and this is the physical world, which she has placed before us to alleviate the misery of our privation. But what is the contemplation of the copy compared with that of the original?[§]

---

[*] *Œuvres Posthumes,* vol. i. p. 207.   [†] Ibid.
[‡] Ibid. p. 209.   [§] Ibid. pp. 224-225.

11

"All is vanity," says Solomon; but let courage, charity, and virtue be excluded from this teaching; rather, let us raise ourselves towards these sublime things, until we are able to say that all is truth, that all is love, that all is felicity.[*]

12

The learned describe nature; the wise explain it.[†]

13

Never persuade yourself that you possess wisdom in virtue of mere memory or mere mental culture. Wisdom is like a mother's love, which makes itself felt only after the labours and pains of childbirth.[‡]

14

Whatsoever is not wisdom only debauches man. With her he is fitted for all things, for the sentiments of nature, for lawful pleasures, for every virtue; in her absence the heart is petrified.[§]

15

It should be regarded as a grace of God when we are stripped successively of all human supports and succours, on which we are always too ready to depend. Thereby He compels us to repose only on Him, and herein is the final and most profound secret of wisdom. How can we be dejected at learning it?[||]

[*] *Œuvres Posthumes,* vol. i. p. 210.   [†] Ibid.
[‡] Ibid. pp. 213-214.   [§] Ibid. p. 226.   [||] Ibid. p. 248.

16

Had we the courage to make voluntarily the sincere and continual sacrifice of our entire being, the ordeals, oppositions, and evils which we undergo during life would not be sent us; hence we should always be superior to our sacrifices, like the Repairer, instead of being almost invariably inferior to them.[*]

17

As our material existence is not life, so our material destruction is not death.[†]

18

Death is the target at which all men strike; but the angle of incidence being equal to the angle of reflection, they find themselves after death in their former degree, whether above or below.[‡]

19

Fear walks with those who dwell upon death, but those who think of life have love for their companion.[§]

20

Death should be regarded only as a relay in our journey; we reach it with exhausted horses, and we pause to get fresh ones able to carry us farther. But we must also pay what is due for the stage already

---

[*] *Œuvres Posthumes,* vol. i. pp. 220-221.   [†] Ibid. p. 230.

[‡] Ibid. pp. 243-244.   [§] Ibid. pp. 246-247.

travelled, and until the account is settled, we are not allowed to go forward.[*]

21

The head of old was subject to the ruling of the heart, and served only to enlarge it. To-day the sceptre which belongs of right to the heart of man has been transferred to the head, which reigns in place of the heart. Love is more than knowledge, which is only the lamp of love, and the lamp is less than that which it enlightens.[†]

22

The man who believes in God can never fall into despair; the man who loves God must sigh incessantly.[‡]

23

Love is the helm of our vessel; the sciences are only the weathercock on the capstan. A vessel can sail without a weathercock, but not without a helm.[§]

24

Science separates man from his fellows by creating distinctions with which prudence often forbids him to dispense. Love, on the contrary, impels men to communicate, and would establish everywhere the reign of that unity which is the principle from which it derives. The Repairer spoke nothing of the sciences, for he came not to divide men; he spoke only of love and the virtues, for he wished them to walk in unison. But science does not divide merely, it tends also to

---

[*] *Œuvres Posthumes,* vol. i. pp. 212-213.   [†] Ibid. p. 212.

[‡] Ibid. pp. 219-220.   [§] Ibid. p. 224.

pride; love, on the other hand, does more than join together, it keeps man in humility. Hence St. Paul said that knowledge puffs up, but charity edifies. [*]

25

Science is for things of time, love for divine things. It is possible to dispense with science, but not with love, and by love will all be fulfilled, for thereby all began, and thereby does all exist. I would that all the teachings of the doctors of wisdom began and ended with these words: Love God, and you shall be learned as all the sages. [†]

26

For our personal advancement in virtue and truth one quality is sufficient, namely, love; to advance our fellows there must be two, love and intelligence; to accomplish the work of man there must be three, love, intelligence, and activity. But love is ever the base and the fount in chief. [‡]

27

Hope is faith beginning; faith is hope fulfilled; love is the living and visible operation of hope and faith. [§]

28

For most men life is made up of two days; in the first they believe everything, and in the second nothing. For some others life also has two days, but what distinguishes them from ordinary men is that in

---

[*]   *Œuvres Posthumes,* vol. i. p. 286.   [†]   Ibid. p. 258.

[†]   Ibid. p. 317.   [§]   Ibid. pp. 231-232.

the first they believe only in illusions, and these are nothing; while in the second they believe in everything, for they believe in truth, which is all.*

29

The Gospel sufficiently impresses on us that the reward of many is with them in this world, whence they have little to expect in the other. This sentence, which, although severe, seems neither cruel nor unjust, has several degrees which it is well not to confound. There are men who will have received their entire recompense here below, others the half only, and yet others a fourth part. Thus the measure of compensations obtained in the present life will regulate the giving or refusing of those in the other. After this the expectations of the rich and happy on earth may be inferred easily.

30

When deliverance has been accomplished, time is still required for self-correction and self-purification. In ceasing to be damned one is not therefore saved, and this is why there are two judgments in the Apocalypse.†

31

Believe not that the joys of the soul are a chimera, and that the goods we acquire in this life are lost utterly. The soul in no way changes its nature by leaving this mortal body. If given over to evil, it receives the punishment thereof by sinking further therein. But if it have loved goodness, and have at times experienced the secret delights of virtue, it will partake of them with increasing rapture. It has known here below the ravishments caused by the contemplation of things which

---

* *Œuvres Posthumes,* vol. i. pp. 314-315.   † Ibid. pp. 298-299.

transcend it. It seems as if nothing on earth can afford it like felicity; it seems even as if earthly pleasures had no existence. It may rely upon the same transports in the superior region; yet more, it may count upon joys beyond measure and uninterrupted delights when this gross material part shall no longer soil its purity. If it be thus, let us by no means neglect life; the greater our care for the soul here, the better shall be our estate hereafter.[*]

32

The law of spirit and of fire is to go up; the law of matter and of bodies is to go down. Hence, from the first moment of their existence, corporeal beings and beings corporised materially tend to their end and reintegration, each in their class.[†]

33

The locality of the soul has been a subject of frequent dispute; by some it has been placed in the head, by others in the heart, by yet others in the solar plexus. Were the soul an organic and material particle, there would be reason in assigning a place for it, as it would be possible that it should occupy one. But if it be a metaphysical entity, how can it be localised physically? Its faculties alone would seem to possess a determined seat-the head for the functions of thought, meditation, judgment, and the heart for affections and sentiments of every kind. As for the soul itself, since its nature transcends both time and space, its correspondences and abode in space escape calculation.[‡]

34

God is a fixed paradise, man should be a paradise in motion.[§]

---

[*] *Œuvres Posthumes,* vol. i. pp. 324-325.　　[†] Ibid. p. 312.

[‡] Ibid. p. 309.　　[§] Ibid. p. 208.

35

Peace is found more often in patience than in judgment; hence it is better that we should be accused unjustly than that we should accuse others, even with justice.*

36

The Holy One quitted that which was above that He might come and restore us to life; we are reluctant to leave that which is below that we may recover the life which He has brought to us.†

37

Work for the spirit before asking the food of the spirit; he who will not work, let him not live.‡

38

The greatest sin which we can commit against God is to doubt His love and mercy, for it is questioning the universality of His power, which is the persistent sin of the prince of darkness.§

39

The most sweet of our joys is to feel that God can wed with wisdom in us, or rather that without Him wisdom can never enter us, nor He without wisdom.‖

---

* *Œuvres Posthumes,* vol i. p. 209. † Ibid. p. 208
‡ Ibid. § Ibid. p. 211. ‖ Ibid. p. 214.

40

All men who are instructed in fundamental truths speak the same language, for they are inhabitants of the same country.[*]

41

Men neglect habitually to study principles; and hence, when they have need to consider the development and functions of principles, they are astonished that they fail to understand them. But they believe themselves to have provided for everything by creating the word "mystery."[†]

42

Man's head is raised towards heaven, and for this reason he finds nowhere to repose it on earth.[‡]

43

All the goods of fortune are given us only to defray our journey through this earthly vale. But those who do not possess pass through it all the same, and this is infinitely consoling for the poor.[§]

44

The keynote of Nature is reluctance. Her unvaried occupation seems to be the withdrawal of her productions. She withdraws them even with violence to teach us that violence gave birth to them.[||]

---

[*] *Œuvres Posthumes,* vol. i. p. 212.   [†] Ibid. pp. 215-216.

[‡] Ibid. p. 211   [§] Ibid. p. 223.   [||] Ibid. p. 224.

45

Who is the innocent man? He who has acquired all things and has lost nothing. *

46

Preserve through all things the desire of the concupiscence of God; strive for its attainment, to overcome the illusion which surrounds us, and to realise our misery. Strive above all things to keep through all things the idea of the efficacious presence of a faithful friend who accompanies, guides, nourishes, and sustains us at every step. This will make us at once reserved and confident; it will give us both wisdom and strength. What would be wanting unto us if we were imbued invariably with these two virtues? †

47

We see that the earth, the stars, and all the wonders of Nature operate with exactitude and following a divine order; yet are we greater than these. O man! respect thyself, but fear to be unwise! ‡

48

The more we advance in virtue the less we perceive the defects of others, as a man on the summit of a mountain, with a vast prospect about him, beholds not the deformities of those who may dwell on the plain below. His very elevation should give him a lively and tender interest in those who, although beneath him, are, he knows, of his own nature. What then must be the love of God for men? §

---

* *Œuvres Posthumes,* i. 224.   † Ibid. p. 227.

‡ Ibid. p. 229.   § Ibid. p. 230.

49

All the impressions which are made on us by Nature are designed to exercise our soul during its term of penitence, to prompt us towards the eternal truths shown beneath a veil, and to lead us to recover what we have lost.[*]

50

The ordeals and oppositions which we undergo become our crosses when we remain beneath them, but they become ladders of ascent when we rise above them, and the wisdom which makes us their subject has no other end than our elevation and healing, and not that cruel and vengeful intent which is commonly attributed to it by the vulgar.[†]

51

It is insufficient to say unto God, "Thy will be done;" we must seek always to know that will; for if we know it not, who are we that we should accomplish it?[‡]

52

The true method of expiating our faults is to repair them, and as regards those which are irreparable, not to be discouraged on account of them.[§]

---

[*]   *Œuvres Posthumes,* i. p. 231.   [†] Ibid. p. 243.

[‡] Ibid. p. 252.   [§] Ibid. p. 16.

53

We are all in a widowed state, and our task is to re-marry.*

54

Purification is accomplished only by union with the true law of our being; all who are outside that law can expiate nothing; they only contaminate themselves more deeply.†

55

That which is true is made by men subservient to the worship of the semblance, whereas the semblance was given them to be subservient to the worship of the true.‡

56

There are for man three desirable things: 1) Never to forget that there is another light than the elementary, of which this is but the veil and the mask. 2) To realise that nothing either can or should prevent him from accomplishing his work. 3) To learn that what he knows best is that he knows nothing.§

57

The spirit is to our soul what our eyes are to our body; without it we should be nothing, even as apart from the life of the body the eyes are useless.‖

---

* *Œuvres Posthumes,* i. p. 17.		† Ibid. p. 17.
‡ Ibid. p. 18.	§ Ibid. p. 21.	‖ Ibid. p. 26.

58

Order thyself aright; that will instruct thee in wisdom and morality better than all the books which treat of them, for wisdom and morality are active forces.[*]

59

As a proof that we are regenerated we must regenerate everything around us.[†]

60

The wise of this world talk incessantly, and that upon all things false. The sages do not talk, but, like wisdom itself, they accomplish unceasingly the living and the true.[‡]

61

The Church should be the Priest, but the Priest seeks to be the Church.[§]

62

Men of this world consider that it is impossible to be a saint without also being a fool. They do not know that, on the contrary, the one way to avoid being a fool is to be a saint.[||]

---

[*] *Œuvres Posthumes*, i. p. 36.   [†] Ibid. p. 102.

[‡] Ibid. p. 103.   [§] Ibid. p. 105.   [||] Ibid. p. 114

63

Mind and not soul is required for human sciences; but for real and divine sciences mind is not needed, for they are the offspring of the soul. Hence no two things can be more opposite than truth and the world.[*]

64

A picture without a frame is offensive in the eyes of the world, so accustomed is it to see frames without pictures.[†]

65

Unity is seldom found in associations; it must be sought in an individual junction with God. Only when that has been accomplished do we find brethren in one another.[‡]

66

Words are given to us in trust, as sheep to a shepherd. If we leave them to go astray, to become famished, or to be devoured by wolves, we shall be called to a stricter account than he is.

67

In order to demonstrate that the principle of any action is lawful, its consequences must be considered; where the actor is unhappy he is infallibly guilty, because he cannot be unhappy unless he is free.[§]

---

[*]   *Œuvres Posthumes,* i. p. 114   [†]   Ibid. p. 135.

[‡]   Ibid. pp. 138-139.   [§]   *Des Erreurs et de la Vérité,* Part i. p. 72.

68

Whatsoever is sensible is relative, and there is nothing fixed therein.[*]

69

Man is one of the arbiters of God, and hence he is ancient as God, though there is not a plurality of Gods on this account.[†]

70

The kingdom of God is a continuous and complete activity. God is not the God of the dead, but of the living.[‡]

71

If man avoids regarding himself as the king of the universe, it is because he lacks courage to recover his titles thereto, because its duties seem too laborious, and because he fears less to renounce his state and his rights than to undertake the restoration of their value.[§]

72

We are nearer to that which is not than to that which is.[||]

---

[*] *Des Erreurs et de la Vérité,* Part ii. p. 7.

[†] *Œuvres Posthumes,* i. 17.   [‡] Ibid. p. 182.

[§] *Des Erreurs et de la Vérité,* Part ii. p. 117.   [||] *Œuvres Posthumes,* i.

73

The prayer of the Spaniard, "My God, defend me from myself," connects with a salutary feeling when we can awaken it within us, namely, that we ourselves are the only beings of whom we need be afraid on earth, whilst God is the one nature who has reason to fear only that which is not Himself We might extend it as follows, "My God, aid me in thy goodness, that I may be spared from destroying thee." *

74

If man, despite his state of reprobation, can still discern within himself a principle which is superior to his sensible and corporeal part, why should not such a principle be acknowledged in the sensible universe, equally distinct and superior, though deputed specially to govern it? †

75

I leave the unenlightened and shallow man to murmur at that justice which visits the trespasses of the parent upon his posterity. I will not even point to that physical law whereby an impure source communicates its impurities to its productions, because the analogy would be false and invidious if applied to what is not physical. But if justice can afflict the children through the fathers, it can also purify the fathers by the children; and though it exceeds the understanding of the ignorant, this should warrant us in suspending our judgment till we are admitted to the councils of wisdom. ‡

---

*   *Œuvres Posthumes*, i. 80.

†   *Des Erreurs et de la Vérité*, Part i. p. 153.   ‡   Ibid. p. 158.

76

The thought of man is expressed in the material world, that of God in the universe.[*]

77

Sensible objects can give us nothing, but can deprive us of all. Our task while they encompass us is less to acquire than to lose nothing.

78

The prayers and the truths which are taught us here below are too narrow for our needs; they are the prayers and the truths of time, and we feel that we were made for others.[†]

79

The universe is even as a great temple; the stars are its lights, the earth is its altar, all corporeal beings are its holocausts, and man, the priest of the Eternal, offers the sacrifices.[‡]

80

The universe is also as a great fire lighted since the beginning of things for the purification of all corrupted beings.[§]

-----

[*] *Tableau Naturel,* Part i. p. 39.

[†] *Le Ministère de l'Homme-Esprit,* p. 39.

[‡] *Tableau Naturel,* Part ii. p. 127.   [§] Ibid. p. 160.

Book VII

The Mystical
Philosophy of Numbers

I

Saint-Martin on
Mathematical Science

THE KNOWLEDGE DERIVED by Saint-Martin from the initiation which took place in his youth was connected with a scheme of numerical mysticism, to which he has recourse very frequently to establish the doctrinal points of his early works; it also occupies an important place in his correspondence, and was the subject of a posthumous treatise. At the same time we do not possess this scheme in its entirety, for the conditions under which he received it made a full presentation impossible, nor do we possess it apparently in quite the same form that he received it himself. It was held by him in very high estimation at all periods of his life, and it was developed by many considerations of his own, considerations which indeed bear all the peculiar signs of his philosophical gift. It would be perhaps too much to say that his entire doctrine is based upon the occult properties of numbers; its arcane portions are more correctly veiled thereby, but as the details are highly technical, they have been so far kept separate in this study, with the intention to deal with them somewhat comprehensively at a later point.

The mystical developments to which numbers have been subjected by the various schools of occultism, Pythagorean, Kabalistic, and so forth, offer in the whole only a slender analogy with the system of Saint-Martin, which, moreover, is connected with peculiar views concerning mathematical science in general. As there is abundant material scattered through his various works to form on this one subject a volume of substantial dimensions, the minor issues must be passed over of necessity and the chief considerations must be compressed into a small shape. I propose, in the first place, to present in outline the views expressed by Saint-Martin as to the fundamental principles of mathematics; in the second place, to collect and condense the scattered statements as to the philosophy of numbers in particular; and, finally, in a third section to tabulate the mystic properties ascribed to the ten numerals.

That Saint-Martin had a tolerable acquaintance with higher mathematics may, I think, be inferred from the familiar style which characterises his references. When, this accepted, it becomes necessary to add that he was a hostile critic of the exact science par excellence, it would seem that in proposing to follow him we are about to abandon altogether the common ground of reason. The criticism is concerned, however, more with the application of the science than with its principles; it is fantastic in the highest degree, but it is well to state at the outset that it does not challenge, for example, the simple calculation that two and two make four. It seems nonsensical enough, in all conscience, but it is refined, not crass in its absurdity. There will be, therefore, no need, as there is indeed no space, to criticise the criticism; its fantasia will be established by its presentation; but I may remind the occult reader how Robert Fludd, the Kentish mystic, more than a century earlier, proved the degeneracy of music because it could no longer influence stones and rocks as it did in the days of Orpheus.[*] That is a consideration which is entirely parallel to the mathematical strictures of Saint-Martin, who was indeed the Fludd of his period, plus a spiritual illumination which we cannot trace in the English Rosicrucian, and for which Saint-Martin is entitled to a permanent place in philosophy when purged of his scientific absurdities; whereas Fludd leaves nothing, after passing through a similar process, except indeed the historical interest belonging to the chief apologist of the Rosicrucians.[†]

---

[*] *Apologia Compendiaria Fraternitatem de Rosea Cruce... abluens et abstergens.*

[†] I believe that he was a man of considerable personal sanctity, and this reference applies only to his philosophical works. If I remember rightly, Ennemoser ("History of Magic") takes much the same view. On the other hand, the late Mr. Hargrave Jennings would have disagreed probably, but then I do not know that he would have understood.

For Saint-Martin mathematical science is only an illusory copy of the true science,[*] as algebra is, in a certain sense, the degradation of numbers.[†] The basis of mathematics is relation, and relation is also its result.[‡] Once the postulates of relations are fixed, the results derived from them are exact and appropriate to the object proposed. In a word, mathematics cannot err, because they never depart from their groove; they turn, so to speak, on a pivot, and all their progress takes them back to that point from which they first started. Mathematical principles not being material, but being still the true law of sensible things, so long as mathematicians confine themselves to these principles, they cannot err; but when they come to the application of the idea derived from them, they are enslaved by the principles.[§] There is nothing demonstrated by mathematics except by reference to some axiom, because axioms alone are true; the ground of their truth is in their independence of the sensible, or of matter; in a word, they are purely intellectual. Did geometricians never lose sight of their axioms they would never go astray in their reasoning, for their axioms are attached to the very essence of intellectual principles, and thus rest on the most complete certitude.[||]

From the confused and confounding criticism which follows this general statement, I have extricated two points which may be accepted as the axioms of Saint-Martin, but there will be no need to say that, whatever their occult value, unlike those of mathematics, they are not self-evidently true. (*a*) Motion is possible without extension.[¶] (*b*) Everything in Nature has its number.[°] Now, there was a time when such paradoxes as the first of these axioms used to be discussed seriously, and, having regard to some extraordinary subtleties put forward by the Spanish theologian Balmes, among other philosophers, we have no right to regard Saint-Martin as distracted because he sustained this thesis. The proposition is, of course, unthinkable, and has no claim on us, because the day of subtlety has ended, but at the period which just succeeded Descartes it had not quite finished, and there was, of

---

* *Des Erreurs et de la Vérité,* Part i. p. 81.

† *Correspondance Inédite,* Lettre xc; Penny, "Theosophic Correspondence," p. 305.

‡ *Des Erreurs et de la Vérité,* Part i. p. 81.   § Ibid. Part ii. pp. 84-85.

|| Ibid.   ¶ Ibid. pp. 101, 102, 130.   ° Ibid. p. 91.

course, an earlier period when such questions were discussed with enthusiasm, when Saint-Martin would have delighted the school-men, would have founded a new method, like Raymond Lully, and would have been burnt, or perhaps beatified if he had not exceeded the limits of ecclesiastical latitude. As to the second axiom, it has no connections in philosophy, unless it be the signatures of Paracelsus; it is, in fact, the exclusive property of Saint-Martin's school of initiation, and will raise no idea in the modern mind except the statement in the Apocalypse that the number of the beast is "the number of a man."

It is, therefore, on all accounts necessary to see how the two axioms are sustained by their enumerator, and this especially that they are the grounds for his impeachment of mathematics.

"Like all other properties of bodies, extension is a product of the generative principle of matter, according to the laws and the order imposed on this inferior principle by the higher principle which directs it. In this sense extension is a secondary production, and cannot have the same advantages as the beings included in the class of prime products." [*] To elucidate this further, we must understand that "there are only two kinds of beings, sensible and intellectual." [†] According to Saint-Martin, the latter are the true source of motion; "they belong to another order than the immaterial corporeal principles which they rule; they must therefore have an action and effects distinct like themselves from the sensible, that is, in which the sensible counts for nothing. Hence also we must suppose their activity both before and after the existence of sensible things. It is, therefore, incontestable that movement may be conceived without extension, since the principle of movement, whether sensible or intellectual, is actually outside extension." [‡]

Now, the failure of geometricians is that they have not recognised this truth. After establishing their axioms in the real world outside the sensible, they have provided for the measurement of extension "some meter derived from extension, or some arbitrary numbers which require a sensible measure before they can be realised by our bodily eyes. [§] They have fallen into the same mistake as that made by the observers of Nature; they have separated extension from its true princi-

---

[*]   *Des Erreurs et de la Vérité,* Part ii. p. 87.   [†]   Ibid. p. 103.

[‡]   Ibid. Part i. p. 104.   [§]   Ibid. p. 86.

ple, or rather it is in extension that they have sought for this principle, confusing distinct things, which, however, are connected inseparably for the constitution of matter." * Put shortly, "the measures taken from extension for the measurement of extension are subject to the same drawbacks as the object which it is proposed to measure," † and thus the extension of bodies is not determined with more certainty than their other properties. "Extension exists only by motion, which is not, however, to say that motion is from and in that which is extended. It is true that in the sensible order movement cannot be conceived outside of extension, but though the principles which produce motion in the sensible order are immaterial, their action is not necessary and eternal, because they are secondary beings receiving the communication of action for a time only from the Active and Intelligent Cause." ‡

The full measure of extension must be sought outside it, in the principle by which it has been engendered, like all other properties of matter. "It is true that geometricians attach numbers to their extended and sensible measure, but these numbers are relative and conventional; with such a scale extension of another kind cannot be measured. To this must be referred the difficulty experienced in the measurement of curves; the measure utilised was made for the straight line, and offers insurmountable difficulties when applied to the circular, or to any curve derived from it." § The conception of the circle as an assemblage of infinitely small straight lines is, in the opinion of Saint-Martin, not a true conception, for it contradicts that which Nature gives us concerning a circumference—a line, namely, in which all the points are equidistant from a common centre. "If the circumference be an assemblage of straight lines, however infinitely small, all its points cannot be equidistant from the centre, since such straight lines will themselves be composed of points, among which the extreme and intermediary cannot be at the same distance from the centre, which is therefore no longer common, while the circumference ceases to be a circumference." ‖

The distinction between the straight line and the circle is established fantastically as follows:—"The object of the straight line is to perpetuate to infinity the production of the point from which it

---

* *Des Erreurs et de la Vérité,* Part ii. p. 87.   † Ibid. p. 88.

‡ Ibid. pp. 101-102.   § Ibid. Part i. p. 88.   ‖ Ibid. pp. 89-90.

emanates, but the circular line limits at all points the production of the straight line, since it tends continually to destroy it, and may be regarded, so to speak, as its enemy. As there is nothing common between these lines, so there is no common measurement of them possible."* Following up this distinction, we must be prepared to regard the circle not as the perfect figure, but as inferior and limited: a paradox which leads us to the second axiom of Saint-Martin, that everything in Nature has its number, by which each can be distinguished; for its properties are results conformed to the laws contained in that number. The right and curved lines being different in their natures, have each their particular number. The straight line bears the number 4, and the circular that of 9, their lesser or greater extent making no difference, because "a large and a small line are each equally the result of their law and their number acting diversely, that is, with more or less power and duration in each, since these numbers remain always intact, though their faculties are extended or contracted in the variations of which extension is susceptible."† From these considerations Saint-Martin concludes that there are no fractions in Nature, and that they are a mutilation of numbers. "The principles of corporeal beings are simple and therefore indivisible, while the numbers which represent and render them sensible enjoy the same property."‡

Saint-Martin applies the number 9 to the circle for the following reasons. The circle is equivalent to zero; its centre may be regarded as unity because a circumference can have only one centre; unity joined to zero makes 10, or the centre with the circumference. The circle, however, can be regarded as a corporeal being, the circumference being the body and the centre the immaterial principle. But this principle can always be separated intellectually from the bodily and extended form, which is equivalent to separating the centre from the circumference, or 1 from 10. The subtraction of 1 from 10 leaves 9; the removal of the unit leaves zero as the circular line, and hence 9 is equivalent to the circle. This correspondence between zero, which is nothing by itself, and the number 9 may be held to justify the view that matter is illusory.§

---

* *Des Erreurs et de la Vérité,* Part i. pp. 91-92.

‡ Ibid. p. 94.

† Ibid. p. 93.

§ Ibid. pp. 120-121.

The number of extension is, according to Saint-Martin, the same as that of the circular line,[*] whence, in his occult phraseology, it has also the same weight and the same measure. The circle and extension are, in fact, one and the same thing, and hence it is that the circular line alone is corporeal and sensible. "Material nature and extension cannot be formed by means of right lines, or, in other words, there are no right lines in nature."[†] The reason assigned for this bizarre statement is, that although the principle of physical things is from fire, their corporisation is from water, and hence bodies are fluid in their primary state. But fluid is an assemblage of spherical particles, and bodies themselves may be regarded as an assemblage of such particles.[‡]

The number 4 is applied to the right line, regarded as a principle and distinct from extension, in accordance with the following reasoning. "There are three principles in all bodies; the circle is a body; the radii of a circle are right lines in the material sense, and by their apparent rectitude and capability of being prolonged to infinity they are the real image of the generative principle. The spaces between the radii are triangles, and thus the action of the generative principle is manifested by triadic production. Join the number, or unity, of the centre to the triad of its production, and we have an index of the quaternary. So also the conception of an intimate bond between the centre or generative principle and the secondary principle, which is proved to be 3 by the three sides of the triangle and the three dimensions, gives us the most perfect idea of our immaterial quaternary. Furthermore, as this quaternary manifestation takes place only by the emanation of the radius from the centre; as this radius always prolonged in a straight line is the organ and action of the central principle; as the curved line, on the contrary, produces nothing, but limits the action and production of the radius, we apply fearlessly the number 4 to the straight line and radius which represents it. As a fact, it is to the number 4 and to the square that geometry refers everything it measures, considering all triangles as a division of the square. Now this square is composed of four lines regarded as right lines, similar to the radius, and quaternary, consequently, like that."[§] From these con-

---

[*] *Des Erreurs et de la Vérité,* Part i. p. 106.

[†] Ibid. p. 107.   [‡] Ibid. pp. 107-108.   [§] Ibid. pp. 126-128.

siderations Saint-Martin concludes that the number which produces beings is that also which measures them, and that the true measure of beings is found in their principle, not in their envelope and extension. Hence also he acknowledges only one square and one square root.*

But 4 is not only the number of the straight line, but also that of motion or movement.[†] "There is, therefore, great analogy between the principle of movement and the straight line." It is not, however, only the analogy of their identical number, but also because "the source of the action of sensible things resides in movement, and the straight line is the emblem of infinity, and the continuity of the production of the point from which it emanates."[‡] The identity of number gives also the identity of law and property, "and hence the straight line directs corporeal and extended things, but never combines with them, never becomes sensible; for a principle cannot be confounded with its production."[§] Collecting the observations on the right line, and referring thence to the question of the circle, Saint-Martin adds: "But if there are no right lines in Nature, the circle cannot be an assemblage of right lines."[||]

If we seek now to discover the purpose of this extraordinary criticism, and to learn how we can attain to the true measurement of things by their principles, I must confess that we glean scant light from the mystic. It is perfectly useless to say that the just valuation of the properties of beings is by means of their principles, unless we can reach their principles. Saint-Martin admits that it may be "difficult to read therein," but that no certitude can be found outside that which "rules and measures all."[¶] Where is the key by which we can unlock the doors of the phenomenal world and communicate with the realities behind it? I do not need to say that Saint-Martin does not surrender it; reason may lead us to the recognition of the noumenal world, but it cannot impart it. The last words of the mystic are either an admission of his impotence and a stultification of his inquiry or a veiled appeal to the fields commanded by a faculty higher than the rational. "Though it is possible by recourse to this principle to judge surely the measure

---

* *Des Erreurs et de la Vérité*, Part i. p. 132.   † Ibid. pp. 105-106.

‡ Ibid. p.110.   § Ibid. || Ibid. p. 111.

¶ Ibid. p. 97.

of extension, it would be profanation to employ it in material combinations, for it can lead to the discovery of more important truths than those which are connected with matter, while the senses suffice for the direction of man in things sensible."[*] Hence, even on the showing of Saint-Martin, the geometricians are not so wrong after all!

Before taking leave of this surprising criticism, the curious may like to be possessed of an argument against the quadrature of the circle which De Morgan would have surely included in his "Budget of Paradoxes," had he been acquainted with the French mystic. "Since the Fall, man has sought to conciliate the right line with the circle; in other words, he has endeavoured to discover what is called the quadrature of the circle. Before his Fall he did not seek the accomplishment of an evident impossibility, the reduction of 9 to 4 or the extension of 4 to 9. The true means of arriving at the knowledge of things is to begin by not confounding them, but by pursuing the examination of each according to its proper number and laws."[†]

There are many inquiries, all leading to more or less amazing conclusions, but all excessively curious, undertaken by Saint-Martin in connection with mathematical science, but into which it is impossible here to follow him. He regarded mathematics as representing the universal law of energy and resistance, because it is occupied in discovering and expressing the relations of dimensions, quantities, and weights, relations which, each in its class, are the expression of resistance and energy acting on all that exists.[‡] In this connection he has some curious remarks on the binomial theorem, and especially on what was then the recent discovery of Descartes, namely, in equations the curve to which they belong, and in curves the equation which expresses their nature.[§] He regarded corporeal existences, general and particular, as a universal and continual quadrature, because the energy or power of co-ordinates cannot yield at any point or leave any opening to the resistance of the curve, and hence this curve or resistance is always combined with and modelled upon the energy in question, and never occupies any spaces but that which it yields to it.[||] Remark-

---

[*] *Des Erreurs et de la Vérité*, Part i. p. 97.   [†] Ibid. pp. 111-112.

[‡] *De l'Esprit des Choses*, ii. 203 *et seq.*   [§] Ibid. p. 305.

[||] Ibid. p. 310.

ing on the old maxim that metaphysics are the mathematics of God, mathematics the metaphysics of Nature, and transcendental or higher geometry the metaphysics of mathematics, he concludes that the right line is the principle and end of all geometry; and that although the general theory of curves, of the figures which they terminate and their properties, constitutes what is called higher geometry, the truly transcendental geometry is that of right lines; for it has generated the geometry of curves, and is more central, more concealed from our knowledge, because it acts within the circle or behind the envelope of things, whilst the geometry of curves acts only at their surface, and is thus their circumference and perimeter.[*] The application of mathematics to the physical sciences, and the attempt to extend them into the domains of medicine, the calculus of probabilities, and the investigation of the law of chances.[†] leads Saint-Martin to the hypothesis of a universal mathematics and arithmetic, accompanying all laws and operations of beings;[‡] but he adds that, in order to attain it, we must be able to number the integral values of things instead of computing only their dimensions and external properties. The mathematician does not in reality possess the fundamental principles of mathematics and the calculus.[§] He observes external laws written on the surface of bodies, on the ostensible effects of motion, on the outward progress of numeration; he has collected all these facts, which, though true, are only resultants, and has erected them into principles. They are principles, but only of a secondary kind, as compared with the fundamental and active laws of things. In attempting to penetrate the sanctuary of Nature equipped only with secondary principles, man has fulfilled his object imperfectly, because his means have been inferior and insufficient. He has the keys of the surface, and he can open the treasures of the surface, but he has not the active and central keys, and the treasures of the centre are interdicted to him.[‖]

---

[*]   *De l'Esprit des Choses,* ii. p. 313 *et seq.*   [†] Ibid. p. 315.

[‡]   Ibid. p. 316.   [§] Ibid. p. 317.   [‖] Ibid. p. 318.

II

The Philosphy of Numbers

THE MATHEMATICAL PARADOXES propounded by Saint-Martin may be regarded almost incontestably as subtleties developed by himself from the occult doctrine of numbers received by him at his initiation. The doctrine itself was probably simple enough in its system and had no thought of impeaching mathematics. We have every reason to suppose that it was confined to attaching certain mystical ideas To certain numbers, and in this respect it is certainly of very high interest to the occult student, because its numerical mysticism is quite opposed to that of any other known school, especially in its treatment of the quinary as an evil number, after all that we have heard in occultism as to the magnificent revelations of the pentagram. It seems also to establish in a fairly conclusive manner that the Martinistic school, in spite of a contrary statement by Eliphas Lévi, had no knowledge of the Tarot system. At the same time I have been unable to avoid concluding, and am therefore bound to state, that Saint-Martin's doctrine of numbers is only a few fragments chipped, so to speak, from an edifice of occult knowledge. It is necessary also to add that he did not, in spite of his devotion, exaggerate the importance of the science which he thus acquired. He states that from his first entrance into his first school, he never thought that numbers gave more than the ticket of the package, and not commonly the substance of the matter itself. [*]

---

[*] *Correspondance,* Lettre lxxiv; Penny, "Theosophic Correspondence," p. 239.

I understand this to signify that they are a method of classification which might in itself be conventional, or that they are agreed symbols which must not be understood literally; so that when we hear of the number of matter, the number of man, and so forth, we must understand an occult essential character or "virtue," more or less arbitrarily labelled or ticketed for readiness of reference. This is, I think, shown very clearly by other words of his own. "Numbers are the sensible expression, whether visible or intellectual, of the different properties of beings, which all proceed from the one only source. Though we may derive by tradition and theoretical teaching a part of this science, regeneration alone shows us the true ground, and therein, each in his own degree, we obtain the true key without masters.* Furthermore, numbers express truths, but do not give them; men did not choose numbers, but discerned them in the natural properties of things." †

Having said this by way of introduction, with the design of indicating the most tolerable mode of regarding an exceedingly obscure subject not over-luminously treated, I propose now to present, collected from a variety of treatises, but substantially in the words of Saint-Martin, his general doctrine concerning the philosophy of numbers.

Numbers are the abridged translation or concise language of those truths and those laws of which the text and conceptions are in God, man, and Nature.‡

We must beware of separating numbers from the idea represented by each, for they then lose all their virtue, and are like the syntax of a language the words of which are unknown.§ The character of every number in the decade may be discovered by the particular operation to which it is united and the object on which it reposes. It follows from this that the virtue of beings is not in numbers, but that number is in the virtue of those beings which derive from it. Immense advantages may be derived by the intelligence of man from the proper

---

* *Correspondance*, Lettre xc; Penny, "Theosophic Correspondence," p. 305.

† Ibid. Lettre xcii. p. 317.

‡ "Numbers are the invisible enveloper of beings, as bodies are their sensible envelopes."—*Tableau Naturel*, ii. 131.

§ *Les Nombres*, p. 18.

use of numbers. The development of the properties of beings is active, and these properties have innumerable increasing and decreasing correspondences between them; hence the combination of numbers, taken in the regularity of the sense discovered in them by reasonable observation, will direct us in uncertain speculations, and will rectify what is false therein, seeing that this true and spiritual calculus or algebra of realities, like the conventional calculus or algebra of appearances, when its values are once known, will conduct us to precise and positive results.* But in the former, numbers receive their value from the nature of things, and not from the will of man; they lead us to truths of the first rank essentially connected with our being. Without the key of numbers, the correspondence between the three regions of true philosophy, divine, spiritual, and natural, cannot be fixed or appreciated correctly.†

Among the marvels offered to those who walk with circumspection in the career of numbers, we are not only taught to admire the magnificence of God, but to distinguish that which we are permitted to know from that which is permanently concealed from our penetration and outside our lights.‡ The mode of our emanation and generation in the divine unity is an interdicted knowledge, because the work of an emanation is reserved for the Supreme Principle, and the knowledge of the mode of that generation is also reserved for Him. By its possession we should be independent of Him, we could perform His work, and, in a word, would be God like Him. Owing to this veil, our Sovereign Principle is the eternal object of our homage and has real claim on our veneration. But while the law of numbers interdicts this knowledge,§ it does offer us the proof that our generation is divine, and it does demonstrate that we come forth directly from God.‖ In the true calculus there are essential roots and roots which are not essential, and it is the same with some of the powers; whilst in arithmetical calculus all the roots are contingent and all the powers variable. In the true calculus, the name of essential power belongs especially to man, but not that of essential root; and it is in the consideration of these two titles that we find at once the proof that

---

* *Les Nombres,* p. 20. † Ibid. p. 21. ‡ Ibid. p. 25.
§ Ibid. p. 28. ‖ Ibid. p. 27.

we have come forth from God and the impossibility of knowing after what mode we have come forth.[*]

At the same time Saint-Martin observes in another place that among the things which man lost at his Fall was the knowledge of the roots of numbers. This knowledge is now impossible to him, as he is unacquainted with the first of all roots. Hence the world does not know what conception to form of numbers. To attain such conception we must reflect on what should be the principle of things; it exists in its weight, its number, and its measure. Number is that which brings forth action, measure that which rules it, and weight that which operates it.[†] These are in the bosom of the Wisdom which accompanies all beings; in their production it imparts to them an emanation of its own essence, and at the same time of its wisdom, that the production may be in its own likeness. Thus all beings have within them a ray of its weight, its number, and its measure.[‡]

---

[*] *Des Erreurs et de la Vérité*, Part i. p. 61.   [†] Ibid. p. 149.

[‡] *Œuvres Posthumes*, i. pp. 244-245.

III

The Mystical Table of the Correspondences Between the Numbers

1 – The Monad

THE NUMBER ONE exists and is conceived independently of other numbers. Having vivified them through the course of the decade, it leaves them behind itself and returns to unity.[*] All numbers derive from unity as its emanations or products, while the principle of unity is in itself and is derived from itself.[†] In unity all is true, and all which is coeternal therewith is perfect, while all is false which is separated from it.[‡] Unity multiplied by itself never gives more than unity,[§] for it cannot issue from itself. Could unity thus produce and elevate itself to its own power, it would destroy itself, as the action which operates in each particular root is terminated by that operation. For unity to produce an essential and central truth there would have to be a difference between germ and product, root and power. Now, according to the law of germs and roots, when they have produced their power they become useless. Hence God could not reproduce Himself without perishing. From principle He would become means, and would then annihilate Himself in His term. But as principle, means, and term are not distinct in Him, as He is at once all of these, without succession in their action or difference iu their qualities, this unity can never produce itself, and hence has never been produced.[||]

---

[*] *Des Erreurs et de la Vérité,* Part i. p. 85.   [†] *Les Nombres,* p. 35.

[‡] Ibid. p. 42.   [§] Ibid. pp. 71-72.   [||] Ibid. p. 73.

Among visible things, the sun is the sign of the unity of divine action, but it is a temporal and composite unity, which has none of the rights belonging to its prototype.[*] In like manner, the continual succession of physical generations forms a temporal unity, which is a disfigured symbol of the simple, eternal, divine unity. Such images are not to be neglected, for they reflect their model from afar. Extremes touch without resembling one another; thus, pure beings live a simple life; those who are in expiation have a composite life, or life mingled with death; sovereignly criminal beings, and those who resemble them, live, and will live, in simple death, or in the unity of evil.[†]

When we contemplate an important truth, such as the universal power of the Creator, His majesty, His love, His profound lights or His other attributes, we aspire with our whole being towards the supreme model of all things; all our faculties are suspended that we may be filled with Him, with Whom we become actually one. Here is the active image of unity, and the Number One is the expression of this unity or indivisible union, which, existing intimately between all the attributes of the divine unity, should exist equally between it and all its creatures and productions. But after having exalted our faculties of contemplation towards this universal source, if we bring back our eyes to ourselves and become filled with our own contemplation, so that we regard ourselves as the font of those lights or of that inward satisfaction which we have derived from the superior source, we thereby establish two centres of contemplation, two separate and rival principles, two disjoined bases-in a word, two unities, of which one is real and the other apparent.[‡]

---

[*] *Œuvres Posthumes,* ii. p. 258.

[†] *Les Nombres,* p. 74.   [‡] Ibid. p. 18.

2 – The Duad

The Number Two has the principle in itself, but does not derive it from itself.[*] It is impossible to produce two from one, and if something issue from it by violence, it can only be illegitimate and a diminution of itself. But this diminution is from the centre, for otherwise it would be apparent only. The diminution made at the centre is made at the middle; to divide anything by the middle is to cut it into two parts. This is the true origin of the illegitimate binary. But the diminution in question does not make unity less complete, for it is susceptible of no alteration ; the loss falls on the being who seeks to attack it. Hence evil is foreign to unity, but the centre, without departing from its rank, is moved to rectify it because there is something of itself in the diminished being. By this we may understand not only the origin of evil, but also that it is not a hypothetical power, since we all virtualise it at almost every moment of our existence.[†]

The duad is therefore the perverse power serving as the receptacle of all the scourges of divine justice, and bound up with material and sensible things for the molestation of its chief and his adherents, who have abandoned voluntarily the divine centre of their spiritual correspondence, and are condemned to exile therefrom despite themselves, and to undergo all the horror of living separation from the source of life. The innate virtues of corporeal forms have been accorded to contain this perverse power, and when man permits the virtues resident in his body to be weakened by his lax and criminal will, the perverse power assumes the empire and operates the destruction of that body.[‡]

The duad is also, according to Saint-Martin, the real number of water.[§]

[*] *Les Nombres*, p. 35.

[‡] *Œuvres Posthumes*, ii. 127-128.

[†] Ibid. pp. 18-19.

[§] Ibid. p. 131.

3 – The Triad

The Number Three does not derive the principle from itself, nor indeed does it possess the principle.* The observations on this number are scattered and obscure, including vague references to a temporal law of the triad on which the dual temporal law is absolutely dependent.† In the divine order, 3 is the Holy Ternary, as 4 is the act of its explosion and 7 the universal product and infinite immensity of the wonders of this explosion.‡ Three belongs to us only by 12 united or added, as 4 is known to us only by its own explosion or multiplication, which gives us 16, and as 7, which is the addition of this 16, describes our temporal (3) and spiritual (4) supremacy, or the immensity of our destiny as man.§ The Number Three operates the direction of forms in the celestial and terrestrial; that is, in all bodies the number of spiritual principles being triadic, every name and every sign which falls on this number belongs to forms or must operate some effect on forms. ‖ In the super-celestial it was the thought of the Divinity which conceived the design of producing this world, and conceived it triadically, because such was the law of forms innate in the divine thought. Now the thoughts of God are beings. The concerted and unanimous action in the Divine Ternary is represented by the three officiating priests when they move together in the Mass.¶

Three is also the number of the essences or elements of which bodies are universally composed. By this number the law directing the production of elements is manifested, and these are reduced by Saint-Martin to three, on the ground that there are only three dimensions, three possible divisions of any extended thing, three figures in geometry, three innate faculties in any being whatsoever, three temporal worlds, three grades in true Freemasonry, and as this law of the triad shows itself universally with so much exactitude, it is reasonable

---

* *Les Nombres*, p. 35.   † *Des Erreurs et de la Vérité*, Part i. p. 10.

‡ *Correspondance*, Lettre lxxvi; Penny, "Theosophic Correspondence," p. 257.

§ Ibid. p. 258.   ‖ *Les Nombres*, p. 67.   ¶ Ibid.

to suppose that it obtains in the number of the elements which are the foundation of bodies.[*] If the Number Three be imposed on all created things, it is because it presided at their origin.[†] Had there been four instead of three elements, they would have been indestructible and the world eternal; being three, they are devoid of permanent existence, because they are without unity, as will be clear to those who know the true laws of numbers.[‡] The reason, whatever it may be, seems to conflict with another statement that there can be three in one in the Divine Triad but not one in three, because that which is one in three must be subject to death.[§] Three is not only the number of the essence and directing law of the elements, but also that of their incorporation.[‖] It is, finally, the mercurial-terrestrial number of the solid part of bodies, in symbolical correspondence with the animal senary soul of which it is the first product, and with all the intermediary principles in all classes. [¶]

4 – The Tetrad

The Number Four is that without which nothing can be known, as it is the universal number of perfection.[°] The Supreme Cause, though connecting with the source of all numbers, proclaims itself specially by the number of the square, which is at the same time the number of man.[**] By reason of the divine virtue in this number he has a direct action on all septenary beings, and it recalls the eminent rank which he occupied in his origin.[††] The square is one, like the root of which it is the product, and the image. It measures all the circumference, as man in the heart of his primeval empire embraced all the regions of the universe. This square is formed of four lines, and the post of man was distinguished by four lines of communication extending to

---

[*]   *Des Erreurs et de la Vérité,* Part i. pp. 122, 124, 125.

[†]   *Œuvres Posthumes,* ii. 160.

[‡]   *Des Erreurs et de la Vérité,* Part i. p. 125.

[§]   Ibid. p. 126.   [‖] Ibid. p. 122.   [¶] *Œuvres Posthumes,* ii. 132.

[°]   *Des Erreurs et de la Vérité,* Part i. p. 133   [**] Ibid. Part ii. p. 229.

[††] *Œuvres* uvres *Posthumes,* ii. 173.

the four cardinal points of the horizon. This square comes from the centre, and the throne of man was in the centre of the land of his domination, whence he governed the seven instruments of his glory. The square is thus the true sign of that place of delights known in all regions under the name of the Terrestrial Paradise.

Four is the number of every centre, and it is therefore that of fire, which occupies the centre of all bodies. So, also, it is that of the temporal spirit granted to man for his reconciliation, but this is the innermost of the three circles which man has to traverse before he completes the days of his reconciliation, which is represented by these three.[*]

The quaternary, represented by the four thousand years at the completion of which Christ was born into the world, is the image of the divine action opposed to the perverse power to contain it within its limits of spiritual privation. Man, to whom it is destined by the Divine Goodness, cannot profit by it except in so far as he has used successfully that first corporeal power given him as a preservation against the first evil action of the quinary chief. If he have allowed this simple inferior power to become degraded, the enemy has much more facility in attacking him with advantage in the active temporal power; and so far from this power turning to the profit of man, to whom it should communicate love, desire, faith, with all true spiritual affections proper for its reconciliation, the evil intellect makes use of this same organ to suggest all the false and ill-regulated passions and affections which can separate it from its object.[†] Hence, also, the avenging spirit of the crimes of human posterity for the maintenance of divine justice is announced by the Number Four.

5 – The Pentad

In the numerical mysticism of Saint-Martin the quinary is the number of the evil principle. It therefore differs, as we have seen, from those systems of occult numeration which regard this number as in an especial way the sign of the microcosm or of man, and seems positive proof that we are dealing here with a school of initiation which

---

[*] *Œuvres Posthumes,* ii. 133.   [†] *Œuvres Posthumes,* ii. 128-129.

derives little from Kabalistic sources. It is also a case in point as to the fragmentary character of the Martinistic doctrine of numbers, for we are really without any details as to the properties of the quinary. It is said that 2 becomes 3 by its minus, 3 becomes 4 by its centre, 4 is falsified by its double centre, which makes 5, and 5 is imprisoned by the measure 6, 7, 8, 9, 10, which forms the corrective and rectifier of the evil quinary.* The number also connects with what Saint-Martin has to tell us concerning the twofold application of all numerals. True numbers produce invariably life, order, and harmony; thus, they always act for, and never against, even when they serve as the scourges of justice. When they undergo mutation in free beings, their character is so changed that it is another number which takes their place, whilst their radical title is always the same in their essence. False numbers, on the contrary, produce nothing; they may ape but cannot imitate the true; they manifest in dismemberment, never in generation, because they have become false by division and have lost the capacity for engendering. A proof is found in the example of the five foolish virgins; they found themselves without oil because their conduct separated them from their five companions, and so also they remained without their bridegroom. As to the wise virgins, they engender only by the bridegroom, and when they shall possess him they will no longer be 5 but 10, since each will possess the spouse, or they will be 6 if the spouse be represented by 1 only. Thus, these five virgins are so little in their true number that, unable by themselves to renew their oil, they are forced to take refuge in prudence and to check charity, which can only be found in the vivifying numbers, the whole force of which flows from the centre of love. We must distinguish, however, between the false numbers when employed to operate restoration and when operating their own iniquities. In the latter case they are given over to themselves and separated wholly from the true line; in the former case, true being assumes their form and character so as to descend into their infected region. But in assuming their form this Being rectifies it, referring it to the true numbers, and by thus opposing the true to the false he visits death upon death.†

---

* *Les Nombres,* p. 20.   † Ibid. pp. 28-29.

6 – The Hexad

This number is the mode of every operation; it is not an individual agent, but it possesses a necessary affinity with all that operates, and no agent brings any action to its term without passing through this number. The senary is the co-eternal correspondence of the divine circumference with God. For this reason, God, who engenders all, embraces and beholds all. The circumference is composed of six equilateral triangles; it is the product of two triangles which actuate one another; it is the expression of six acts of divine thought manifested in the days of creation and destined to effect its reintegration. Thus this number is the mode of creation, though it is neither its principle nor agent. It is in the theosophical addition of the Number Three that we find proof of senary influence in corporisation. Scripture traces the senary from the origin of things and takes it beyond their term. Having shown the work of the six days, it presents in the Apocalypse, before the throne of the Eternal, four animals having six wings, and twenty-four ancients, prostrating themselves before Him. By this we see that the senary is the universal mode of things, because it has the same character in the universal order, and hence our trine faculties must follow it to obtain the completion of their action: Thought, 1; Will, 2; Action, 3 = 6. The 24 ancients of the Apocalypse equal 6, namely, 1, 3, 4, 7, 8, 10. These numbers added give 33, including zero, the image and evidence of corporeal appearances. But they give 24 without zero. Hence these six numbers alone have acted, are real, and will act eternally; that is to say, there are eternally two powers, that of God and that of the Spirit. The senary suffered in the several prevarications which caused the Regenerator to descend here; it was necessary that He should repair its virtuality. For this reason He changed into wine the water contained in six ewers at the marriage of Cana.

It is not less true that the senary, being only the mode of operation of all agents, cannot be regarded precisely as a real and active number, but rather as a co-eternal law impressed on all numbers. It is also that over which man had dominion formerly, and will again rule after his restoration.* Finally, the number 2 acts in the senary of forms which are of themselves only a passive addition of the two kinds. The root of these is two, and it is the agent of their modes and sensations by the multiplication of its own elements.

7 – The Heptad

The spiritual septenary number signifies the Divine Power itself † This is the number of the universal forms of the Spirit; its fruit is found in its multiplication. The square of 7, or 49, is 7 in development, while in its root it is 7 in concentration. Development is also necessary before it can proceed to 8, which is the temporal mirror of the invisible, incalculable denary. While it passes from 7 to 8 by means,of the great unity with which it unites, it also passes from 49 to 50 by means of the same unity, and it draws the quaternary or human soul into this reunion by making it traverse and abolish the novenary of appearances, which is our limit and the cause of our privation. This shows that 5 is equal to 8 and 8 equal to 5 in the great wonder which the Divine Repairer has wrought for our regeneration. ‡

Seven is known only by the temporal 4 x 4= 16 = 7. But at the same time it is clearly the number of the Spirit, because it comes from the Divine and gives 28, on account of its double power opposed to the lunary power. It should be observed that the number 28 indicates that the Word had no place till the second prevarication. But these are merely images, because 7 coming from 76 is not root, nor is it the essential power of 4, for it enters into its root only by way of addition§

Independently of the numerical root 16, which expresses the septenary power of the soul, we find it in its powers over the ternary of the elements and the ternary of the principles of the central axis. The soul is the centre of these two triangles. If, instead of this centre, we

---

*   *Les Nombres,* pp. 60-62.   †   *Œuvres Posthumes,* ii. 129.

‡   *Correspondance,* Lettre xc; Penny, "Theosophic Correspondence," pp. 306-307. Saint-Martin states that this point came directly to his intelligence, and that it was not received from man.

§   *Les Nombres,* p. 70.

count the power of the soul over the celestial, we shall find in a more active manner the soul's septenary power over the physical and spiritual both.[*]

But $7 \times 7 = 49 \times 7 = 343$. Man was established at his post, or, more correctly, emancipated only when his power attained its cube. It is in the elements of this cube that we see clearly the destination of primitive man, since he was placed between the superior triangle, from which he derived everything, and the inferior triangle, which he ruled. To know the true properties of a being, the cube of its power must be considered, for there only is the scheme of its faculties developed.[†]

The Number Seven also indicates that the temporal epoch, or manifestation of universal justice, must be visited on all prevaricators. But the Number Four is that of the agent who exercises this justice. As this agent is the Spirit and spirit cannot appear in time without a corporeal envelope, it is made known sensibly by the septenary, which is the body of the quaternary, as the senary is the body of the septenary, and as the material ternary is the body of the senary which has operated it, or as, finally, the quaternary is the body of unity, which cannot manifest here in its simple nature, but must subdivide for us the powers which it has placed in creation.

8 – The Ogdoad

It is only after the complement of the square of the Spirit that the operation of the octonary can be consummated, while its work can only be known clearly in the spirit of the number 50, because then the number of iniquity and the number of matter are dissipated by the living and regenerating influence of the unity which replaces them. As to the absolute Unity, or the Father, no one has seen or shall see Him in this world, save in the octonary, which is the sole way whereby we can attain to Him.

The number 50 disappeared on the approach of the Holy Octonary, because they two could not subsist together. iniquity and appearance could not remain before unity and its power. This is that

---

[*]   *Les Nombres,* p. 78.   [†]   Ibid. p. 86.

Divine Church outside of which no man can be saved and against which the gates of hell shall not prevail; this is the key which opens and no one shuts, shuts and no one opens.*

Christ is triadic in his elements of operation as in his essential elements his number is 8, and his mystical extraction teaches us that in his temporal work he was at once divine, corporeal, and sensible, though when considered in the eternal order he is divine in his three elements. He was the way, the truth, and the life. It was necessary that he should comprise within him the divine, a sensible soul, and the corporeal, to operate here below on the sensible order and all creation, because even as our thinking soul cannot be joined to our grosser individual envelope without the mediation of an individual sensible bond, so the Divine Repairer could not be joined to his corporeal though pure form without the medium of a sensible soul. This soul invests him with the number 4, his divine being bears the number 1, his body the number 3. In us the divine soul bears the number 4, the body that of 9, while the number of our sensible soul, Saint-Martin says, was unknown to him, but he had reason to think that it was not the same as that of the Saviour, because in all other elements which he possessed like to our own, he bore invariably superior numbers. In this sensible soul the whole key of man consists; thereby he is joined to the sensitive or corporeal animal, but as he is not placed willingly, like Christ, in this prison, he cannot be expected to know the key which secures it. Saint-Martin thought, however, that the number was 6.†

9 – The Ennead

Nine is the number of every spiritual limit, as the material circumference is in the limit of the elementary principles which act therein. Hence it represents the general and particular course of all the expiations inflicted by divine justice on the posterity of man. Man fell by proceeding from 4 to 9, and can only be restored to himself by returning from 9 to 4. This law is terrible, but it is nothing in comparison

---

* *Les Nombres,* pp. 54-56.   † Ibid. pp. 40-41.

with the law of the number 56, which is frightful for those who face it, since they cannot arrive at 64 until they have experienced all its severity. The passage from 4 to 9 is the passage from spirit to matter, which in dissolution according to numbers gives 9. As to the law of 56, it depends upon the knowledge of the properties and conditions of the number 8, which were part of the light given by initiation to Saint- Martin and not further explained. The criminal remains in the number 56, while the just and purified will attain to 64 or unity.[*]

To whatever powers the number 9 is raised, it always remains 9, because, like 3 and 6, it has only a tertiary power, while 4, 7, 8, 10 are secondary powers, unity alone being the first power. Hence unity, in all possible multiplications, gives only one, because, as already seen, it cannot issue from or duplicate itself It manifests outside itself by its secondary and tertiary powers, co-eternally bound therewith. Could we know the active way by which it effects the manifestation of its powers we should be its equal. We are assured, however, that it operates its expansions only in its decade. The expansions themselves operate only outside the decade. There are spiritual expansions and expansions of form which work by different laws and produce different results. The secondary powers connect immediately with the centre, but the tertiary only mediately, and hence they produce forms alone, having no creative law, for this belongs to unity, and no administrative law, for this is confided to the secondary powers.[†]

---

[*]   *Correspondance,* Lettre xiii; Penny, "Theosophic Correspondence," pp. 55-56. Saint-Martin states that he received this teaching from the school of Pasqually.

[†]   *Les Nombres,* pp. 70-71.

10 – The Decad

By the reunion of the spiritual septenary to the temporal ternary, we have the famous denary ever present to our thoughts. As the image of Divinity itself, it accomplishes the reconciliation of all beings by causing them to return into unity. The temporal denary is composed of two numbers, 7 and 3, but its type connects with unity itself and is not subject to any division.[*] So long as numbers are united to the decade, none of them present the image of corruption or deformity; these characters manifest only in their separation. Amongst the numbers thus specialised some are absolutely bad, such as 2 and 5, which alone divide the denary. Others are in active operation, suffering, or curative operation, as 7, 4, and 8. Yet others are given only to appearance, such as 3, 6, 9. Nothing of this is seen in the complete decade, for in that supreme order there is no deformity, illusion, or suffering.[*]

---

[*] *Œuvres Posthumes,* ii. pp. 187-188.   [†] *Les Nombres,* p. 68.

Appendices

I

Prayers of Saint-Martin

1

Eternal source of all which is, Thou who sendest spirits of error and of darkness to the untruthful, which cut them off from Thy love, do Thou send unto him who seeks Thee a spirit of truth, uniting him forever with Thee. May the fire of this spirit consume in me all traces of the old man, and, having consumed them, may it produce from those ashes a new man, on whom Thy sacred hand shall not disdain to pour a holy chrism! Be this the end of penitence and its long toils, and may Thy life, which is one everywhere, transform my whole being in the unity of Thine image, my heart in the unity of Thy love, my activity in the unity of the works of justice, and my thought in the unity of all lights. Thou dost impose great sacrifices on man, only to compel him to seek in Thee all his riches and all his delights, and Thou dost force him to seek all these treasures in Thee only because Thou knowest that they alone can make him happy, for Thou alone dost possess them, who hast engendered and created them. Truly, O God of my life, I can find nowhere save in Thee the root and realisation of my being. Thou also hast said that in the heart of man alone canst Thou find Thy repose. Cease not, therefore, for one instant thine operations upon me, that not only may I live, but that Thy name may be known among the nations. Thy prophets have declared that the dead cannot praise Thee; let death then never come near me, for I burn to offer Thee immortal praise; I burn with desire that the Eternal Son of Truth may never have to reproach the heart of man with the smallest clouding of Thy splendour, or the least diminution of its fullness. God of my life, the utterance of whose Name accomplishes all things, restore to my nature that which Thou didst first impart to it, and I will manifest that Name among the nations, and they shall learn that Thou alone art their God, Thou alone their essential life, as Thou only art the movement and motive principle of all beings. Do Thou sow the seed of Thy desires in the soul of man, in that field where none can contest with Thee, since it is Thou who hast brought it into existence. Sow Thy desires therein, that the soul, by the force of Thy love, may be snatched from the depths which hold it and would swallow it up forever. Abolish for me the realm of images; scatter the fantastic barriers which place an immense interval and spread thick darkness between Thy living light and me, entombing me in their folds. Show unto me the sacred character and the divine seal of which Thou art the custodian; pierce the centre of my soul with the fire which burns in Thee, that my soul may burn with Thee till it knows Thine ineffable life and the inexhaustible delights of Thine eternal existence. Too feeble to endure the weight of Thy Name, I leave in Thy hands the task of erecting its complete edifice, and of laying Thyself its first foundations in the depths of that soul which Thou has given me for a torch, showing light to the nations, that they may no more dwell in darkness. Thanks be unto Thee, O God of peace and love! thanks be unto Thee, because Thou hast been mindful of me, and hast not willed that my soul should want, lest Thine enemies should say that the Father forgets His children or is unable to deliver them.

2

I will approach Thee, Thou God of my being; I will approach Thee, all unclean as I am; I will show myself with confidence before Thee; I will come unto Thee in the name of Thine eternal existence, in the name of my life, in the name of Thy holy alliance with man. This threefold offering shall be for Thee an acceptable sacrifice, on which Thy Spirit shall send down its divine fire, to consume and transport it to Thy sacred abode, all charged and filled with the desires of a needy soul sighing only after Thee. Lord, Lord! when shall I hear Thee utter in the abyss of my soul that consoling and living word which calls on man by his name, proclaiming his enrolment in the heavenly army, and Thy will that he should be numbered among Thy servants? By the power of that holy word shall I find myself speedily encompassed by the eternal memorials of Thy power and love, with which I shall boldly advance against Thine enemies, and they shall flee before the dread lightnings flashing from Thy victorious word. Alas, O Lord! shall a man of misery and darkness cherish such high aspirations, such proud hopes? In place of smiting the enemy, must he not seek only a shield from their blows? Furnished no longer with shining arms, is he not, as a despicable object, reduced to tears of shame and ignominy in the thickets of his retreat, unable to show himself before the day? In place of those triumphant anthems which once followed him in his conquests, is he not doomed only to be heard amid sighs and groans? Vouchsafe at least one boon, O Lord, that whensoever Thou searchest my heart and my reins, Thou shalt never find them void of Thy praise and love. I feel, and would feel unceasingly, that all time is not enough for Thy praise, that to accomplish this holy work in a manner which is worthy of Thee, my entire being must be possessed and set in motion by Thine eternity. Grant, therefore, O God of all life and all love, that my soul may reinforce its weakness with Thy strength; permit it to enter into a holy league with Thee, by which I shall be invincible in the sight of my enemies, which shall bind me so to Thee by the desires of my heart and of Thine, that Thou shalt ever find me as zealous for Thy service and glory as Thou, O Lord, art eager for my deliverance and beatitude.

3

Spouse of my soul! by whom it has conceived the desire of wisdom, aid me Thyself to give birth to this well-beloved son, whom I can never cherish sufficiently. So soon as he beholds the light, immerse him in the pure baptismal waters of Thy life-giving Spirit, and be he ever numbered among the faithful members of the Church of the Most High. Like a tender mother, do Thou take him in Thine arms till his feeble limbs have strength for his support, and shield him from all that is harmful. Spouse of my soul! unknown except by the humble, I do homage to Thy power, and I would not confide to other hands than Thine this son of love whom Thou hast given me. Nourish him Thyself, watch over his early steps, instruct him when he grows in the honour which he owes to his Father, that his days may be long on the earth; inspire him with respect and love for the might and the virtues of Him who hath given him being. Spouse of my soul! inspire me also, me first, to nourish this precious child unceasingly with spiritual milk, which Thou hast formed Thyself in my breast. May I ever behold in my son the image of his Father, in his Father the likeness of my son, and of all those whom Thou mayst engender within me through the unbroken course of the eternities. Spouse of my soul! known only to the sanctified, be Thou at once the mentor and model of this child of Thy Spirit, that in all times and places his works and example may proclaim his heavenly origin. Place Thou also at length on his head the crown of glory, and he shall be an everlasting monument before the peoples of the majesty of Thy Name. Spouse of my soul! such are the delights which Thou preparest for those who love Thee and seek for union with Thee. Perish everlastingly him who would tempt me to break our sacred alliance! Perish everlastingly him who would persuade me to prefer another spouse! Spouse of my soul! take me Thyself for Thine own child; let me be one with him in Thine eyes, and pour on us each all graces which we cannot both receive from Thy love. I can live no more if the voices of myself and my son be forbidden to unite for the eternal celebration of Thy praises in canticles, like inexhaustible rivers ever engendered by the sense of Thy wonders and Thy power ineffable.

4

How should I dare, O Lord, for one instant to gaze on myself without trembling at the horror of my misery! I dwell in the midst of my own iniquities, the fruit of all manner of excesses, which have become even as a vestment; I have outraged all my laws, I have misused my soul, I have abused my body; I have turned, and do turn daily, to an ill account all the graces which Thy love showers continually on Thine ungrateful and faithless creature. To Thee should I sacrifice all, giving nothing unto time, which in Thy sight is like an idol, void of life and understanding; yet I devote all unto time and nothing unto Thee. Thus do I cast myself beforehand into the abyss of confusion, given over to idolatrous worship, where Thy name is not known. I have acted like the senseless and ignorant of this world, who expend all their efforts to annul the dread decrees of justice and to render this place of probation no longer one of toil and suffering in their eyes. God of peace and God of truth, if the confession of my faults be insufficient for their remission, remember Him who took them on Himself, washing them in the blood of His body, His soul, and His love. Like fire, which consumes all material and impure substances, like this fire which is His image, He returns to Thee, free from all stains of earth. In Him and by Him alone can the work of my purification and rebirth be fulfilled. In Him alone can Thy sacred majesty endure to regard man, through whom also Thou willest our cure and our salvation. Gazing with the eyes of His love, which cleanses all, Thou dost see no longer any deformity in man, but only that divine spark which is in Thine own likeness, which Thy sacred ardour draws perpetually to itself, as a property of Thy divine source. O Lord, Thou canst contemplate only that which is true and pure as Thyself; evil is beyond the reach of Thine exalted sight, and hence the evil man is like one whom Thou rememberest no more, whom Thine eyes cannot fix, since he has no longer any correspondence with Thee. In this abyss of horror I have, notwithstanding, dared to dwell; there is no other place for man who is not immersed in the abyss of Thy compassion. Yet no sooner does he turn his heart and eyes from the depths of iniquity than he finds himself in that ocean of mercy which encompasses all Thy creatures. So will I bow myself before Thee in my shame and the sense of my misery; the fire of my suffering shall dry up within me the abyss of my sinfulness, and there shall remain for me only the eternal kingdom of Thy mercy.

5

Take back my will, O Lord, take back my will; for if I can suspend it one instant before Thee, the torrents of Thy life and light, having nothing to resist them, shall pour impetuously within me. Help me to break down the woeful barriers which divide me from thee; arm me against myself; triumph within me over all Thine enemies and mine by subduing my will. O Eternal Principle of all joy and of all truth! when shall I be so renewed as no longer to be conscious of self, save in the permanent affection of Thine exclusive and vivifying will? When shall every kind of privation appear to me a profit and advantage, by preserving me from all bondage, and leaving me ample means to bind myself to the freedom of Thy spirit and wisdom? When shall evils appear to me as favours extended by Thee, as so many opportunities of victory, so many occasions of receiving from Thy hand the crowns of glory which Thou dost distribute to all those who fight in Thy name? When shall all advantages and joys of this life become to me as so many snares, unceasingly set by the enemy that he may establish in our hearts a god of lying and seduction in place of that God of peace and truth who should reign there forever? When, in fine, shall the holy zeal of Thy love and the ardour of my union with Thee rule me to renounce with delight my life, my happiness, with all affections foreign to this sole end of Thy creature man, so loved by Thee that Thou hast given Thyself all for him, that he might be inflamed by Thine example? I know, O Lord, that whosoever is not transported by this holy devotion is not worthy of Thee, and has not yet made the first step in Thy path. The knowledge of Thy will and the solicitude of the faithful never to depart from it for a moment, herein is the one, the true resting-place for the soul of man; he cannot enter therein without being filled immediately with rapture, as if all his being were renewed and revivified in all its faculties by the springs of Thine own life, nor can he withdraw there from without beholding himself given over forthwith to all the horrors of uncertainty, danger, and death. Hasten, God of consolation, hasten, God of power, to communicate to my heart one of those pure movements of Thy holy and invincible will! One only is needed to establish the reign of Thine eternity, and for constant and universal resistance of all alien wills which combine in my soul, mind, and body to give battle thereto. Then shall I abandon myself to my God in the sweet effusion of my faith, then shall I proclaim His wonderful works. Men are not worthy of Thy wonders, or to contemplate the sweetness of Thy wisdom, the proflmdity of Thy counsels; and I, vile insect that I am, can I even dare to name them, who merit only visitations of justice and wrath? Lord, Lord! may the star of Jacob rest for a moment upon me; may Thy holy light be kindled in my thought, and Thy will most pure in my heart!

6

Hearken, my soul, hearken, and be consoled in thy distress! There is a mighty God who undertakes to heal all thy wounds. He alone has this supreme power, and He exercises it only towards those who acknowledge that He possesses it and is its zealous administrator. Come not before him in disguise like the wife of Jeroboam whom the prophet overwhelmed with reproaches; come rather with the humility and confidence which should be inspired by a sense of thy frightful evils, and of that Universal Power which willeth not the death of a sinner, since it is He who created souls. Let time fulfill its law upon thee in all the things of time; speed not thy work by disorders; delay it not by false desires and vain speculations, the heritage of the fool. Concerned alone with thine interior cure, thy spiritual deliverance, collect with care the scant forces which each temporal period develops within thee; make use of these secret motions of life to draw nearer daily unto Him who already would possess thee in His breast, and share with thee the sweet freedom of a being who enjoys fully the use of all his faculties without ever encountering a hindrance. Whensoever these happy ecstasies transport thee, raise thyself on thy bed of sorrow, and cry unto this God of mercy and almightiness: Lord, wilt Thou leave to languish in bondage and shame this former image of Thyself, whom the ages may have buried under their dust but have never been able to efface? It dared to misconceive Thee in those days when it dwelt in the splendour of Thy glory. Thou hadst only to close the eye of Thine eternity, and it was plunged from that instant into darkness, as into the depths of the abyss. Since that deplorable lapse it has become the daily scorn of all its enemies, who, not contented to cover it with derision, have filled it with their poisons, have loaded it with chains so that it could no longer defend itself but became an easier prey to their envenomed darts. Lord, Lord! is not this long and humiliating ordeal sufficient for man to recognise Thy justice and do homage to Thy power? Has not this infected mass of its enemy's contempt enervated long enough the image of Thyself to open his eyes and convince him of his illusions? Dost Thou not fear that in the end these corrosive substances may entirely efface its imprint and place it beyond recognition? The enemies of Thy light and Thy wisdom would not fail to confound this long chain of my degradations with Thine eternity itself; they would believe their reign of horror and disorder is the sole abode of truth; they would claim themselves victorious over Thee and possessed of Thy kingdom. Permit not, therefore, longer, O God of zeal and jealousy, the profanation of Thine image; the desire of Thy glory fills me more than any desire of my own happiness apart from that glory of Thine. Rise on Thy throne immortal, the throne of Thy wisdom, ablaze with the marvels of Thy power; enter for a moment that holy vineyard which Thou hast planted from all eternity; pluck but one of those vivifying grapes which it produces unceasingly; let the sacred and regenerating juice flow upon my lips; it will moisten my parched tongue, it will enter into my heart, it will bear to it both joy and life, it will penetrate all my members and will make them strong and healthy. Then shall I be quick, agile, vigorous as on that first day when I came forth from Thy hands. Then shall Thine enemies, frustrated in their hopes, blush with shame and tremble with fear and rage to see their opposition against Thee made vain and the accomplishment of my sublime destiny despite their daring and persistent efforts. Hearken then, O my soul! hearken, and be consoled in thy distress! A mighty God there is who hath undertaken the healing of all thy wounds.

7

I present myself at the gates of the temple of my God, and I will quit not this humble asylum of the indigent till I have received my daily bread from the Father of my life. Behold the mystery of this bread! I have tasted thereof, and I will proclaim its sweetness to unborn nations. The Eternal God of Beings; the sacred title taken by Him who is made flesh that He might be manifested to the visible and invisible nations; the spirit of Him at whose Name every knee shall bow, in heaven, on earth, and in hell; such are the three immortal elements which compose this daily bread. It is multiplied unceasingly, like the immensity of beings who are nourished thereby, and, whatsoever be their number, never can they diminish its abundance. It has developed in me the eternal germs of my life, and has enabled them to circulate in my veins the sacred sap of my original and divine roots. The four elements which compose it have dispelled darkness and confusion from the chaos of my heart; they have restored to it the living and holy light; their creative force has transformed me into a new being, and I have become the custodian and administrator of their sacred characters and life-giving signs. Therefore, as His angel and minister have I shown myself in all regions, to make known the glory of Him who hath chosen man; I have reviewed all the work of His hands and have distributed to each of them those signs and characters which He has impressed on me in order that they might be transmitted to them, and to confirm the properties and powers which they have received. But my ministry has not been confined to operation on the regular works of Eternal Wisdom; I have approached whatsoever was deformed, and have set on these fruits of disorder the signs of justice and vengeance attached to the secret powers of my election; those which I could snatch from corruption I have offered as a holocaust to the supreme God, and I have composed my perfumes of the pure praises of my mind and heart, so that all which lives may confess that the homage, the glory, the honour are due unto this sole supreme God as the source of power and justice. I have exclaimed in the transports of my love: Blessed is man, because Thou hast elected him as the seat of Thine authority and the minister of Thy glory in the universe. Blessed is man, because Thou hast permitted him to feel, even in the depths of his essence, the penetrating activity of Thy divine life. Blessed is man, because he may dare to offer Thee a sacrifice of thanksgiving founded in the ineffable sentiment of all the wishes of Thy holy infinity. Powers of the material world! powers of the physical universe! not thus hath God treated you! He has constituted you the simple agents of His laws and the forces operating for the fulfillment of His designs. Hence is there no other being in Nature which does not second Him in His work and cooperate in the execution of His plans. But He is not made known to you as the God of peace and the God of love; at the moment when He brought you into being ye were disturbed by the consequences of rebellion, since He ordained man to subdue and govern you. Still less, ye perverted and corrupt powers, has He dispensed to you those favours with which He has deigned to overwhelm man. Ye have failed to preserve those which were granted you by virtue of your origin; ye dreamed of a brighter lot and a more splendid privilege than to be the objects of His tenderness, from which moment ye have deserved only to be the victims of His justice. To man alone has He confided the treasures of His wisdom; on this being after His own heart has He centred all His affection and all His powers. Sovereign Author of my spirit, my soul, and my heart! be Thou blessed forever and in all places, because Thou hast permitted man, Thine ungrateful and criminal creature, to recover these sublime truths. Had the memory of Thine ancient and sacred covenant bound not Thy love to restore them, they would have been lost unto man forever. Praise and benediction to Him who hath formed man in His image and after His own likeness, who, despite all the endeavours and all the triumphs of hell, hath reclothed him in his splendour, in the wisdom and the beatitudes of his origin. Amen.

8

Men of peace and men of aspirations! let us contemplate in unison, with a holy fear, the vastness of the mercies of our God. Let us confess to Him together that all the thoughts of men, all their purest desires, all their ordered deeds, could not, when combined, approach the smallest act of His love. How should we therefore express it? for it is confined to no individual deeds or times, but manifests at once all its treasures, and that in a constant, universal, and unhindered way! God of truth and God of love! so actest Thou daily with man. Amidst all mine infection and vileness Thy hand untiring extracts what still remains of those precious and sacred elements of which Thou didst form me at first. Like the thrifty woman in the Gospel, consuming her light to recover the dime which she lost, Thy lamps are ever lighted, ever Thou stoopest to earth, ever hopest to recover from the dust that pure gold which has slipped from Thy hands. Men of peace! how should we contemplate otherwise than with holy fear the extent of the mercies of our God! We are a thousand times more guilty towards Him than, in the sight of human justice, are those malefactors who are dragged through cities and public places, loaded with the of infamy, and forced to confess their crimes aloud at the doors of the temples and in the presence of the powers which they have defied Like them, and a thousand times more deservedly than they, should we be dragged ignominiously to the feet of all the powers of Nature and the Spirit; we should be paraded like criminals through all the regions of the universe, both visible and invisible, and should receive in their presence the terrible and shameful chastisements which are invoked by our appalling prevarications. But in place of finding stem judges armed with vengeance, behold a venerable Monarch whose eyes publish His clemency, whose lips utter pardon only for all those who do not blindly hold themselves guiltless. Far from willing that we should wear henceforth the vestments of opprobrium, He commands His servants to give back to us our primeval robe, to set a ring on our finger and shoes on our feet. For all these favours it is enough, like later prodigal sons, to confess that we have not found in the house of strangers the happiness of the house of our Father. Men of peace! say, shall we contemplate except with holy fear the infinite love and mercy of our God? Say, shall we not make a holy resolution to remain faithful for ever to His laws and to the beneficent counsels of His wisdom? O God! incomprehensible in indulgence and past understanding in love, I can love but Thee alone; I would love none but Thee, who hast forgiven me so much. I desire no place of repose except in the heart of my God, who embraces all by His power, my support on every side, my succour and my consolation. From this divine source all blessings pour on me at once. He pours Himself into the heart of man continually and forever. So does He engender within us His own life; so does He establish within us the pure rays and extracts of His own essence, whereon He loves to brood, and they become in us the organs of His endless generations. From this sacred treasury, through all the faculties of our nature, He directs kindred emanations, which repeat in turn their action through all that constitutes ourselves, and thus our spiritual activity, our virtues, our lights are unceasingly multiplied. Behold, it is exceeding profitable to erect Him a temple in our hearts! O men of peace! O men of aspiration! say, shall we contemplate without a holy fear the vastness of the love and of the mercies and of the powers of our God?

9

How should it be possible, O Lord, to sing here below the canticles of the Holy City? Amidst such streams of tears, can we raise the hymns of jubilation? I lift up my voice to begin them, but I utter sighs only and tones of pain. I am overwhelmed by the length of my sufferings; my sin is ever before me, threatening instant death, with the chill of its poisons freezing all my being. Even now it lays hold of my members; the moment comes when I shall lie like a corpse which is left by hirelings to putrefaction. Yet Thou, O Lord, who art the universal source of all that exists, art also the font of hope. If this spark of flame be not already quenched in my heart, I still cling unto Thee, I am still bound to Thy divine life by that deathless hope which springs for ever from Thy throne. From the depth of my abyss I dare therefore to implore Thee, to pray that the hand of Thy loving-kindness may heal me. How are the cures of the Lord effected? By humble submission to the wise counsel of the Divine Physician. With gratitude and ardent desire must I drink the bitter draught which His hand offers; my will must be joined with that which animates Him towards me; the length and sufferings of the treatment must not prompt me to reject the good which the Supreme Author of all goodness seeks to effect in me. He is penetrated with the sense of my sufferings, and I have only to be enkindled myself with the sense of His loving interest; then shall the chalice of salvation profit me; then shall my tongue be strengthened to sing the canticles of the Holy City. Lord, with what hymn shall I begin? With one to His honour and glory who has restored me to health and effected my deliverance. From the rising of the sun to the going down of the same will I chant this canticle over all the earth, not only to celebrate the power and love of my Liberator, but to communicate to all desiring souls, to the entire human family, the certain and efficacious means of recovering health and life forever. I will teach them thereby how the spirit of wisdom and truth may abide in their own hearts and direct them in all their ways. Amen.

10

My soul! hast thou strength to consider the enormity of that debt which guilty man has contracted with Divinity? If thou hast found strength for crime, thou hast good reason to contemplate it in all its horror. Measure, therefore, in thy thought the vineyard of the Lord; remember that man should tend it; conceive the wealth of the harvest which it should produce under his care; think how all creatures under heaven await their sustenance from its culture by thee, that the vineyard of the Lord awaits in like manner its adornment at thy hands, that the Lord Himself awaits from thy fidelity and watchfulness all the praise and glory which should accrue from the fulfillment of His plans. But thou hast fallen; the dominion of the enemy is upon thee; thou hast made barren the Lord's ground, brought the dwellers therein to want, and filled God's heart with sadness. Thou hast dried up the source of wisdom and of increase in this lower world, and still thou dost hinder daily the productions of the Lord. Consider the extent of thy debt, the impossibility of its payment. The fruits of each year are owing from the moment of thine infidelity, the wages of all the hours which have passed since that fatal hour. Where is the being who shall acquit thee in the sight of that eternal justice whose dues cannot be cancelled, whose designs must attain their fulfillment? Herein, O God supreme, are exhibited the torrents of Thy mercy and the inexhaustible abundance of Thine eternal treasures. Thy heart is opened towards Thy hapless creature: not only his debts are discharged, but a surplus remains with which he may succour the needy. Thou hast ordained Thy Word itself to cultivate the vineyard of man; that sacred Word whose soul is love has come down into this barren place; the fire of His speech has consumed all the parasitic and poisonous plants which choked it; He has sown the seed of the tree of life in their place; He has opened up health-giving springs, and it has been moistened by living waters; He has restored strength to the beasts of the earth, wings to the birds of heaven, light to the starry torches, sound and speech to every spirit which abides in the sphere of man. To the soul of man itself He has restored that love of which He alone is the source, which has inspired His holy and wonderful sacrifice. Eternal God of all praise and grace, one only being, Thy Son Divine, could thus repair our disorders and acquit us in the sight of Thy justice. The creative being alone could make restitution of that which we squandered, for it needed a new creation. If, therefore, O universal powers! ye strive to chant His praises who has reinstated you in your rights and restored your activity, what thanks are not due from me, since He has become the hostage for my debts Himself towards you, to all my brethren, and has discharged all? It was said of the penitent woman that much was forgiven her because she had loved much. But for man all has been remitted, not only prior to his love, but while he was steeped in the honors of ingratitude. O men! O brethren! let us give ourselves wholly to Him who has begun by forgiving all to us. Each one of God's movements is universal and is manifested in every universe. Now, like unto this God supreme, be the movement of love universal in all our nature, at once embracing all the faculties which compose us. Amen.[*]

---

[*] *Œuvres Posthumes,* vol. pp. 444-482.

II

Metrical Exercises of Saint-Martin

THE LITERARY REMAINS of Saint-Martin include "Phanos: a Poem on Poetry"[*] and a number of occasional verses, some reference to which will be found in Appendix III. He also published during his lifetime a metrical pamphlet entitled "The Cemetery of Amboise," while in his posthumous works there is a prose essay on "Prophetic, Epic, and Lyrical Poetry."[†] As in the order of criticism the last is curious rather than of high value, so his verse is generally to be admired for anything except its execution. He regarded prophetic poetry as belonging to the first order, because it drew from the first principle of inspiration and emotion. The true theme of poetry is the divine law in all the classes to which it extends, not human love, and still less material nature. Therefore most epical and nearly all lyrical poetry is a deflection and an impertinence. As regards the laws of verse, he lays down an axiom which is completely characteristic, for, like many views of Saint-Martin, it had never entered into the mind of man to conceive it previously. "Supreme music has no measure, and poetry is of this kind,"[‡] which, it will be observed, is much more than to say that poetry is to be rather valued for its spirit than for its form. Both views are in a sense impossible, or at least intolerable, at this day, when we have agreed that the divine word must assume a

---

[*]   *Œuvres Posthumes,* vol. pp. 287-313.

[†]   Ibid. pp. 271-282.   [‡]   Ibid. p. 277.

divine shape in order to be worthy of itself Saint-Martin's definition is much the better of the two, because it is unthinkable; the other is a vulgar fallacy. Perfect poetry is a perfect spirit wedded to a perfect form. When it is not so wedded it is not poetry. Just as the spirit of man is not man without the form of man. There is no need, however, to enlarge upon a point about which nobody now disputes, and as on the understanding that Saint-Martin's metrical exercises are not poetry, there is something occasionally in their matter which commends itself to his admirers, I have ventured to give one specimen of his verses, also on the understanding that the translation has no higher claim than a reasonably faithful rendering.[*]

---

[*]   *Œuvres Posthumes,* vol. i. pp. 331-336.

Stanzas on the Origin and Destiny of Man

I

The Voice of the Soul.

Supernal torch, thy light descends on me,
My life's enigma is explain'd by thee.
'Tis not because thy kindly warmth I hail
As ire derived from fonts that never fail;
Torch which enlightens, in thy splendours bright
I see myself derived from thy pure light;
Immortal townsman of a heavenly place,
From the Eternal Day my days I trace.

II

My shining birthright makes all glories fade,
No light shall cast the inner light in shade;
Who seeks to shroud or dim that sacred beam,
I hold thereby would God Himself blaspheme;
Attest it, Laws, which Truth's most holy plan
Graved deep within the incorporeal man
When first engender'd from that virtue's breast
Words in Truth's temple heard, ye too attest!

III

The Divine Voice.

Resplendent type of mine almighty power,
Of my pure essence the most perfect flower
Majestic man, thy high election know I
If forth on thee my secret unction flow,
'Tis to confirm the mission of thy birth,
My justice making known through all the earth,
Bearing my light through falsehood's dark domain,
By thine own self declared my grandeur's reign.

IV

The Voice of the Soul.

Ye elements, in all your actions bound,
Still blindly follow your unending round—
Not yours the functions of the gods to share;
Man of that right divine alone is heir;
Exclusive minister of Wisdom's laws,
Beams from the sun supreme he only draws.
Their splendours darting all the dark disperse,
And God in man shines o'er the universe.

V

Is man a god? What strange deceit is here!
Behold this prodigy divine appear
Vested in weakness, with disgrace his crown—
What foe has stripp'd him of his old renown?
Not king but captive now, to sense a thrall,
And, exiled far from his imperial hall,
The sacred accents of the heavenly shore,
The harp's harmonious strains, he hears no more.

VI

The Divine Voice.

O'er all that lives his once establish'd right
Peace to its empire gave beneath my sight;
Ye slaves who now your ancient lord subdue,
Peace when he seeks must be implored of you!
Once from life's stream he drew, which heard my voice,
And, leaping down, did earth with fruits rejoice;
What waters now will make that desert bear?
Tears from his eyes alone, descending there!

VII

To him alone this agony refer
Who did my justice and its stripes incur,
My law renounced, invoked to aid his reign
Foul falsehood's hosts, and 'gainst me arm'd in vain
For hope on crime establish'd soon betray'd,
The priest of idols was their victim made,
Death the one fruit such service bears its slave,
And life the costly sacrifice he gave.

VIII

The Voice of the Soul.

Eternal God, did man's most hapless race
For aye Thine image and Thy work debase?
Say, are Thy sons brought down so deep in shame
That they can rise not in Thy virtue's name?
Is Thy most sacred character destroy'd?
Thy highest title-that of Father-void?
And must that name of child, whose powers transmit
Life without end to them, turn void with it?

IX

Oh, when Thy glory was my home of yore
I learn'd Thy love endured for evermore,
Unfathom'd and unbound Thy mercy's sea!
Ah, Holy God, confirm Thy first decree!
With favours fresh increase Thy former grace—
Lo, they shall teach me yet my steps to trace
Beneath Thy wings, and compass that design
For which my nature first was drawn from Thine.

X

The Divine Voice.

Volcanic forces, in their gulfs compress'd,
By rocks and torrents are denied all rest,
But the 'fierce flame leaps round them and subdues—
Do thou, O timid man, like forces use!
A constant power direct to rend the chain,
To burst the bar, and thus thy freedom gain;
Inert are they, nor shall withstand thy strength,
Far from their fragments shalt thou soar at length!

XI

When the swift lightning, ere the thunder's peal,
Doth all the vault of heaven by fire reveal,
It manifests a master to the air;
Such work is thine; discern thy symbol there.
Lo, I have launch'd thee from the starry height,
'Tis thou who dartest downward trailing light,
And flash-like striking on the earthly ground,
Dost with the shock to thy first heaven rebound.

XII

Man is the secret sense of all which seems;
That other doctrines are but idle dreams,
Let Nature, far from all contention, own,
While his grand doom is by her day-star shown.
To vaster laws adjusted, he shall reign,
Earth for his throne, and his star-crown attain,
The universal world his empire wait,
A royal court restore his ancient state.

XIII

The Voice of the Soul.

That voice restores me I Angels free from sin,
Agents of God, who dwells your hearts within,
My transports share I A jealous lord is He,
But for my wisdom and felicity—
To justify mine origin sublime—
To bare the treasures of my natal clime—
That I with you may draw from springs above
The draughts of science and the draughts of love.

XIV

O if such love, despite the void between,
Impel you sometimes towards this earthly scene,
Will not its virtues and its powers upraise
Us earthly dwellers towards your heavenly ways?
O friends at least, whatever chance betide,
May nought your natures from mine own divide,
May my poor hymns to mix with yours be meet,
And in your council may I find a seat!

XV

Sacred and saintly Truth! Thy voice I hear,
Thine is the victory, Thy world comes near;
Its beams divine transmute the sense of sight
Till scene and eye diffuse the same rich light.
O founts divine, with darkness all unmix'd,
For God therein His holy place hath fix'd,
Time's twisted paths beneath my feet swim by,
I lose them leaping towards eternity.

III

Bibliography of the
Writings of Saint-Martin

Based on the Collection of M. Matter,
with additional Information, and Summaries of each Work

1

Of Errors and of Truth; or, Men recalled to the Universal Principle of Knowledge. In which work the uncertainty and incessant mistakes of their Researches are made plain to Inquirers, and the True Road is indicated for the acquisition of physical evidence on the origin of Good and Evil, on Man, on Nature, material, immaterial, and sacred, on the Basis of Political Governments, on the Authority of Sovereigns, on Civil and Criminal Jurisprudence, on Sciences, Languages, and Arts. In two Parts. Edinburgh, 1775. 8vo, pp. 230, 236.

The date on the title-page of this, the original edition, rests on the authority of Matter, who also states that it was reprinted without alteration of date or place, but with the addition of a table of contents, which refers, however, to the paging of the first or some previous edition. It is also suggested by Matter that Edinburgh was Lyons, and that the imaginary place of publication was a whim of the philosopher, which was followed also in his second work *(Saint-Martin... sa Vie et ses Œuvres,* 2me edition, p. 106). The edition of 1775 is also mentioned by T. B. Genoe, who was a personal friend of Saint-Martin. An impression dated 1782 (Edinburgh) is apparently unknown to previous bibliographers. There is no table of contents, and no indication that it is a reprint.

The treatise "Of Errors and of Truth" is divided into two parts and subdivided into seven sections, each part paged and titled separately, and hence it is sometimes described as in two volumes. It is preceded by a preface, which describes it as written with certain reservations and under certain veils, because it deals with truths and principles handed down from the beginning and in the custody of a small number of elect persons. The spiritual and natural philosophy of the author is developed in the first part; the second is, broadly speaking, concerned with the political questions enumerated in the title.

The work has once been translated into German, with a preface, by Matthew Claudius, Breslau, 1782.

Published at Salomonopolis, by Androphile, at the sign of the Immoveable Pillar, there appeared in the Masonic year 5795 a bulky volume entitled "Sequel to Errors and Truth, or Development of the Book of Men recalled to the Universal Principle of Knowledge, by an Unknown Philosopher," which is not, however, the work of Saint-Martin, but is declared by him to be stained with "the very vice of the false system which he combated." It has been sometimes referred to Holbach and even to Condorcet, but the authorship remains unknown. It has also been suggested that it was only a clever burlesque, but the work itself will not bear this innocent interpretation. It may be characterised more accurately as a malicious fraud designed to discredit the Martinists. It reviews in succession a number of the questions treated in the genuine work, as, for example, good and evil, liberty and necessity, the fall of man, will as a fundamental faculty of human nature, and so forth, developing in every case the antithesis of Saint-Martin's teaching, and yet pretending to be his production, and referring back to the original work. Five years later, that is to say in 1789, and at Hersalarm, appeared a "Key of Errors and of Truth, or Men recalled to the Universal Principle of Reason," by a Known Locksmith, which must not be confused with the foregoing. The two works are occasionally bound together, but their authorship appears to be distinct. The second has been referred to the Chevalier de Suze (Barbier) on grounds of which I am unaware. Matter says that it has escaped notice rather than passed into oblivion. It has at least the merit of being the work of an open enemy, and is to that extent honourable; nor is it altogether unworthy of remark by the discriminating student of Saint-Martin at the present day. It is in any case a testimony to the extraordinary vogue obtained by the book which it was intended to refute, and of which the authorship seems to have been still generally unknown. The place of publication seems also to have deceived the critic, who states that the materials of *Des Erreurs et de la Vérité* were drawn from a number of MSS. "communicated by the Royal Society of Edinburgh," and even hints that much of its inspiration may be traced to Warburton's "Divine Legation of Moses." The key is the work of a fatalist speaking the philosophical language of French free-thought at the period, and chiefly attacking the alchemical side of Saint-Martin's speculations, together with his numerical mysticism. The writer had evidently some first-hand acquaintance with the Freemasonry of his period; and among the many constructions placed upon the work which he criticised, he mentions that it was regarded by the fraternity as an allegorical presentation of their system. By the theologians it was attributed to the devil, and by some others to the theologians, that is to say, the Jesuits. In the *"Portrait Historique et Philosophique de M. De Saint-Martin, fait par lui-même,"* there is the following note, numbered 165: "It was at Lyons that I wrote the work 'Of Errors and of Truth,' partly by way of occupation and because I was indignant with the Philosophers so called, having read in Boulanger that the origin of religions was to be sought in the fear inspired by the catastrophes of nature. I composed this work about the year 1774; it was written in four months by the kitchen-fire, for there was no other at which I could warm myself. One day the saucepan containing the soup overturned on my foot and burned me somewhat seriously." This was the period of the author's thaumaturgic experiences with the Comte d' Hauterive; it was also one of some activity in connection with the Order of the Elect Cohens at their Lyons Lodge of Beneficence, at which he delivered some discourses extant in his posthumous works.

2

The Red Book. This work is described by Matter as so rare that it is almost unattainable As he does not mention it in his life of Saint-Martin, and gives no account of its contents, I infer that he had never seen a copy. He states that the authorship is denied by every critic, but that it was acknowledged by Saint-Martin; not, however, so far as I can trace, in any of his published writings. All attempts to secure an example for the purposes of this bibliography have ended in failure. Within recent years it has, I understand, been met with at public auctions in London. Assuming that it is correctly attributed, it is at least certain that Saint-Martin was anxious to conceal his connection with it, for he states that the epigraph of each of his works is derived from the one which preceded it. Now *Le Livre Rouge* is assigned by Matter to the period intervening between *Des Erreurs et de la Vérité* and the *Tableau Naturel,* but the epigraph of the latter occurs in *Des Erreurs,* &c, and not in the intermediate publication. Having regard to the marked characteristics of Saint-Martin's genuine works there ought to be no difficulty in determining the claim of the Red Book whenever a copy is procurable.

3

A Natural Picture of the Correspondences which Exist Between God, Man, and the Universe. Two parts in one volume; pp. 276 and 244. Edinburgh, 1782. 8vo.

The epigraph reads: "To explain material things by man, and not man by material things." It occurs in *Des Erreurs et de la Vérité,* as already stated, and will be found on p. 19 of the first part. The publisher's advertisement observes that it was received from the hands of a stranger, and that the MS. had numerous annotations which seemed foreign to the text, and were therefore printed within brackets. Baron Kirchberger questioned Saint-Martin as to the second point, and he replied: "The passages inter-parenthesis in 'Le Tableau' are mine. The editor thought he could not see in them a sufficient coherence with the rest of the work, which induced him to prepare the reader concerning them in the way he did, and I allowed him to act as he liked." The passages thus distinguished are the most bizarre portions of the book, and seem to veil some of the strange knowledge which he had derived from his initiation.

Saint-Martin tells us that the *Tableau Naturel* was written at the suggestion of some friends, and partly at the abode of Madame de Lusignan in the Luxembourg, partly at that of Madame de la Croix, also a resident of Paris. M. Gence expresses the general opinion of critics when he observes that "it is more closely logical in its course, more methodical and more continuous than the first work." As the personal friend of Saint-Martin, and himself a mystic, I am glad that he adds these words concerning the enigmatical parts: "It is not by these purely allegorical figures that his doctrine must be judged." Without questioning their importance, when properly understood, the reader can afford to dispense with these in favour of the luminous instruction of the text itself. He will find that this is more than a sequel to the work which preceded it; it is, in fact, the key to its obscurities, and, I might add, also the atonement for its defects. It is, in particular, a triumphant vindication of Saint-Martin from the charge of pantheism which has been preferred against him by the loose criticisms invariably passed upon mystics. It does indeed regard man as an emanation from God, "but not after the physical analogy of something given off and therefore lost to its source." Nor is man a limitation or specification of divinity which must be drawn back ultimately into the being from which he originated "The true analogy is to be sought in man himself, who communicates his thought, and thus his life, to his fellow-man, but experiences no deficiency in consequence." The correspondences described in the title are those which man in his present state of privation receives naturally from the physical universe by his senses and from the First Cause intellectually.

A translation of the *Tableau Naturel,* with a commentary by an anonymous writer, appeared in German at Reval in 1783, and seems to have been reprinted at Leipzig in 1785. Baron Kirchberger was at the pains of procuring a copy, the receipt of which was acknowledged by Saint-Martin, but it evoked no criticism.

4

The Man of Aspiration, by the author of *Des Erreurs et de la Vérité*. Lyons, 1790. 8vo.

The epigraph is taken from p. 90 of the first part of the "Natural Table": "If bright evanescent rays gleam at times in our darkness, they make our situation more frightful, or abase us further, by showing us what we have lost." It was written partly at London and the rest at Strasbourg at the instigation of Thiemann. Another friend, Salzmann, superintended its passage through the press, and it was sold by Sulpice Grabit. M. Matter says that, according to Petillet, a famous bookseller at Lausanne, this work was frequently reprinted. M. Gence makes the same statement, adding that it was revised. An edition in 2 vols. 12mo appeared at Metz in 1812. When enumerating his writings at the request of Baron Kirchberger, Saint-Martin speaks (*a*) of an edition, presumably the original, which was "few in number, and there are none left"; (*b*) of one recently issued, namely, by Grabit of Lyons, at the bookseller's own cost. It was translated into German by Wagner, Leipzig, 1813, 2 vols. M. Gence describes it as a book of "aspirations in the style of the Psalmist, in which the human soul presses towards its first estate, which the way of the spirit can help it to recover through the Divine Goodness." M. Matter qualifies it as the work of a profoundly religious philosopher, with some inspired pages. It was much admired by Lavater, who testified in public to its excellence. Saint-Martin himself says: "I confess that there are germs scattered in this work, the properties of which I knew not when I sowed them, but they now open daily before me, thanks to the providence of God and our authors." There is evidence, I think, that it was the author's favourite work, and perhaps the only one which he was accustomed to carry with him in his numerous migrations. It is also frequently referred to in his correspondence. On one occasion he was asked for the key to its meaning, and he replied with the following lines:

"Avant qu' Adam mangeât la pomme,
Sans effort nous pouvions ouvrir.
Depuis, l'œuvre ne se consomme
Qu' en feu pur d'un ardent soupir;
La clef de l'Homme de Désir
Doit naitre du désir de l'homme."

5

Ecce Homo. Paris, 1792. 8vo. Printed and apparently published at the press of the Cercle Social, Rue du Théâtre Français.

Saint-Martin says: "I wrote the *Ecce Homo* at Paris, in accordance with a lively inspiration which I received at Strasbourg." Its object was to warn people against the wonders and the prophecies of the time, especially those of somnambulists. The Duchesse de Bourbon, though he bore witness that none could surpass her in the virtues of piety and the desire of all that is good, had an inclination towards phenomena of this "lower order," and she was one of his friends whom he had partly in view. He regarded such interests and such experiences as examples of the degree of infirmity and abasement into which man had fallen.

An anonymous translation of *Ecce Homo* was published at Leipzig in 1819.

6

The New Man. Entirely anonymous, but bearing on its title this motto from *Ecce Homo:* "We can read ourselves only in God, and comprehend ourselves only in His light." It was published at Paris in the Year 4 of Liberty, by the Directors of the *Cercle Social* press, 4 Rue du Théâtre Francais. 8vo, pp. 432. Though issued subsequently to *Ecce Homo,* the period of its composition was prior to that work. It was written, says Saint-Martin, at Strasbourg at the suggestion of my dear Silverhielm, formerly almoner of the King of Sweden and nephew of Swedenborg," and elsewhere observes that its object is "to describe what we should expect in regeneration." He adds: "I should not have written it, or I should have written it differently, if I had then had the acquaintance I have since formed with the works of Jacob Böhme." He, however, excused himself from supplying Kirchberger with the corrections he had in his mind. "It would be beyond my ability to do so. I have sat long enough at my desk; I must not again busy myself in work of this kind, and, in future, I desire to write only from my substance. Moreover, the work in question is rather an exhortation, a sermon, than a work of instruction, although something of this may be derived from it here and there. I wrote it at the request of one who wished something from me in the way of exhortation. I did it in haste; it has been printed from the first draft, and I am glad to have it off my hands." This passage is important, because it establishes the exact relation in which Silverhielm stood to the "New Man," into which, one would almost infer from M. Matter, he had infused not only the system of his illustrious uncle, but his own particular notions as to its plan and composition. Saint-Martin, we now see, was the instructor, not the disciple.

7

Letter to a Friend, or Philosophical and Religious Considerations on the French Revolution. Published at Paris by Louvet, Palais-Egalite, 1796.

Though described as a pamphlet by Saint-Martin, this work is a treatise of considerable dimensions. It is, on the whole, the least ultra-mundane of his political writings, though it regards the French Revolution as the beginning of the Last Judgment, and, as it were, a summary of its content. He suggested to Kirchberger its translation and publication in Germany, if the latter thought it would be calculated to check the "infernal doctrines" then spreading in that country. The Baron, ever enthusiastic over any production of his correspondent, declared that it was the most profound work which had been written on its subject, and that it solved the greatest difficulties in the theory of social order, yet so wisely that it did not wound deeply. But he dissuaded Saint-Martin from the idea of translation, as he did not think it suitable to the peculiar necessities of his country. Saint-Martin says that in France it was a rejected corner-stone, adding: "I do not the less believe that I have done a good work which the Master will accept, and this is all that I desire." I think there is evidence that he remained anxious for its translation, and this ultimately took place, but it was not till long after his death, namely, in 1818, that the version of Varnhagen von Ense appeared at Carlsruhe.

8

Light on Human Association, by the author of the work entitled "Of Errors and of Truth." Paris, 1797. 8vo. Published by Marais, Cour des Fontaines, Palais-Royal.

A recurrence to some political problems discussed in *Des Erreurs et de la Vérité.* M. Matter says that excepting the "Letter on the French Revolution" he knows nothing which more completely reveals Saint-Martin himself or is more thoroughly his own. At the same time he establishes its analogies with Rousseau. It is a further protest against seeking the elements of human association in the mere needs of our material being. The true end must be a return to that point from which humanity has descended, and, as in the "Letter," so here, he maintains that the earliest human associations were theocratic, and that such should be all governments.

9

The Crocodile, or the War of Good and Evil which took place during the Reign of Louis xv. An Epico-Magical Poem in 102 cantos, comprising long voyages free from mortal accidents, a little love without its madness, great battles devoid of bloodshed, instruction apart from pedantry, and seeing that it includes both prose and verse, it is therefore neither in verse nor prose. The Posthumous Work of a Lover of Secret Things. Paris, Imprimerie du Cercle Social, year 7 of the French Republic (*i.e.* 1709). 8vo, pp. 460.

The new pseudonym, and the pretence that publication was posthumous, make it evident that Saint-Martin did not wish a performance of this kind to be associated with the serious and transcendent purposes of the "Unknown Philosopher." It is a comedy without laughter and a "facetious allegory" in which the fun seems exceedingly

laboured. It seems, however, to rank high in the opinion of some mo-
dem Martinists, who regard it as a veiled account of Saint-Martin's esoteric doctrine and an exposition of the mysteries of the Astral Light,

10

**An Observer's Reflections on the Question Proposed by the Insti-
tute: What Institutions are most Fitted to Ensure the Morals of a
People?** Paris, 1798.

From the standpoint of Saint-Martin, it is obvious that there could
be but one institution, and that is religion theosophically and not
officially understood. M. Matter, whose criticism of this pamphlet
and the circumstances which occasioned it is replete with kindly insight, discusses this point, and recognises also the qualifications of
Saint- Martin for the treatment of the subject at large. That the mystic himself dismisses it in a few pages and describes it as a trifle to
Kirchberger, is, he considers, because Saint-Martin knew too well
that the solution would not be acceptable. He was not, however, usually deterred by probabilities of this kind. It is needless to add that
the Institute did not crown his answer. There was, in fact, no serious
competition and no award.

11

**A Discourse in Reply to Citizen Garat, Professor of Mental Philoso-
phy at the Normal Schools.** Printed in the *Débats de l'Ecole No'rmale,*
t. Paris, 1801.

Originally read at the Conferences by Saint-Martin himself. There
was a reply by Garat and a rejoinder by the mystic. This ended the
debate, which from all accounts created a considerable impression, as
much from the position of the disputants as from the subject at issue.
On the one side was a pupil who, from the curious constitution of
the Normal Schools, was older, as it chanced, than the professor, and,
moreover, "a former military officer and Chevalier of Saint-Louis, as
well as a writer much admired in more than one country of Europe,
and a spoilt child of the former regime of society;" on the other, a

brilliant orator, having also a ready pen, "a former Minister, and future ambassador and President of the section of Moral and Political Sciences at the Institute." Saint-Martin desired the absolute recognition of the existence of a moral sense in man, of a primeval speech imparted to man at his creation, and the relegation of unthinking matter to its proper place.

12

The Influence of Signs upon Thought. Paris, 1799. A second edition appeared in 1801.

Originally inserted in the "Crocodile," this little work is, in the opinion of M. Matter, a pearl of some price in that dubious parable. For Saint-Martin, as for Emerson, the whole world was an omen and a sign, and every sign a sacrament, that is to say, "a representation or indication of a thing concealed for us." As to the conventional signs made use of among men, they are substitutes for others, more real and more positive, of which we are now deprived. Signs are indispensable for the development of ideas in man, but these signs are the fruit of the ideas, and although they may stimulate the latter do certainly not create them. The thesis was proposed by the Institute and drawn up by Garat, but Saint-Martin for the second time failed to obtain a hearing.

13

The Spirit of Things, or Philosophical Survey of the Nature of Beings and the Object of their Existence. Two vols. Paris, 1800. 8vo. Published by Debray, in the Palais-Égalité, and by Fayolle, Rue Honoré, over against the Temple of Genius. pp. iv, 326 and v, 345.

The epigraph for once is in Latin: *Mens hominis rerum universalitatis speculum, est.* It is established by M. Gence that this work is identical with the "Natural Revelations" projected in 1797, as appears from a letter to Kirchberger in that year. The German patrician advised him earnestly to suppress everything that savoured of mystery. As this work has been sufficiently considered in the text, I need only quote the description which is given by Saint-Martin:— "Partly of my own accord, and partly on the solicitation of some friends, I have undertaken a work to be entitled 'Natural Revelations,' in which I am ingarnering from my notes, and from anything new that may come to me, several points of view which appear likely to be useful to the hearts and minds of my fellow-creatures. According to some who have seen it, it presents even now some wholesome waters at which the burning thirst may be quenched. I shall go on with it, if God favour me; and when it is done, if it is judged to be worth printing, and our pecuniary means permit, I shall publish it." Later on he describes it as outlines only, "because it embraces the whole circle of things physical and scientific, spiritual and divine, and it would be impossible to exhaust each subject in the space devoted to it." When he adds that it is a preparatory introduction to the works of Jacob Böhme, we may accept this view of the volume without being forced to acknowledge that it contains much of Böhme's influence. The Revolution had reduced Saint-Martin to poverty, and for the first time he endeavoured to interest his friends in the circulation of one of his works.

14

The Cemetery of Amboise. 8vo. By the Unknown Philosopher. A pamphlet of 16 pages, republished in the second volume of the Posthumous Works.

The versification of this poem is so exceedingly careless that it is placed almost outside the pale of any criticism which pays its chief regard to form. And yet it is redeemed by its aspirations. The cemetery of Amboise was the resting-place of the ancestors of Saint-Martin, towards which a religious fascination attracted him, and he remembers how in their neighbourhood Burlamaqui sanctified the morning of his life. He pauses at the grave of a young villager named Alexis, and, musing as usual on the apotheosis which men call death, the spirit of the dead youth rises to speak to him, encouraging him in the path he has taken, and foretelling the woes of France. It ends, like all visions of Saint-Martin, with Wisdom seated on a throne, the time when Ezekiel restored life to the dead bones of Israel; man has his treasures given back to him, the captive tribes of the true Jordan regain its banks, and Jerusalem again beholds her children.

15

The Ministry of Man the Spirit. By the Unknown Philosopher. Paris, 1802. 8vo. Printed by Migneret, Rue du Sepulchre, 28. pp. xvi, 422.

The epigraph is taken from "The Spirit of Things," and is one of those striking aphorisms which occur so frequently in Saint-Martin: "Man is the word of all enigmas." The work, in three parts, treats of Nature, Man, and the Logos. M. Matter calls it "the Swan's song of the theosophist of Amboise;" and though his acute critical judgment is a little deranged by an exaggeration of the influence of Böhme, he gives us the best means of appraising that influence when he says that the work contains nothing which has not been previously sketched or indicated in preceding writings. He adds, what is exceedingly true, that it bears the seal of an unusual recollection and clearness, and that its dream of the palingenesis of nature accomplished by the reintegration of man in his principle, if it be indeed nothing more than a dream, is at least of a sublime order. Mr. E. B. Penny, the theosophic translator of Saint-Martin, has not done full justice to the sympathies of M. Matter when he represents him as an academic reviewer, with a touch of patronage towards his subject; and I think that, all things considered, next to being a mystic like Saint-Martin, one could wish to be a critic like his biographer. The "Ministry" had the misfortune to be published almost simultaneously with Chateaubriand's "Genius of Christianity" and was, of course, eclipsed by that brilliant work. Saint-Martin, however, was, as usual, a dispassionate critic of his last achievement. "Though this work is clearer than the rest, it is too remote from human ideas for me to count upon its success. I have often felt in writing that it was much as if I took my violin and played dance-music in the cemetery of Montmartre, where, scrape as I might with my bow, the corpses would neither foot it nor hear my strains."

16

Posthumous Works of M. de Saint-Martin. Two vols. Tours, 1807. 8vo. Printed and Published by Letourmy, Rue Colbert, No. 2. pp. xxxii, 406 and 482.

A collection of priceless interest, it is not too much to say that in its absence we should have been without the means of understanding Saint-Martin. It contains his "Historical Portrait" and an ample selection from his "Thoughts," discourses pronounced by him at the Lyons Lodge of Beneficence, a collection of private prayers, all his extant poems, and a variety of small treatises on the Source of our Knowledge and Ideas, the Location of the Reasonable Soul, Divine Government, the Ways of Wisdom, &c. As regards the memorial notes, M. Matter suggests that the selection is not intelligent, and, in the absence of the original, the statement cannot be challenged, but to possess it in any shape demands our gratitude.

17

Of Numbers. By L. C. de Saint-Martin, called the Unknown Philosopher. A Posthumous Work, together with Light on Human Association. Including an unpublished Portrait of the Author, and an Introduction by M. Matter, Hon. Inspector-General of Public Instruction. Collected and published by L. Schauer. Paris, 1861. Royal 8vo. pp. xvi, 107 and 47.

As this curious treatise has been the subject of a special study, I need only say that M. Schauer was introduced to the works of Saint-Martin by the MS. of this treatise, which he purchased at a public auction. He admits ingenuously that he acquired it on the supposition that it was a translation of the Biblical Book of Numbers. It led him to the study of the mystic, and he was fortunate enough to obtain copies of his works corrected by his own hand. He proposed to republish them all, and began with this posthumous treatise, which in the first instance was lithographed and then printed in a somewhat awkward shape.

18

Unpublished Correspondence of L. C. de Saint-Martin, termed the Unknown Philosopher, and Kirchberger, Baron de Liebstorf. From May 22, 1782, to November 7, 1797. Collected and published by L. Schauer and Alph. Chuquet. Paris, 1862. Royal 8vo. pp. 330.

The subject of such frequent reference in the text of the present study, there can be no need to describe further this precious volume. Nor is it necessary to do more than mention the useful translation which has made it known to English readers, of which the full title is as follows:—"Mystical Philosophy and Spirit Manifestations." Selections from the recently published Correspondence between L. C. de Saint-Martin and Kirchberger, Baron de Liebistorf Translated and edited by E. B. Penny. Exeter, 1863. Crown 8vo.

19

The following tracts, enumerated without description in the Bibliography of Matter, are now wholly unobtainable, and I have failed to meet with examples.

A) The New Age, or the Hope of the Friends of Truth, 4 pp.
B) The Religious Awakening, Stanzas and Canticles.
C) The Union of God and Man; Spiritual Advent of the Word. A Discourse pronounced in a religious assembly, February 2, 1798.

20
Translations of Jacob Böhme

Aurora Breaking, or the Root of Philosophy, Astrology, and Theology. Translated from Gichtel's Amsterdam edition of 1682, with a Notice of Jacob Böhme, by the Unknown Philosopher. Two vols. Paris, 1800. 8vo.

The first work of the German theosophist, never completed, and usually regarded as a sublime chaos, much inferior in value, and much more difficult to grasp than his later and fuller illuminations. With this verdict Saint- Martin seems generally in agreement, but at the same time considers that the "Aurora" contains all the germs which were developed subsequently in the "Three Principles" and other treatises. Though the first to be published, it seems to have been the last translated by Saint-Martin, and may thus indicate his intention to present all the writings of his "beloved author" in their chronological order.

The Three Principles of the Divine Essence, or the Eternal Unoriginated Engendering of Man; for what he has been created and unto what end; after what manner all things began in time, how they pursue their course, and to what they shall return at the end. Translated (from the Amsterdam edition, as above) by the Unknown Philosopher. Two vols. Paris, 1802. 8vo.

Referring to this treatise by Böhme, Saint-Martin exclaims: "My astonishment becomes boundless when I see that such wonders are in the world" (*Correspondance,* Lettre lxxiv.). It was in the fifteenth chapter of the "Three Principles," No. 7, taken in connection with No. xii. that Saint-Martin discerned an indication of the resipiscence of the evil principle. The absence of more explicit teaching on this subject in his favourite author was evidently a source of regret. The translation of this work was begun by Saint-Martin in December 1795 (*Correspondance,* Lettre lxxxiv.), under great difficulty, owing to his failing sight. He regarded it as one of Böhme's most important works, and one which, if need be, might stand for the whole.

Questions on the Origin, Essence, Being, Nature, and Property of the Soul, together with the Profound and Sublime Basis of the Six Point and the Nine Texts. Translated from the German by an Unknown Philosopher. Published posthumously at Paris in one vol. 8vo, 1807.

Some copies are furnished with a curious full-page plate, showing the "Philosophical Globe, or Eye of Eternity." The text was revised by M. Gilbert. Saint-Martin recommends this treatise to Kirchberger for its information on the intercourse between souls *(Correspondance,* Lettre lxxxiv.). On this subject Saint-Martin himself made a very keen observation, namely, that we look for the souls of the departed in "the sensible principles in which they no longer are," while they seek us in "the spiritual and divine principle in which we are not yet." Hence the difficulty of communication between the two sides of the gate of death.

The Threefold Life of Man, according to the Mystery of the Three Principles of Divine Manifestation, written in accordance with a Divine Instruction. Followed by the "Six Points" and the "Nine Texts." Translated from the German into French in 1773, by an Unknown Philosopher. Published posthumously at Paris in 1809.

The text was revised by M. Gilbert The date to which the translation is attributed by the title is an egregious mistake. Writing to Kirchberger on May 23, 1794, Saint-Martin observes: "Thank God, I begin to be tolerably familiar with our author's German; and I go on, when I have time, with my translation into French of the 'Threefold Life,' which I have undertaken as a provision for my old age, for my eyesight is failing, and if I were to lose it, I could find no one in this place able to read it to me in German." The translation was completed in November of the same year.

21

Unpublished Writings

(Enumerated in the Bibliography of M. Matter)

Family Correspondence, comprising 63 letters, at that time in the possession of M. Toumyer, together with several works in MS.

Several unpublished treatises on the Conferences between Saint-Martin and the Comte d'Hauterive, at Lyons; on Astrology; on Magnetism and Somnambulism; on Signs and Ideas; on the Principle and Origin of Forms; on the Holy Scriptures, &c.

Note: M. Alfred Erny, a writer on transcendental subjects, and an occult student of many years' standing, informs me that the son of M. Matter is said to possess numerous MSS. of the Unknown Philosopher. These are perhaps the treatises referred to above. Matter was a descendant of Rodolph de Salzmann, and was acquainted with Chauvin, the friend of Fabre d'Olivet and executor of Joseph Gilbert, to whom all Saint-Martin's MSS. were bequeathed, according to my informant.

Projected Works

The New Tobias, a poem sketched as follows in the "Historical Portrait": "Name of my country written on the dust. An eagle effacing it with his wings, as the unfortunate attempts to read it, unable to recover what it has lost until it has deciphered this name. Search after him who inscribed it." The reader will observe the analogy between this idea and that of Matthew Arnold's mournful verses, beginning, "Before man parted for this earthly strand."

An Unnamed Tragedy. I include this on the authority of Matter, who had access to the MS. of the "Historical Portrait," a considerable portion of which was suppressed in the "Posthumous Works." I find no reference to it in any published writing of Saint-Martin.

22

One Hundred Unpublished Letters in the possession of the Supreme Council of the Martinist Order at Paris, forming part of the Archives of the Chevaliers Bienfaisants de Lyons. Forty-eight of these letters are addressed to J. B. Willermoz. Mention is also made of other works in MS. from the pen of Saint-Martin, which have passed into the custody of the Council.

IV

Martinism and the
Masonic Rite of Swedenborg

WHILE THIS WORK was passing through the press, the President of the Martinist Order in France has published a
contribution to its subject, based on documents in possession of the Supreme Council,* the existence of which archives I
have had occasion to mention previously. Much of the information is
not only new but valuable, and yet it may be necessary to distinguish
that which rests indubitably on the authority of the documents from
some things which seem to depend less certainly from the construction placed by the writer on his materials. Our respect is due to Papus
for many years of zealous and strenuous work in the cause of transcendentalism, and it is with some reluctance that I venture to differ
from him, even over documentary criticism or the appreciation of
historical aspects. It seems advisable, however, in the present instance:
(*a*) to read his presentation of Saint-Martin in the light of what we
have learned certainly concerning the Unknown Philosopher by the
testimony of the mystic's published works, and (*b*) to bear in mind
that upon historical questions the criterion of evidence is not invariably so rigorous in France as it is in England.

As regards the first of these points we know indubitably and precisely the kind of value set by Saint-Martin on the initiation which he

---

* *Martinésisme, Willermosisme, Martinisme et Franc-Maçonnerie. Par* Papus.
Paris, 1899.

received from Pasqually; that he abandoned the physical communication with the unseen which was taught by his master, partly on the ground of the dangers, but more conspicuously of the hallucinations to which it tended; and that this course was mainly the consequence of an early bias towards the interior life, to which Saint-Martin devoted himself subsequently, and by this means elaborated a doctrine of knowledge which was largely personal to himself, yet in a measure derived from Pasqually, and including later on certain theosophic additions from Jacob Böhme. We know that he consistently and always deprecated recourse to the outward way-by which he meant intercourse with spirits-on the part of those who had received any call to the inward life; that he never swerved from this position thenceforward; that it fills all his writings, and appears in a most especial manner in the intimate interchange of sentiments which took place between himself and Kirchberger, a friend evidently most dear to him. We know, finally, by his own express statement that he had abandoned all initiation save that of union with God, and that though he had conceived a certain respect for Swedenborg, he treated him most lightly as compared with Jacob Böhme.

When, therefore, Dr. Papus indicates-more or less on the authority of secret documents-that Saint-Martin was engaged secretly in a propaganda which he discountenanced openly; that he was less or more connected with the "physical communications" of which he gave with so much apparent earnestness so very indifferent an account; and that we are to look through Pasqually to Swedenborg for the grounds of his philosophical systems; it is indispensable that we should take these new facts in the light of what we know already, and that both must be somehow brought into proper line and harmony. We are promised at a fitting moment the publication of the documents concerned, and shall then, no doubt, be able to them their true place without sacrificing the Unknown Philosopher, whom we have learned to know and love, to the somewhat evasive personality which has thus emerged suddenly from concealment. In the absence of these documents we shall do well to suspend our judgment so far as Saint-Martin is himself concerned. It is possible, however, to speak somewhat definitely as to the connection between Martinism and Swedenborg, and this leads me to the second point which I proposed to develop. Those who are familiar both with the writings of Swedenborg and Saint-Martin will not readily admit the derivation of one from the other as deducible from any ordinary consideration of the two systems, and it must be confessed that a more ill-starred and disillusionising choice was seldom made than this attempt to invoke the Swedish seer to explain the fascinating mystery of Pasqually's occult knowledge. The warrant of the explanation is a fact already known to us, and authenticated, so far as I can judge, by the archives of Martinism, namely, that Martines de Pasqually was at one period a disciple of Swedenborg. On what considerations Dr. Papus bases his further views I am unable to say, but there is no reason to suppose that they derive from official documents. He affirms (*a*) that the illumination of Swedenborg was supplementary to that of the Rosicrucians, and that the seer himself was an adept of occult science; (*b*) that his propaganda was opposed to the Jesuits, and that as part thereof he supplemented his written revelations by a religious practice involving a ritual—in other words, he founded a corporate Church; (*c*) that he instituted the Masonic Rite which bears his name, and was indeed the actual creator of High-Grade Masonry.

Let me point out first of all that there are fewer opportunities in France for a first-hand acquaintance with the work of Swedenborg than exist in this country, where his writings are fully translated and readily accessible. While, therefore, the views enumerated above must be unacceptable in England, we can account naturally for their appearance in Paris, and excuse it also on the ground of insufficient opportunity for acquaintance with the facts of the case. Every student of Swedenborg—and here there are life-long students who are acquainted also with the literature of occultism—is well aware that the Swedish seer had no familiarity with the occult sciences, and gives no indication of such in any of his works; that what is now known as the New Jerusalem or Swedenborgian Church was not started until after his death; and that his connection with Masonry is little more than a matter of report. On the other hand, students of Masonry in England are equally well aware that the origin of Continental High-Grade Masonry was the Templar Chapter of Clermont. The Grand Master of the Rite of Swedenborg in England is Mr. John Yarker, and I have his assurance: (*a*) That as to whether Swedenborg was initiated into Masonry we are very much in the dark. (*b*) That he knows of no proof supporting the asserted participation of Swedenborg in the French High Grades. Now, I submit that, when stripped of all its adornments, the bare fact of an early connection between Pasqually and the Swedish seer possesses few consequences, and that having regard to the peculiar system of the Spanish occultist we are fully justified in concluding that he drew from other sources than the doctrine of the New Jerusalem, in which case it may, I think, be admitted that the influence of Swedenborg upon Saint-Martin has been neither understated nor exaggerated in the section which I have devoted to this subject.

Index

Made in the USA
Thornton, CO
11/23/24 21:24:12

73597854-d1fe-4727-82f4-f614859b8fcbR01